Studies of the New Testament and Its World

EDITED BY JOHN RICHES

Contents

Preface to the English Edition

I would first like to express my great pleasure at the decision of T. & T. Clark, Edinburgh to publish an English translation of my book *Law in Paul's Thought*. For this my sincere thanks, especially to the editor of the series, John Riches of Glasgow University. I am also grateful for the translation which, as far as I am able to judge as a German, works very well.

I would of course like to see the decision to make an English translation as symptomatic of the great sympathy with which a number of New Testament schholars in Great Britain have engaged in discussion of my work on Paul's theology and have indeed in different ways declared themselves in agreement with fundamental elements of my hypothesis. If I am not wholly mistaken it is above all in Great Britain that there is to be found a readiness to accept the idea of some development in Paul's thought.

Göttingen, April 1984   Hans Hübner

From the Preface to the German Edition

The thesis which I wish to advance in this monograph, that there was a development in Paul's understanding of the Law and, in consequence, in his theology, is based above all—how could it, in an exegetical work, be otherwise?—on the interpretation of the relevant utterances of the apostle. It should therefore be clear that, for the author, it is the philological arguments together with the theological arguments which arise out of them which have the greatest weight (e.g. for Gal 5.14), as opposed for example to the attempts to derive historical reconstructions from such arguments. The attempts at historical reconstruction, above all in Sections 1.2 and 2.2, are in the way of things the most hypothetical sections of the book. They in no way lay claim to providing the groundwork for the overall presentation. Thus I would ask the critical reader to read the book in the awareness that, for its author, the historical reconstruction of suppositions as to *why* Paul's thought developed in this way and not another is not the heart of the matter. My concern is that the reader should perceive how above all the argumentation in Section 1.4 represents a crucial phase in the development of my case.

My heartfelt thanks are due to my student Hannelore Hollstein for the preparation of the bibliography and finally, and above all, to my wife for her care in the typing of the manuscript.

The original intention was that the book should have appeared in October 1976 and included greetings for the 70th birthday of Prof. Heinrich Greeven D. D. However, as is so often the case with spiritual children, the birth was delayed. So the book is dedicated belatedly to my colleague, Prof. Greeven.

Christmas 1977   Hans Hübner

INTRODUCTION

0.1 The Problem

Did Paul undergo a development in his understanding of the Law? This
question is not new. As early as 1850, Albrecht Ritschl had pointed out, in the
first edition of his monograph, *Die Entstehung der altkatholischen Kirche*,[1] that
the two conceptions of the Law in Galatians and Romans were not entirely
compatible with each other – did not wholly tally: in Galatians Paul equated
elements of the Law with paganism, the governing factor being the dominant
concern for the ceremonial ordinances; while the statements in Romans, on the
other hand, had a predominantly ethical interest, so that there the ceremonial
law appears to be left out of account. The point is again made, but more
clearly, in the second edition, in 1857.[2] Ritschl maintains the same standpoint
as late as the second edition (1882) of his main work on dogmatics, *Die
christliche Lehre von der Rechtfertigung und Versöhnung*:[3] an excursus on Gal
3.13 'serves in passing to make the point how differently at different times Paul
assessed the Mosaic Law'; for 'in Galatians and Colossians he viewed the
Mosaic Law as a whole in accordance with the predominant impression made
by the ceremonial commandments as material out of keeping with
Christianity, whereas in Romans he viewed it in terms of the predominant
impression made by the ethical material.'[4] In Galatians (3.21), Paul declares
the Mosaic Law to be intrinsically out of keeping with the saving purpose of
life, but in Romans (7.10) he concedes that in itself the Law is indeed endowed
with such characteristics.[5] In Romans, where it is the ethical content of the Law
that is predominantly in view, there is nothing to suggest 'that Paul both
previously and later derived the Law from the angels and denied its solidarity
with God.'[6] Thus Ritschl can speak of the *'two incompatible chains of ideas
about the Mosaic Law'*.[7] Both arise out of Paul's personal experiences. On the
one hand the harassments emanating from the Law are in mind, as described
by Paul in Rom 7 (which Ritschl understood autobiographically): the moral
ideal was unattainable; but on the other hand Paul considered himself above
reproach in the Pharisaic practice of the Law.[8] 'Paul's alternation of these two
series of assessments of the Law shows how individual, and indeed path-
ological, his views are in this area.'[9]

That Ritschl nevertheless did not posit any *development* in Paul's theology of

1

the Law is probably connected not least with his view that Colossians was an
authentic letter of Paul's. He was thus able to speak of Paul's 'alternating'
between the two series of judgements; thus in Colossians he picks up what he
had initially said in Galatians but had then not developed in the interval, i.e., in
Romans, because of a change of perspective. Friedrich Sieffert, however, does
speak of the 'organic development and vivid forward movement' of Pauline
thought and of the 'development of Pauline doctrine' in his dissertation,
*Bemerkungen zum paulinischen Lehrbegriff, namentlich über das Verhältniß des
Galaterbriefs zum Römerbrief.*[10]
    In Galatians the dominant idea was that of independence from the Mosaic
Law. This was something which the apostle had to lay hold of with all his might
after his conversion, which had come as a bolt from the blue. It is 'still the
source and foundation for all his convictions'. Consequently Paul also seeks to
guide his readers towards this objective; they too should come 'to a recognition
of the complete (!) irrelevance of the Mosaic Law for the Christian life.'[11] Thus
in Galatians 'ἐλευθερία is the concept which dominates the entire argument.'[12]
In Romans, on the other hand, 'the paramount concept is correspondingly the
δικαιοσύνη θεοῦ, man's legal standing as established by God.'[13] However, this
leads Sieffert to suggest the following chronology: 'If we first of all consider
that in Pauline teaching ἐλευθερία is only the consequence of the δικαιοσύνη
θεοῦ we will find it entirely understandable that the exposition of doctrine
which starts from ἐλευθερία as its fundamental concept is the earlier one.'[14] In
other words, Galatians has chronological priority. Consequently the concept
of the δικαιοσύνη θεοῦ has its place 'only on the way to the ethical objectivity
of Christianity', and 'therefore has much more positive links with Old
Testament religion than has the idea of Christian ἐλευθερία', to the extent that
the former concept indicates 'an objective relation of man to God, and one of
such a character as had already been sought within Old Testament religion as
the highest objective of moral and religious life; only there it had been sought
in the wrong way and consequently in vain.'[15]
    In this context Sieffert appeals to Ritschl, who, as we have already noted,
regarded the Law as being considered in Galatians primarily with reference to
its ceremonial regulations, and in Romans primarily in relation to its ethical
side. From this Sieffert concludes as follows: 'But that is to say in effect that
Paul assessed the Mosaic Law as a whole variously and from a variety of
perspectives...'[16] It is precisely this variation in perspective which led the
apostle to extend the concept of δικαιοσύνη in Romans in both a positive and
at the same time in an ethical direction. Thus in Romans there is also 'a genuine
Christian δικαιοσύνη which is the expression *not of a relation* but of a *mode of
behaviour*, and which is the ethical fruit of the δικαιοσύνη θεοῦ.'[17]
    One thing Sieffert does not seek to do is to claim that the pronouncements of
the two letters are mutually incompatible. His point was simply to indicate the
direction in which the theological interest of the apostle developed. It was not
in the least his desire to declare all those concepts which are not in Galatians

but can be found in Romans to have been still foreign to Paul when Galatians was written.[18] This conclusion is somewhat surprising. At all events, many of Sieffert's formulations can be better understood if they do not presuppose merely a process of explanation pure and simple in Paul's theological development: that is, if they consider the development not only from the standpoint of continuity but also from that of discontinuity. One wonders, at the end of the essay, whether Sieffert has not softened the real thrust of his argument by feeling himself compelled, for whatever reasons, to harmonise in this way.

Carl Clemen takes the opposite position. He puts Romans chronologically before Galatians. Statements such as we find in 2 Cor 5.16 or Gal 5.11 point to a Judaistic period in Paul after his conversion, a period in which his approach was to a greater extent related to that of the original apostles. Paulinism as we know it developed out of this earlier position.[18a] Where Sieffert assumed a development in Paul to a more positive evaluation of the Torah, Clemen thinks rather of a movement from a relatively moderate to a relatively more intransigent assessment of it. For him the result of his investigation was 'that the acknowledged *dependence of Galatians on Romans*, asserted in his day by Bruno Bauer (!) and then by Steck, is *undeniable*, specifically, as it happens, in the matter of the status of the Law.'[19] Sieffert deals critically with this view, which was later retracted by Clemen himself,[20] in a further essay.[21] This too is allowably of such importance for our subject that we may fittingly dwell on it for a little.

Sieffert agrees that his first essay was not entirely free from exaggeration of the idea of the forward movement and development of Pauline teaching in the four main letters; nevertheless this view now seems to him more assured than ever in the light of further scrutiny. He therefore welcomes Clemen's 'sureness of touch and rare shrewdness' in taking up this subject, the more so as his other colleagues had 'reacted to the assertion that there were traces of such a development...only with the greatest reserve.'[22] But perhaps it was not merely the subject which prompted Sieffert to enter into detailed discussion with Clemen, but also the two men's affinity in their way of thinking, which made them sensitive to thought *processes*. Thus it may well be significant that Sieffert characterises Clemen's hypothesis as follows, even though Clemen came to precisely the opposite conclusions from him, and that he certainly did not do so merely by way of wrapping up his criticism in a polite disguise; here is what he says: (Clemen's view was) 'by no means unattractive'; it is a 'dazzling edifice, the discerning execution of which is at all events extremely stimulating.'[23] Why then is it nonetheless 'not tenable'?[24] His answer is that one cannot infer from Gal 5.11 any initial Jewish-Christian preaching of the Law on Paul's part,[25] for his conversion to Christianity led, more in his case than with others, to a breach with all legalism.[26] Modern research on Paul, of course, regards this notion almost as an axiom. Thus Galatians is on a level with the Damascus experience. But this then has the consequence for the relation of Galatians to Romans that: 'it is probable that once the sharp, dialectical, rigid formulation of his teaching on freedom from the Law, as we find it in Galatians, had been brought into being by the struggle the apostle found himself having to engage in against Judaism-within-Christianity, there then followed in Romans at a later date a *more comprehensive* and *profound*, but at the same time *more moderate development* of that teaching;[27] but the reason for this was, rather, that Galatians brings out that circle of ideas which is linked to freedom from the Law more as a separate element in itself, whereas Romans represents more an interweaving of the two groups of ideas.'[28] The modifications which Sieffert thinks he can discern in Romans as compared with Galatians cannot all be listed here, but we may refer to the following points which he mentions. In Romans we no longer hear of the Law's origin as partly from a source subordinate to God (Gal 3.19); and the bald expression in Gal 3.19 that the purpose of the Law was to provoke offences is not repeated in Romans. On the other hand, Romans does contain most of the thoughts in Galatians relating to the Law.[29] The different natures of the two letters also show up in the fact that according to Rom 7.10 the purpose of the Law is meant in itself to lead as such to life, whereas Gal 3.21 expressly denies that the Law has the purpose of bringing life.[30]

Sieffert explains the differences between the two letters as an 'apparent contradiction': in Galatians one chain of ideas predominates, viz., the Law seen in terms of its outward, national expression, but in Romans it is the other chain, viz., the Law in terms of its inward, moral content.[31] 'However, as this distinction, and therefore the resolution of the contradictions mentioned, has not been fully carried through, the difference between Galatians and Romans comes out sharply, with the different approaches that predominate in them.'[32] All in all, it is the particular circumstances at the time of writing and not the alternation of momentary moods in Paul that have 'given rise to real *conceptual development* in Paul's teaching on the Law, in one specific direction.'[33] Concretely this means that there emerged a 'moderating attitude which along with the proclamation of salvation granted a certain status to Judaism and the Law.'[34]

Here is a final example from the period prior to the First World War. Paul Wendland writes in his monograph on Hellenistic-Roman civilisation (second edition, 1912): 'In Romans the natural knowledge of God is the correlate of the Jews' possession of the Law, but in Gal 4.8-10 the apostle is carried away by his polemical zeal into making idolatry – which after all followed from the distortion of that knowledge – a phenomenon parallel to the Mosaic religion of the Law, and into dealing with it under the common notion of worship of the elements.'[35] Thus Wendland also notes that there is a difference between the two letters but explains it not by a development in Paul's thinking, but in psychological terms.

In recent literature, Ritschl's and Sieffert's views no longer have any great influence. Today exegesis of Galatians is largely carried out on the basis of

Romans, and that of Romans on the basis of Galatians. Yet in many commentaries and monographs we still learn of the difference between Galatians and Romans in asides.[36] Only a few authors, however, go into the matter in any detail. Among them is Ulrich Luz. He sums up his detailed exegetical studies as follows: 'The opposition between Gal 3f. and Rom 9.1-5 and 11.16-32 seems to be insurmountable.'[37] But how did this opposition come about? Do we have to reckon with a basic change in Paul's thinking? Luz does not think so. In his view Romans and Galatians are not so far apart chronologically that we would be obliged to opt for such a radical solution. He explains the difference in the line of argument in the two letters from the difference in the situation in each case to which the two letters are addressed.[38] From this, it follows for him that 'we have seen the extent to which Paul's statements require to be understood in terms of the situation to which they address themselves, or to which the Pauline letters are to be explained not as expositions of items which are correct in themselves but as a pronouncement in and in terms of the situation.'[39] He continues with the dialectical comment: 'or, to put it otherwise, we have seen that Paul can say things which are quite contrary in his letters in order to say nevertheless the same thing.'[40]

When we look back on this rather selective[41] review of the expositors of the two Pauline letters, it is striking that there is one conclusion they have not drawn, namely that Paul in Romans no longer wanted to say what he once said in Galatians. Ritschl explains the remarkable circumstance of their difference in terms of the apostle's psychological situation. Sieffert explains it by means of the category of 'development', though of course using the word simply in the sense of an explanatory development of points already made. Luz explains it in terms of the different situations to which Paul was addressing himself. It is hard to escape the impression that there was a reluctance to explore the solution which had at least been considered by all three authors, viz., that one should distinguish Romans from Galatians in terms of their content.

The present essay is addressed to the question whether the difference between Galatians and Romans as to their pronouncements about the Law is not so serious that it cannot be accounted for either as an explication continuous with what went before, or simply in terms of the different situations of the addressees – disregarding, among others, Ritschl's psychologising interpretation. At all events, one thing is clear: the discrepancy in the two letters as to their ideas on the Law is manifest. It calls for an exegetical solution. And a second point should likewise be clear: the question broached in the nineteenth century has not yet been clearly perceived, let alone dealt with as fully as it might deserve, in the twentieth. The present investigation has been written with the intention of taking up this question. I say deliberately 'taking up' the question. For decades it has been something of a Sleeping Beauty, and there has scarcely been even a brief, twilight interruption of that sleep. Consequently it would be presumptuous were an exegete to seek to present a definitive answer (even quite apart from the fact that *every* historical pronouncement implied in an exegetical statement involves presumptuousness, to the extent that one is saying, 'That's how it was at that time!' Perhaps anyone who says of the past, 'That's how it was!' - even for good reasons - should be just a little disconcerted by his temerity). Thus here we are first and foremost concerned to recall to the consciousness of New Testament scholars this question *as a question*.

When therefore we read Galatians or Romans from the perspective of what each of them has to say as a unique contribution of its own, we should perhaps not be so very surprised if we experience a growing apprehensiveness, first vague, then increasingly decided, as we note how on all sides the one letter is explained on the basis of the other and *vice versa*.[42] We are not saying there could be no justification for this procedure under conditions which would require precise specification - but in no circumstances can it be a methodological presupposition. The historian must reckon with the fact that the historical constellation he is handling does not at all times say the same thing. If however we are to let each of these two letters of Paul's say what is unique to it this also means that we have to 'hear out' this characteristic element in each case. The word 'hear' is being used as literally as possible here, for Paul really did dictate his letters and did so with the intention of their being read out and therefore 'heard'. So the exegete has the duty of also hearing the texts of the New Testament if he does not wish to apprise himself of their contents only in an extremely alien mode. Anyone who 'hears' Galatians, or who 'hears' Romans, will register something that has been said independently of the other letter in each case.[43] Of course the question arises whether we still can 'hear' in this way, as unfortunately we do always associate the one letter with the other in some way. And the fact that, again, in the end only written material is set down in a scholarly investigation regarding what is to be or has been read *out*, simply demonstrates the inadequacy - of necessity a fundamental inadequacy - in such an enterprise. It should also be noted that naturally it was not possible to make the 'hearing' of the Pauline letters into a methodological principle in this present study.

The title of the study is *Law in Paul's Thought: A Contribution to the Study of the Growth of Paul's Theology*. In writing the work it was necessary to avoid two possible dangers. The first was that of having too wide a spread. Anyone writing a monograph involving Paul's theology has to take into account the wide-ranging discussions on, say, his doctrine of justification, his christology, or the problem of history and salvation-history (*Heilsgeschichte*) in Paul. However, as here we are not concerned with the presentation of Pauline theology as such but rather with a specific perspective from which this theology can be viewed, some limitation of our field was necessary. Many questions which the author would like to have considered have had to be excluded. For the subject was simply to work out that particular contribution which the 'Law' as a variable makes to the problems which here await treatment. Consequently we have phrased the title 'A *Contribution* to the

Study of the Growth of Paul's Theology'. The reason for speaking in the title of Paul's theology as a definable entity lies in the conviction that the doctrine of justification which finds expression in Romans does in fact constitute the core of Paul's theology. In the apostle's thought, justification certainly is not simply one individual subject among others. 'Justification by faith' is what Paul is ineluctably concerned to talk about. But this means that the real centre of his theology is to be seen in his endeavours to think this through, i.e., in his theology of justification. It is certainly not just a 'secondary crater'! But if that is so, then it is all the more imperative to try to see his intellectual endeavours as a *process*, specifically as one in which he is also striving to get at the sense and meaning of the Mosaic Law. The view that those efforts to understand the Law which terminate finally in Romans contributed *a fortiori* to the definitive shape of his doctrine of justification is responsible for the methodological procedure which I have largely followed of comparing Galatians and Romans with each other at specific points in each case. (Thus there is a correspondence between Sections 1.1 and 2.1; 1.2 and 2.2; 1.3 and 2.3 and 1.4 and 2.4 of this study. Only occasionally were 1 and 2 Corinthians taken into account, e.g., in Section 3.2.) However, within the framework of this particular study it was enough to have shown how the apostle's definitive doctrine of justification received its shape as a result of his ultimate understanding of the Law, without having given extensive treatment to the whole range of theological problems relating to the justice of God or to the question of history and salvation-history in Paul. To repeat: the *growth* of Paul's theology, not its final state, is the subject of this investigation.[44]

The other danger was that by concentrating on that particular perspective which revealed itself as the right one to the author, one might avoid discussions of secondary literature which though necessary fell outside the purview of one's chosen perspective. On the other hand, a consciously chosen perspective naturally also means that there is a consciously sought constriction of one's field of vision. But it is only in the methodical pursuit of the presentation to its end that we can concretely discover whether this intentional constriction was justified, i.e., whether in fact nothing essential has been lost from the field of vision.

0.2 Addendum to Introduction

Section 0.1 was intended to lead us into the subject-matter of this study. For this reason, too, only a few scholars were mentioned, for whom differences of sense between Paul's various pronouncements on the Law have been or are a real problem. There was never any question of providing a survey of the literature which would be bibliographically complete. However, for this

English edition, I should like to draw attention explicitly to two British scholars whose works I had not as yet taken into account on completing the first impression of the German edition, but who ought without question to be mentioned here. In 1974 there appeared Anthony Tyrrell Hanson's book, *Studies in Paul's Technique and Theology*. Hanson, of course, does not – as I do – assume that there was a really substantial modification of Paul's view of the Law; but nevertheless he does go so far as to allow for Paul's learning from experience that his line of argument in Galatians required correction. Thus the author brings out the following distinction: '...in Galatians Paul writes quite freely of the covenant which God made with Abraham.... It is...really part of the new covenant. But in Romans, when he is dealing with essentially the same material, he drops the covenant language.'[1] Hanson offers two suggestions in answer to the question why Paul allowed the covenant language to drop in Romans. The first of these is that such language was confusing, for it spoke first of all of a new covenant with Abraham but then of an old covenant with Moses! The second suggestion is that experience of discussion with Jews showed Paul that it was difficult to separate the conclusion of a covenant in Gen 15 from the institution of circumcision in Gen 17. 'So he decided in Romans to insist on only two covenants as far as Christians were concerned, the old one on Sinai and the new one on Golgotha.'[2] (Moreover, the problem of the relation of Gen 15 to Gen 17, within the framework of Paul's theological reflections, will be of no mean significance even for our deliberations; see Section 1.1 and Section 2.1.) Pp.70ff. of Hanson's book also merit attention – especially the distinction of 'κατάρα and the figure of the victim hung on a tree in Galatians' and 'ίλαστήριον and the figure of the sacrifice on the Day of Atonement in Romans.'[3] I agree with Hanson that 'the sheer fertility of Paul's mind' is shown in this.[4] But does Hanson not over-harmonise by suggesting that the differences arise from varying subject-matter in the two letters? 'The figure of the victim' in Galatians is regarded by him, in fact, as governed by Christ's victory over the powers, whereas he thinks that Paul uses 'the figure of the sacrifice' in Romans because he is 'perhaps more' preoccupied in that letter with the universal character of salvation.[5] At all events, however, the point should be noted that Hanson clearly discerns the nature of the problem – he recognises the question awaiting solution with all clarity.

The book which is of greatest importance for our subject and which was not taken into account in the German edition is the thesis by John W. Drane, who is a pupil of Bruce's. It is entitled *Paul, Libertine or Legalist? A Study in the Theology of the Major Pauline Epistles*, and it appeared in 1975. I did of course already quote with approval an essay by Drane (see Note 47 of Section 2.2) but his book is allowably even more significant than that essay was.

Drane takes really seriously the idea of a development in Paul's theology. Entirely in line with our own methodological approach he writes, 'If we interpret Galatians in total independence of Romans (as its original readers had to do), it appears more likely that Paul intended the mention of angels to disparage the Law, and on the basis of this particular passage we can only conclude that here he was meaning to issue a categorical denial of the divine origin of the Torah.'[6] Of course Drane is not dealing specifically with Romans in this book – he touches on it always only in regard to other letters of the apostle, as it were *en passant*. Nevertheless the distinction between Galatians and Romans as regards the question of the Law is brought out. Thus on the difference between Gal 3.19 and Rom 5.20ff. we read (if the reader will permit somewhat lengthy quotation because of the nature of the subject-matter): 'But there is a great difference here from what Paul says in Romans. Here he simply makes a bare, factual statement about the Law's function, whereas in Romans he goes on to draw out the positive implications of this function in terms of the ultimate saving purpose of God. There he makes it plain that, since God's purpose was to overcome sin, and since the Law was the means by which unconscious wrongdoing could be shown up as defiance of God's will, the introduction of the Law was a gracious and benevolent action on God's part. But here in Galatians the same thought is applied to show almost the very opposite! What follows in the rest of the verse almost cancels out what Paul has said of the Law's positive function.'[7]

However, Drane's book has been mentioned, not primarily because of the discussion relating to the Law, but because it proffers a thesis which runs parallel to our own in an interesting way. For Drane is concerned to show how Paul's attitude alters in relation to the complex of questions on 'tradition, freedom, and the norm for action'. He assumes in this the same chronological sequence for the four main letters as is done in the present study: Galatians, 1 Corinthians, 2 Corinthians, Romans. Here again are a few quotations relating to this point:

'The different attitude which Paul displays here' (scil. 1 Corinthians) 'to the question of tradition' (Drane is thinking primarily of 1 Cor 11.23ff. and 15.3ff.) 'over against his teaching in Galatians' (above all Gal 1.11ff.) 'is clear enough. But when we look to Paul's ethical teaching in 1 Corinthians, we move in what at times seems to be a different world from that of Galatians.'[8] Whereas in Galatians the point is that the work of the Spirit is what creates the perfect Christian character, according to Drane Paul is concerned in 1 Corinthians to formulate in very precise ways how the principle of a Christian ethic is to be applied.[9] Drane finds in 1 Corinthians (e.g., 7.10ff.) a tendency to 'law direction'.[10] 'We find precisely the same pattern in 1 Cor 7.19, where Paul actually takes up in the first half of the verse a statement out of which he had made great spiritual capital against his opponents in Galatians, but quite unexpectedly he now modifies it in such a way that he appears to be saying exactly the opposite of what he had said in Galatians!'[11] 'We need not suppose, of course, that it was necessarily the Old Testament commandments that Paul had in view here. But the least we can do is to observe that whereas in Galatians Paul was able to reject legalism in all its forms, here in 1 Corinthians he reintroduces the *form* of legal language, which in turn leads him into an ethical

position in 1 Corinthians not so very much different from the legalism he had
so much deprecated in Galatians.'[12]

Corresponding to this we have the idea that Paul's uncompromising
behaviour in relation to Peter as to the *factum Antiochenum* in Gal 2.11ff. 'runs
quite contrary to Paul's instruction on the very same thing (!) in 1 Corinthians
8.1-13, and his statement of his own procedure in 9.19-23.'[13] With regard to
this passage and then also 1 Cor 10.32 we read: 'The contrast with Paul's own
attitude at an earlier stage in his ministry is obvious. Whoever they were, the
non-eaters in Corinth had almost certainly been influenced by Jewish thought.
They may even have been former Jews or proselytes. This means they were in
precisely the same situation as Cephas at Antioch (Gal 2.11ff.), though Paul's
method of dealing with them was very different.'[14] I am very ready to agree
with Drane here because I admit that these were precisely the passages which
had led me to investigate the subject of the Law in Paul to see if there might be
any traces of development in it, even if I went into 1 Corinthians only
peripherally at the time. So then from Galatians to 1 Corinthians there is a
development in the direction of tolerance!

The high point of Drane's thesis is in the assumption that Romans should be
looked upon as a synthesis of thesis (Galatians) and antithesis (1
Corinthians).[15] At the moment I would not wish to give a detailed reaction to
this here, but simply to note briefly that I do not find the synthesis theory
entirely plausible. I see Romans rather on the line of development from 1
Corinthians and I have reservations when in relation to 1 Corinthians Drane
assumes that 'Paul has made a significant shift in the direction of what, for
want of a better term, we can only (!) describe as "early catholicism".'[16]
However, these critical remarks cannot and should not diminish the great
significance which this book ought to have for Pauline research.

Appendix to 0.2

Hans Dieter Betz's[17] commentary on Galatians is distinguished by the fact that
Galatians is carefully analysed, particularly from the standpoint of Graeco-
Roman rhetoric and epistolography. Thus he assigns Gal 2.15f. to the
propositio, while Gal 3.19-25 is a 'digression on the (Jewish) Torah' within the
probatio and Gal 5.14 belongs to the *exhortatio*. Betz too repeatedly notes
differences between Galatians and Romans, e.g., on Gal 3.13: 'The parallel
passage in Rom 7.7-12 reveals a different position compared with Galatians; in
Romans Paul does not repeat what he said in Gal 3.19-25, but emphasises the
positive role of the Torah. In Galatians, this positive role remains implicit (cf.
5.14; 6.2).'[18] Like myself he asks, 'How is the entirely negative view of the Law,
expressed up to 5.12, related to the positive interpretation of the concept in

5.14-6.10?'[19] However he does not go as far as I do because he consciously detaches himself from the view that the angels in Gal 3.19 are evil demons – 'This doctrine may begin with Cerinthus...'[20] – and on the other hand he distinguishes Gal 5.3 and 5.14 as 'doing' and 'fulfilling' of the Torah.[21] In any event however it should be emphasised as noteworthy that Betz is concerned about the relation of the two passages to each other. Pauline research will no longer be able to overlook this excellent commentary in so far as the subject-matter of Galatians is somehow or other involved. Betz too, by his penetrating analyses, raises the question, partly explicitly and partly implicitly, of the difference between Galatians and Romans, and thus at least implicitly also raises the question of theological development in Paul. (See my forthcoming review in *ThLZ*.)

It had been hoped that the English translation of this book would appear some years ago. The delay however has its advantages, for it now means that it is possible to enter into some discussion of publications that have engaged critically with my study. I would recommend however that the reader, before turning to my rejoinder to these publications, should first read the full account of my position in the book itself. For this reason I reserve my discussion of E. P. Sanders's and H. Räisänen's work till the end of the present volume.

Notes for Introduction

1. Ritschl, *Altkath. Kirche*, 1st ed., 76f.
2. Ritschl, *Altkath. Kirche*, 2nd ed., 73.
3. In the third edition (1889) Ritschl to a great extent did of course withdraw this viewpoint.
4. *Rechtfertigung und Versöhnung* II, 2nd ed., 252; but II, 3rd ed., 255: '...this is how he seems (!) to have viewed...the Mosaic Law'; significantly II, 3rd ed., 314: 'Now the statements about the Law are always (!) related literally to the entire content thereof without any distinction even being hinted at between the moral and the ceremonial items. Nor can it be shown that the pronouncements in the one letter call to mind more the one type of item while those in the other call to mind the other type.' (However, the letters referred to here are Phil and Rom.)
5. Ibid. II, 254; slightly altered II, 3rd ed., 255: '...here it is admitted that the Law itself does possess this characteristic...'
6. Ibid. II, 2nd ed., 313; no longer in II, 3rd ed.!
7. Ibid. II, 2nd ed., 313, my italics; no longer in II, 3rd ed.! Instead of this Ritschl tries now to harmonise Gal and Rom in regard to the statements of the Law; see above all II, 3rd ed., 312f.
8. Ibid. II, 2nd ed., 313; see also II, 3rd ed., 314-316.
9. Ibid., 320; greatly attenuated in II, 3rd ed., 321: 'The divergent judgements on the Law which the Christian apostle makes his own prove how individual his views in this field are.'
10. Reprinted in *JDTh* 14 (1869), 250-275; quotations: 257.

11. Ibid., 262.
12. Ibid., 263.
13. Ibid., 264.
14. Ibid., 267.
15. Ibid., 267.
16. Ibid., 268.
17. Ibid., 273; my italics.
18. Ibid., 274.
18a. Clemen, *Chronologie*, 49ff.
19. *JDTh* 14(1869), 263; my italics; see also Clemen, 'Die Reihenfolge der paulinischen Hauptbriefe', *ThStKr* 70, 219-270. However, he later admitted that the reasons adduced by him for the dating of Gal and Rom were not compelling: *ThLZ* 27 (1902), 233. More recently, Foerster has again championed the thesis of the priority in time of Rom to Gal: 'Abfassungszeit und Ziel des Galaterbriefs' = *Apophoreta*, 135-141.
20. See n. 19. It is with some little surprise that I read in Lüdemann, *Paulus der Heidenapostel*, 21, n. 11, that while I could blame Suhl (n. 41 of Section 0.1) for not having taken into account Pauline research of the nineteenth century and in particular that of Clemen and Sieffert, I myself would seem to have no knowledge of the two-volume monograph on Paul by Clemen in which he retracted most of his earlier views! In this connection I have explicitly drawn attention to Clemen's retraction, viz., that in *ThLZ* 27 (i.e., in 1902, which was two years *before* his monograph on Paul!). As I intended in the Introduction merely to draw attention to random points I have of course – deliberately! – provided no exhaustive survey of the literature. Unfortunately, in the German edition of my book on Paul, a misprint has crept in: n. 20 of the Introduction should read: 'see n. 19' (not 'see n. 18a').
21. Sieffert, 'Die Entwicklungslinie der paulinischen Gesetzeslehre nach den vier Hauptschriften des Apostels' = *Theologische Studien*,332-357.
22. Ibid., 334.
23. Ibid., 340.
24. Ibid., 340.
25. Ibid., 341; twice wrongly there Gal 5.15 instead of 5.11.
26. Ibid., 342. Admittedly today we would formulate somewhat more precisely, the conversion of Paul *is* his breach with the Law.
27. Ibid., 343; my italics.
28. viz., the Christian proclamation among the Gentiles which appears in 1 and 2 Th and the question of the Law.
29. Ibid., 345.
30. Ibid., 346f.
31. Ibid., 347.
32. Ibid., 348.
33. Ibid., 356; my italics.
34. Ibid., 356.
35. Wendland, *Die hellenistisch-römische Kultur*, 245.
36. E.g., Eichholz, *Die Theologie des Paulus im Umriß*, 247: 'If we compare Rom with Gal then we must notice that Paul in Gal comes to the most *abrupt* formulae *in criticism of the Torah* – so abrupt that by contrast the expressions in Rom seem objective and mild by comparison. Perhaps(!) it may also be said that in Rom Paul is *correcting* his position in relation to Gal or has *gone beyond it*, as regards the radical nature of certain formulae which he does not repeat in Rom; Dietzfelbinger, *Paulus und das Alte Testament*, 12, n. 24; Bammel, Νόμος Χριστοῦ = *StudEv* III, 127f.
37. Luz, *Geschichtsverständnis*, 285.

38. Ibid., 285f.

39. Ibid., 286.

40. Ibid., 286.

41. A good historical survey of exegetical discussion of the question of the Law in Paul from about the beginning of the last third of the 19th century is given by Otto Kuss in his essay 'Nomos bei Paulus' (*MThZ* 17, 177ff.). This review sketches these attempts independently of our particular question and thus provides an excellent supplement to the review conducted here on the basis of a quite specific intention. The extent to which at times the 19th century threatens to escape our field of vision is shown, for example, by the latest investigation of Paul and his letters by Alfred Suhl (1975). This very discussion omits consideration of Clemen and Sieffert, to mention only these two!

42. Just one of the typical examples from most recent times: MacGormann, 'Problem Passages in Galatians', *SouthWestJTh* 15, 43: 'It (sc., the translation of Gal 3.19b in the RSV) sounds as through the law they came into a situation in which there were transgressions, to hold them in check. But this seems to ignore some of the insights of the *Roman letter, ever the best commentary on Galatians*' (my italics).

43. Deissmann, *Paulus* 10, n. 1, cf. E.T. 11-13: 'That these letters are letters which were read out aloud is a perspective which is still not adequately noted in exegesis.' (This note is not in the English edition.) This warning holds good even today despite Deissmann's exaggerated psychologising.

44. The development of Pauline theology has been recently considered also from a completely different perspective. According to Georg Strecker, Paul's proclamation at the time when he wrote 1 Th should not be identified with the later message of justification ('Das Evangelium Jesu Christi' = *Jesus Christus in Historie und Geschichte*, 525). It is not until Gal that Paul unfolds his 'Gospel' as a message of justification (ibid., 528). The relationship between the gospel and the message of justification as expounded in Gal is elaborated further in Rom (ibid., 529). This idea is developed further by Strecker in 'Befreiung und Rechtfertigung. Zur Stellung der Rechtfertigungslehre in der Theologie des Paulus' = *Rechtfertigung*, 479-508. However, we cannot go into this idea here. Let us ask just one question: What is meant by *the unfolding* of the gospel as a message of justification? To my mind it is at this point that we have to enter into discussion with Strecker.

Notes for 0.2

1. Hanson, *Paul*, 142.

2. Ibid., 142.

3. Ibid., 72.

4. Ibid., 72.

5. Ibid., 72.

6. Drane, *Paul*, 34: 'this particular passage' = Gal 3.19.

7. Ibid., 34.

8. Ibid., 62.

9. Ibid., 64.

10. Ibid., 64.

11. Ibid., 65.

12. Ibid., 65.

13. Ibid., 67.

14. Ibid., 68.

15. Ibid., 135; 161, n. 8.

16. Ibid., 131.
17. Betz, *Galatians, A Commentary on Paul's Letter to the Churches in Galatia* (*Hermeneia*), Philadelphia, 1979, 433, n. 9.
18. Ibid., 149, n. 106.
19. Ibid., 274.
20. Ibid., 169, n. 64.
21. Ibid., 275.

1 NOMOS IN GALATIANS

1.1 First approach: Abraham

In Galatians, Paul reproaches the Galatian congregations with being on the point of placing themselves under the dominion and bondage of the Law, or, more precisely, of renewing such bondage. He considers that the Galatians are in danger of seeking to be justified by the works of the Law. Because he perhaps assumes, or, it may be, has been informed, that in Galatia Peter's behaviour and attitude were being cited in support of the way of the Law, he reports among other things on his conflict with Peter at Antioch, during which he had to remind all those who belonged to the contrary party of their common basis in the faith: justification is not something which results from the works of the Law but solely from faith in Christ Jesus. Everything for Paul depends on the exclusiveness of the contrast: there can be no kind of justification on the basis of works of the Law; not a single person is justified by these (Gal 2.16: ἐξ ἔργων νόμου οὐ δικαιωθήσεται πᾶσα σάρξ, i.e., ἐὰν μὴ διὰ πίστεως Χριστοῦ Ἰησοῦ)! Again the essential point for Paul is that this presupposition was something that both he and Peter had to share (both as *Jews*!) if they were to come to believe in Jesus as the Messiah: 'even *we* (emphatic ἡμεῖς!) have come to believe in Christ Jesus, *in order* (ἵνα!) to be justified by faith in Christ but not by works of the Law' – to which might well be added, 'because *we* had seen through the false approach of justification through the Law' (cf. 2.16). The incapacity of the Law to justify is indeed not directly enunciated here, but is nevertheless plainly presupposed: one is not justified through works of the Law for the simple reason that the Law is not capable of justifying.

In Gal 3 the proof from Scripture is adduced as to why no one is justified by the Law. However, this argument is not a direct continuation of the programmatic thesis presented in 2.16ff. on justification by faith alone and not by the works of the Law. It is rather embedded in the *higher order argument* that believers are the sons of Abraham. We must formulate it still more precisely, viz., that only those who have faith can reckon themselves as sons of Abraham. Note the syntactical drift in the sentence: οἱ ἐκ πίστεως, οὗτοι υἱοί εἰσιν Ἀβραάμ (3.7). That the third chapter ends with the conclusion, 'if you are Christ's, then (ἄρα) you *are* Abraham's offspring, you *are* heirs according to promise' (3.29), may well reveal what the main concern of the Galatians

15

was. Paul's line of argument leads us to suppose that they were concerned to ensure that their status was indeed that of sons of Abraham. But if so, then we can assume that it was the opponents of Paul agitating in the Galatian congregations who in the course of their polemics against the apostle and his preaching had troubled the Galatians on the following lines: 'we will not participate in being sons of Abraham if we do not practise circumcision. But those who have no share in being sons of Abraham will lose the salvation which is bestowed in Christ. Therefore faith in Jesus Christ is of use only if the basis for such faith is circumcision.'[1] The trend of Paul's argument therefore leads us to suppose that his opponents in Galatia were saying: 'Only those could be sons of Abraham who, like Abraham himself, were circumcised, and who were circumcised along with Abraham.' After all, they could appeal to Gen 17.9ff., 'And God said to Abraham, "As for you, you shall keep my covenant, you and your decendants after you throughout their generations. This is my covenant, which you shall keep, between me and you and your descendants after you: Every male among you shall be circumcised...and it shall be a sign of the covenant between me and you." ' But this is to assert unequivocally that circumcision is a constitutive element in being a son Abraham. Paul's opponents were therefore in a strong position when they appealed to this passage. But if the Old Testament is the common ground of Paul, his opponents, and the Galatian congregations, then his opponents did in fact have an easy task: they had only to point to Gen 17 and to say, 'Thus it is written – in Scripture, which Paul also quotes!'

There is therefore much to be said for the suggestion that it was not Paul who initiated the discussion about Abraham but that he took it up as a pressing question which had been raised by others.[2] One does not have to strain one's imagination to see how the reference to Gen 17 could disturb (ταράσσειν 1.7) the Galatians.[3] Such a reference could be understood as an accusation against Paul at this very point where eternal salvation and what was ultimately decisive were at stake; as if to say, He has deceived us as to the essentials. Jost Eckert rightly draws attention, along with Carl Holsten, to the Galatians' 'interest in eternal bliss'.[4]

Thus Paul does admit that being a son of Abraham is of decisive importance. He specifically does *not* deny that the continuity from Abraham which his opponents asserted is decisive. Nor is there any statement by which he in any way plays down Abraham's importance. But everything depends on what it is that *constitutes* being a son of Abraham. As in all probability his opponents had previously done, Paul also points to Genesis – *not* of course to Gen 17 *but* to Gen 15: he believed the Lord and he reckoned it to him as righteousness (Gen 15.6 = Gal 3.6).[5] From this he *concludes*: 'So (ἄρα) you see that it is "men of faith" who are the real sons of Abraham!' It is scripture, to which indeed his opponents also appealed, which foresaw that God justifies the Gentiles by faith. This scripture announced in advance to Abraham, 'In you shall all the nations be blessed'. And again Paul *concludes*: 'So then (ὥστε), those who are "men of faith" ' – again the stereotyped οἱ ἐκ πίστεως formula – 'are blessed with Abraham who *had faith*, who in fact are blessed "in community with" the believing Abraham.'[6]

Paul's argumentation can therefore be briefly summarised as follows, as a syllogism:

1st premiss: Abraham was justified because of his faith.

2nd premiss: In Abraham all peoples are blessed.

Conclusion: If all the peoples are blessed in Abraham (in the sense of being justified) then this can only be, as in the case of Abraham, because of their faith.

Paul's failure to mention the programmatic passage in Gen 17 is worthy of note inasmuch as the concept of διαθήκη introduced in Gal 3.17 (but understood by Paul in the sense of 'will' or 'testament' and not 'covenant')[7] is treated not only in Gen 15 (where it occurs only once) but also specifically in Gen 17 (in verses 1 to 14 alone it occurs *15 times*). Above all, however, in Gen 17 this treatment occurs, as has already been said, in the context of circumcision. Circumcision is the sign of the διαθήκη between God and Abraham! And between God and Abraham's posterity (ἀνὰ μέσον τοῦ σπερματός σου; Gen 17.10)! Paul does of course interpret the singular, 'thy seed', in arbitrary fashion: thy specific descendant, viz., Christ.[8] Is Paul therefore of the opinion that his argument on the basis of Gen 15.6, with its reference to the faith of Abraham that justifies, is so compelling that he can afford simply to pass over the connection mentioned in Gen 17 between the enduring covenant that embraces God and all Abraham's posterity, and the covenant sign of circumcision?[9]

There is yet a further striking point. The promise given to Abraham in Gen 18.18 (= Gal 3.8) is linked in the section in Gal 3.15ff. with the giving of the Law by Moses, but not, as one might have expected from the situation, with circumcision. This shows clearly that for Paul the *demand for circumcision* acquires relevance immediately *from the standpoint of the Law*, that is, simply, of the demands of the Law. The διαθήκη, i.e., God's will or testament interpreted as promises (ἐπαγγελίαι) is immediately set against the Mosaic *nomos*. The law cannot annul a will made four hundred and thirty years earlier by God. Thus the promises to Abraham acquire temporal and therefore substantive priority over against the *nomos*. It is therefore not Moses but Abraham who has relevance for salvation! This is what Paul is saying to the Galatians, with their ardent interest in salvation.

Once the function of the Mosaic Law has been set forth, in a further stage in the argument in which it is shown to operate in conjunction with the enslaving power of sin (see below); and once in contrast to this the liberating status of being a son of God 'in Christ Jesus' has been emphasised, the statement is then made that – I paraphrase – you are all *one* in Christ Jesus who is the *single* offspring of Abraham. All of you who are now Christ's *are* therefore (ἄρα) (also) this single offspring of Abraham's, who is heir according to the promise

(Gal 3.28f.).[10] In other words, why do you therefore seek to take the circuitous route by way of circumcision and *thus* by way of the Law when it is not in the least necessary, nay more, when it is not in the least possible? Within the framework of *this* particular line of argument[11] the question is now raised *why* the Law cannot justify. (What follows is intended as an initial 'approach', as indicated in the heading to this section. Thus to a great extent it is provisional and suggestive. The decisive points will be treated later.) In 3.9f. those who are 'men of faith' and 'those who rely on the works of the Law' are contrasted. The 'men of faith' are those who as Schlier says 'have their basic way of life in faith and whose *pistis* is the principle by which they live'.[12] They are therefore such as base their self-understanding on faith, in their own existence. The source of their existence is for them faith. In their understanding of themselves they do not see their existence as believers ultimately as conditioned by immanent factors. 'Those who rely on the works of the Law' on the other hand are such as understand their existence in the fulfilment of the requisite total of works of the Law which are to be added up together. The basis of their existence is not constituted by their being rooted in God but rather, as they understand themselves, by the quantity of the individual works (of the Law) they have performed. Their existence is 'on the basis of' (ἐκ) quantity. But since these men of Law regard the works of the Law which are required of them as being capable of fulfilment, they regard as something that is feasible this existence of theirs which has been established on a quantitative basis. *Existence* becomes something which is *at the disposal* of the person existing. Its constituent elements are reduced to things to be done – *facienda* – which are localised in the sphere of immanence and as such are capable of being done – *facibilia* – because the sphere of immanence is the sphere which is at their disposal. Paradoxically, however, these immanent *facibilia* are said to guarantee acquittal in the tribunal of the transcendent God!

The scriptural proof 3.10ff. makes clear Paul's assumption that for those who are dependent on the Law there is a quantitative factor in their self-understanding and indeed that in his eyes this quantitative factor is the essential one and is that which actually delimits or defines their self-understanding. Those 'who depend on the works of the Law' and whose being is therefore an existence made up of individual deeds or achievements are under the curse. That is, they stand under God's radical negation. Not a blessing, but a curse – these are the ancient Old Testament categories according to which already in the old Shechemite liturgy of Deuteronomy 27 in Israel those who are rejected by Yahweh were separated from those accepted by him. But why are those who understand themselves and therefore their being on the basis of their deeds, and who conceive of their being as constituted on the basis of individual works, why are they under the curse? Paul replies precisely by appealing to that old Shechemite liturgy: 'For (γάρ) it is written, "Cursed be every one (ἐπικατάρατος πᾶς) who does not abide by all (πᾶσιν) things written in the book of the Law, to do them" ' (Gal 3.10 = Deut

27.26 LXX). But if the basis for the maxim in 3.10a (all who rely on the works of the Law are under a curse) is Deut 27.26 LXX, the *tacit presupposition* is that there is *no single* person who follows the Law in *all* its prescriptions.[12a] Of course in using Deut 27.26 LXX[13] Paul is expressing something wholly different from what the Hebrew text intended. Translated, this runs: 'Cursed be he who does not fulfil the words of this law, to do them' (concluding the Shechemite dodecalogue). However, the requirements of this dodecalogue are thought of as being altogether capable of achievement. Furthermore it is expected of everyone in Israel that he will act accordingly. If he does not, Yahweh's curse will overtake him! However, as in the LXX text the Greek words πᾶς and πᾶσιν have been introduced, Paul is able to deduce from this version the theologoumenon which is important to him and according to which *each one* is guilty because there is no individual person who has done everything that is commanded in the Law. Thus neither is it astonishing that we nowhere so far as I know find the view based on Deut 27.26 that someone who transgresses the Torah even just in a single point is accursed.[14]

Gal 3.11 should be rendered, 'For it is evident that no one is justified before God by the Law, for (we should supply: it is written) "he who through faith is righteous shall live".'[15] This verse constitutes the proof for the supposition we arrived at when considering verse 10 that the apostle is making the tacit assumption that no one realises the extreme, quantitative ideal demanded by the Law, viz., fulfilment without remainder of *all* the prescriptions of the Law, so that anyone who fails even just in a single point counts as being completely unrighteous.[16] Because nobody matches up to the requirement in question,[17] and therefore because nobody becomes righteous in this way, there must necessarily be another possibility of making a person righteous: not justification through his own acts, but justification through God's action, which is laid hold of in faith. When verse 10 states that 'manifestly' (δῆλον) no one is justified by the Law, this is not to be understood as discernment of a set of circumstances which can be empirically verified. The general sinfulness from which no individual is excluded cannot be recognised on the basis of an analysis of men's actual behaviour.[18] Paul, in fact, bases the idea of δῆλον on the well-known quotation from Habakkuk, i.e., on a scriptural quotation: 'for only he who through faith is righteous shall live.' Consequently he is able later (3.22) to make the theological judgement that 'the scripture has consigned all things (τὰ πάντα = all men, οἱ πάντες) to the power of sin.'

3.12 once again contrasts the *intrinsically* dual, but *in actuality not* dual possibility of existence for the righteous man: either life on the basis of what he does or life on the basis of his faith. In principle a life based on his deeds would be conceivable: according to Lev 18.5 the one who will live (ζήσεται as in Hab 2.4; so that ζήσεται is the *tertium comparationis*) is he who keeps the Law. But in reality this is not the case. However this actual impossibility is deduced from scripture. It can be recognised *only* in faith. In Section 1.4 this idea, to which attention is here drawn for the first time within the framework of an initial approach, will be treated in relation to the principles on which it is based.

In 3.13 we find the final step in this particular line of argument: in order for justification by faith instead of by works to become possible Christ took upon himself the curse which overtakes those who have been unable to exhibit any righteousness on the basis of works. This is again substantiated from scripture: 'Cursed (ἐπικατάρατος as in Deut 27.26!) is every one who hangs on the cross' (Deut 21.23). Thus also in the framework of the argument dealing with Abraham we reach the final conclusion that Christ took upon himself the curse, in order that even the Gentiles might in Christ Jesus participate in the *'blessing which was Abraham's'*.[19]

1.2 A second line of approach:
the Synod on the Gentile Mission. A misunderstanding on Paul's part?

How is it that Paul in his discussion with the Galatians treats the Law as if it were the real point of contention, although it nowhere clearly appears from Galatians that what concerned Paul's opponents in their mission or their polemics against Paul was the Law as such? On Schmithals's view that Paul's opponents were not Judaists but Gnostics, Gal 6.13 even gives proof of their fundamental abandonment of the Law.[20] Let us again try, by way of an answer to this, to see how the argument of the letter hangs together.

Directly after the introduction, Paul reproaches the Galatians for apostatising: 'I am astonished that you are so quickly deserting him (God) who called you in the grace of Christ and turning to a false gospel which however is no Gospel' (1.6) – i.e., away from God and into the sphere of what is godless (ἀπό – εἰς). In connection with this reproach, the apostle provides the autobiographical data which then follow.[21] He who was over-zealous for the traditions of the fathers (and therefore for the Law!) was called by God. God revealed to him his son (in the context of the argument this must mean: the Son *instead of* the Law!) *so that* he might proclaim him (again: *instead of* the Law) to the Gentiles (1.12-16). The Gospel, which is free from the Law, or still more plainly the Gospel of which the content is freedom from the Law (this of course emerges only from the argument of Galatians as a whole), originates with God. He therefore has no need of any human mediation – not even through the Jerusalem authorities. On the contrary it is he who has persuaded them on the basis of his missionary success (2.7-9: ἰδόντες, γνόντες!)[22] that the Gospel essentially implies freedom from the Law.[22a]

The apostasy of the Galatians into legalism is concretely demonstrated in their intention to have themselves circumcised (5.3; 6.13). Paul therefore reports that at the 'Apostolic Council' – which for preference should be called the 'Synod on the Gentile Mission' since on the one hand the subject of the

Gentile mission was the point of dispute which was to be dealt with by the Synod[23] and on the other hand one cannot strictly speak of a council of the apostles – Titus the Greek was not compelled to be circumcised (2.3). But if Titus was not compelled, then he remained free, that is, free from the Law. However, at this Synod there were 'lying brethren' who had 'crept in' illegitimately (παρεισάκτους ψευδαδέλφους, 2.4). They and they alone were those who wanted to 'spy out (κατασκοπῆσαι) our freedom which we have in Christ Jesus' in order to 'bring us into bondage' (καταδουλώσουσιν)....[24] In his argument with his opponents in Galatia Paul is therefore concerned to emphasise that it was not the official members of the Synod nor the Jerusalem authorities (to whom nevertheless these opponents were seemingly appealing!) who had the intention of suppressing freedom. The official Church was not guilty of this. It was people who were wrongly seeking somehow or other to gain a hearing for their quite unauthoritative views, and who did so at the Synod in a manner which was wholly out of order. This was the 'extra-synodal opposition' which as Paul saw it was appealing in reactionary fashion to a past age's doctrine of salvation. Not recognising the signs of the times, they were seeking artificially to keep alive what had once held good prior to the resurrection of Christ, in the 'former aeon', and were trying to do so by suppressing freedom. Paul stresses that he had not yielded even for a moment to these enemies of freedom, 'that the truth of the gospel might remain with you' (i.e., with the Galatians, who are here being addressed![25] 2.5).[26] Paul is thus emphasising that at the Synod on the Gentile Mission what was at stake was circumcision as a requirement of the Law, and in this connection the authorities in Jerusalem had not laid any injunction on Paul and Barnabas (οὐδέν). For Paul, this οὐδέν means 'no legal stipulation'.

However Paul specifically does not say of the Synod that the Law as such was the point at issue. And yet, where Paul mentions circumcision in connection with the Synod, he is of course thinking of it as pars pro toto legis – the part for the whole. For the intention which he is here pursuing is to show that since the Gentile Christian, Titus, was not compelled to be circumcised, Gentile Christians must not be compelled to obey the Law nor to observe it. Titus represents all Gentile Christians,[26a] and circumcision stands for the whole Law. Of course we must be clear here that the danger in which the Galatians stood, or in which Paul saw them, was not that of seeing the Law as a factor in salvation. Initially, in Galatia, only circumcision was involved. But from Paul's standpoint circumcision means a fortiori an obligation to obey the whole Law. But this is what he is trying to make clear to the Galatians, 5.3.[27] Galatians is an attempt to restrain the Galatians from circumcision. Theologically this happens not by his arguing from circumcision as such but from the consequences of circumcision, i.e., from the Torah and enslavement to it. Thus circumcision is rejected in order to reject the Torah.

It is perfectly obvious that in Jerusalem it was difficult to discuss freedom from circumcision without at the same time discussing the Law. At all events, circumcision is mentioned not only in Gen 17, a book attributed to Moses, but also in Lev 12.3, i.e., in the actual Mosaic Law. It can hardly be doubted that the debate at the Synod dealt with circumcision *as* an obligation of the Law, and Paul's reference to Peter's Gentile way of life at Antioch prior to the arrival of 'certain men from James' (2.12) may well allow us to suppose that the food laws of Lev 11 were also discussed, from Paul's standpoint, successfully. Doubtless, *for Paul* the express acceptance at the Synod on the Gentile Mission of freedom for Gentile Christians from the duty to be circumcised and to keep the food laws was a solemn ratification, by all those participating in the Synod, of freedom from the Law as such for the Gentile Christians. But we may perhaps ask whether all the participants really understood the *releasing* of the Gentile Christians from circumcision and the food laws as *freedom* in principle from the Torah.[28] It may very easily be supposed that James and his party and perhaps even Peter too were certainly not of the opinion that when the question of liberation from certain prescriptions of the Torah, albeit very central ones, was raised, the Torah *itself* was under debate. By analogy, say, with the Jewish mission, where not only proselytes in the strict sense of the word were won, but also 'God-fearers' (σεβόμενοι or φοβούμενοι τὸν θεόν),[29] they could regard the uncircumcised Gentile Christians as Christian σεβόμενοι or φοβούμενοι τὸν κύριον ' Ιησοῦν Χριστόν.[30] What was good for the goose was good for the gander: what was right for the Jewish mission should also be acceptable for the Christian mission!

However, Paul, who sees the principles implicit in every question of detail and sees every decision in detail as reflecting a decision in principle,[31] has a different understanding of this (presuming always that the Jerusalem authorities may not have understood the Synod as Paul did): if freedom from circumcision is conceded, this can be understood only as freedom *in principle* from the Torah. (Let us at this stage in our reflections leave aside for the present the question whether, despite freedom from the Torah or elimination of the Torah as a means of salvation, this Torah nevertheless remained the binding standard for moral behaviour. Even if what Schrage[32] says generally of Paul – 'freedom from the Law as a means of salvation is at the same time freedom *for* the Law in respect of its ethical content' – holds good for Romans, we may nevertheless ask whether this differentiation is appropriate to the sense of the argument in Galatians.) Circumcision, at all events, is among the most important requirements of the Law. It is specifically circumcision which implies the obligation to obey the whole Torah. But if the obligation to obey that prescription falls, then so does the stipulation that one is obliged to keep the Law! If there is a dispensation from circumcision, then the Torah itself comes to lack any foundation. And conversely, anyone who nevertheless continues to consider circumcision as binding on him is obliged to keep the whole Law. Thus Paul can positively adjure the Galatians thus: 'I testify again to every man who receives circumcision that he is bound to keep the whole Law' (ὅλον τὸν νόμον ποιῆσαι, Gal 5.3). If Paul, prior to his call to be a missionary to the Gentiles, really had been a member of the strict Pharisaic school of Shammai, we could then easily attribute to him the view that he who speaks of circumcision is at the same time speaking of the whole Law.[33] For the Law is on this view indeed indivisible. Anyone who takes away even just one particular item from it destroys it utterly. But at the Synod not only a little but a great deal indeed, and of a decisive nature, had been taken away from the Law. Thus the former Shammaite Paul could not but deduce that the Law *had* been allowed to fall by his interlocutors. For anyone who breaks out from the edifice of the Torah the very cornerstone of circumcision brings about the collapse of the entire structure. But this is not in any way to say that the Jewish Christians at the Synod, however, would necessarily have accepted such presuppositions as a basis for their own thought. Even for James as a strict observer of the Law [34] it need not be assumed that he was living in the world of Shammaitic reasoning.[35]

Regarding the weight to be given to these reflections we may say that our concern was not to prove that Paul and the Jerusalem authorities were actually at cross purposes in the way indicated. The purpose here was solely to raise the question whether Paul *could* have taken the decisions of the Synod and incorporated them into a different theological framework, and *whether* therefore the picture of the Synod given in Gal 2 *might* not require some correction as a consequence. What is clear is the intention of the argument in Gal 2. It can be summarily presented as follows. At *that* time, i.e., at the Synod on the Gentile Mission, it was agreed with the Jerusalem authorities that circumcision and therefore *eodem actu* obedience to the Torah were not requisite for Gentile Christians. Now however, Jewish Christians are appealing to Jerusalem as the justification for making circumcision and, as a necessary concomitant, the Law binding on Gentile Christians. Thus they, but not Paul, were at odds with the decisions taken by the Jerusalem authorities. It is not Paul who was against Jerusalem, but his opponents, who were seeking to turn the Galatians from the Gospel. Thus the tenor of the letter is that Paul is at one with the acknowledged Jewish Christian authorities. His opponents do indeed reproach him for being in dissent from the Jerusalem authorities although he owes his apostleship to them. But in reality he is at one with them although he does not in fact owe his apostleship to them.[36] This agreement with them does not consist, say, just in a readiness to make concessions towards Gentiles who wish to become Christians. On the contrary, Peter – and then assuredly James too! – shares with Paul the conviction, the *conviction of faith*, no less, that the Law is powerless to justify (Gal 2.16ff.!). Unhappily we have no information whether Peter and James really did share the theological judgement of 2.16 or whether they did not rather desire that the freedom of Gentile Christians from circumcision (and from the Law?) should be understood *only* as a permitted dispensation, i.e., as a concession.

One thing in fact gives cause for reflection: if the Jewish Christian members of the Synod at Jerusalem, including James, had with Paul understood conversion to Christ as *in principle* a turning away from the Law, why did *they* go on practising the Law? Was it *just* out of opportunism lest they should fare as previously the persecuted 'Hellenists' in Jerusalem had fared (Acts 6ff.)? Might it have been only for sociological and ecclesiastical political reasons, and in no sense theological reasons – just to enable them to remain within the fold of Jewish Judaism, which was a necessity of life? But to all appearances it was not pure opportunism, although this perhaps should not wholly be denied. For otherwise Paul would not have had to sustain his struggle at the Synod at all. The fundamental implications of the theological judgement which was in fact formulated in fundamental terms – οὐ δικαιοῦται ἄνθρωπος ἐξ ἔργων νόμου, 2.16, or even ἐξ ἔργων νόμου οὐ δικαιωθήσεται πᾶσα σάρξ (not a single individual!) – will hardly have been advocated in the circles around James and Peter.

But even in the development of Paul's argument there is a further *break* at this point. If indeed Paul evaluates as a fall from grace (5.4) the intention of the Galatians to have themselves circumcised and so, as he saw it, to put themselves under the Law; and if he interprets this as separation from Christ; and if he understands life under the Law as enslavement to the Law; if in brief he assesses existence under the enslaving power of the Law (and therefore of sin!) as having the effect of separating men from Christ (and by implication from the Church), then the question is necessarily raised, why he sees himself as still united, ecclesiastically speaking, with the Jewish Christians who without doubt saw themselves as bound to the Law (in his eyes the enslaving power of the Law!).

In fact, if, according to the theological argument of Galatians, being in Christ Jesus is identical with freedom from the Law, it is truly remarkable that Paul does not deny membership of the Church to James, and that, if he regards freedom from the Law not as a tactical step for the Gentile Mission but as being of the essence of the Christian faith, he does not condemn and scourge as unbelief the faith of the Jewish Christians who were holding fast to the Law. We cannot initially escape noting at this point not merely a lack of balance, but an actual illogicality in his argument and in his attitude.

1.3 The function of the Nomos

In our first approach to the subject it became clear how decisive the quantitative element in Paul's argument is: only total obedience to the Law is obedience to the Law at all. This postulate of the fulfilment of the contents of the Law as a whole means that even if just a single prescription of the Law is transgressed against, the effect is as if the entire Torah had been disregarded, i.e., total loss of righteousness – entirely in the sense of the exclusive alternative 'all or nothing'.

If Paul now suggests that thc Galatians wcrc rcady or at least almost ready to fulfil *some* demands of the Law, then the strict implication is that he means they would not fulfil *other* demands of the Law, for this in fact is the presupposition on which his argument is based, namely that all, and therefore the Galatians too, fail to practise complete observance of the Law. But then we have to ask: *what* demands, according to Paul, are the Galatians capable of conforming to and *what* are they *not* capable of conforming to? To all appearances, in the Galatian congregation *the demand for circumcision* is on the point of being accepted (5.3; 6.13). At all events this is a requirement which can be fulfilled even if it is a highly painful one for those involved. Furthermore, there is a reference to the observation of *cultic times* (4.10). Now it may be, as Schmithals has suggested,[37] that where the Galatians and Paul's opponents are concerned we should not be thinking of requirements of the Mosaic Law, that is, that in Galatia, Gnostic or at least syncretistic Jewish practice was involved; nevertheless Paul's line of argument – and this is what we are concerned with here – still makes it clear that for him cultic observance of sacred times was understood as observance of the Law. Requirements relating to cultic observance of sacred times are however also, like circumcision, perfectly capable of being correctly fulfilled.[38] Dietary laws and the *Levitical laws of purity* are referred to only in regard to Peter's behaviour at Antioch (2.11ff.). It is not possible to say whether such requirements were made in Galatia or whether Paul simply assumed that they were made, but we cannot exclude the possibility that they were. On the contrary, the fact that Paul goes into the *factum Antiochenum* would lead one rather to suppose that the Galatians were also conforming to food and purity regulations. But again if dietary laws were also in force in Galatia misgivings regarding the impossibility of their fulfilment would hardly have been appropriate.

All the requirements just enumerated – circumcision, observance of sanctified times and possibly dietary legislation – belong to the cultic stipulations of the Torah; does Paul therefore mean that while its cultic part can be fulfilled, its moral requirements cannot? And yet, at least in Galatians, this is precisely what Paul does not say – quite apart from the fact that we are importing a distinction into the Mosaic Law here which cannot be found as such in ancient or at least in Jewish thought, where, in fact, there is no clear-cut distinction made at all between the cultic and the moral aspect. We have only to think of Qumran. There observation of the cultic order takes place in the context of the observation of the order of creation. Life in accordance with the Torah is lived out as something that is in accord with the laws of creation and the course of history.[39] Thus so far we can say only that in Galatians Paul asserts the unfulfillability in practice of the Law for man and that he sees love as the fulfilment of the Law (5.14). This will require fuller treatment subsequently. As it would seem that the question of the specific content of the Torah will, at least at this stage of our reflections, lead us no further, let us turn instead to a consideration of the *function* of the *nomos*. Paul asks: τί οὖν ὁ νόμος; Since in what follows he answers this primarily by referring to the function of the Law, let us translate: 'What purpose then does the Law serve?' In 3.19ff. Paul gives two answers to the question of the function of the *nomos*: (1) that the Law provokes transgressions, (2) that the Law enslaves.

(1) τῶν παραβάσεων χάριν προσετέθη is to be translated as a final and not a causal clause: the Law is added (to the promises) and has been given 'for the sake of transgressions' or more pointedly 'to provoke transgressions'.[40] Schlier is right in rejecting the answer of the later Luther or of Calvin that Gal 3.19 expresses the idea that the Law makes transgressions recognisable.[41] The theologoumenon expressed in Romans 3.20, 'knowledge of sin occurs because of the Law, ἐπίγνωσις ἁμαρτίας...', is not to be found *here*! Of course that still leaves the question how provocation to sinful deeds is to be understood. Is it to be taken, as Lipsius put it, as: 'in order to call them forth, in order to give sins (which already existed) the stamp of positive transgressions of the Law'?[42] This in fact would mean only that the true character of the sinful deeds would become clear.

The purpose of the Law is thus to provoke sinful deeds, i.e., transgressions of the Law itself; more precisely, the purpose of the giving of laws – or in personal terms the purpose of the law-giver (or law-givers? see below) – is to make men transgress the Law. But it should be noted that this says nothing about the immanent intention of the Law; according to the latter, of course, its stipulations are meant 'to be carried out', and in this way one is meant 'to live' (Gal 3.12 = Lev 18.5). Accordingly a clear distinction has to be made between the *immanent intention of the Jewish Law* and *the intention of the legislator*.

But this then raises the question of the legislator. *Who* is it who thus intends that humankind should be provoked to sinful deeds through the giving of Law – and this means in the context *all* men and women? The answer given by most commentators is 'God'. Thus, for example, according to Sieffert God intends that sins should come into being in the punishable, moral form of transgressions which merit wrath: 'for evil had to be extremely great, so that grace could surpass it all the more (Rom 5.20).'[43] Of course this has a very cynical note about it: a God who – although he is the Holy One! – puts men in the (literally!) damnable and immoral situation of sinning only so that he can show his divinity through his kindness and unsurpassable grace! This consequence would of course no longer result if not God but the angels were the legislators. In the same verse, indeed, we read: the Law...instituted by angels, διαταγεὶς δι' ἀγγέλων. Now it is practically uncontested that the intention of this pronouncement is to emphasise the inferiority of the Law.[44] There is however debate whether by the phrase δι' ἀγγέλων the direct or indirect origin of the Law is expressed. Most scholars take the angels to be only mediators of the *nomos*, whereas God is its originator and actual promulgator.[45] The preposition διά does indeed initially tell in favour of mediation by angels of the Law given by God. Angelic authorship, however, would lead us to expect διά. With Schlier, we may concede that διά, in accordance with its actual meaning, should be understood here instrumentally,[46] but even Schlier supposes a certain activity of their own by the angels in the act of mediation of the Law. Perhaps, suggests Schlier, Paul saw in the tradition of the mediation of the Law by the angels a hint that this Law was 'really only a rather indirect and *therefore* corrupt divine Law'.[47] But if we take in verse 20 which continues the argument of verse 19, we may go a step further.

The much-debated verse 20 – Sieffert was already talking of more than three hundred explanations and Oepke even of four hundred and thirty![48] – is best understood in my view if we read it in the light of the view that a mediator is by definition the mediator of a plurality: as God is only *one* – and later Paul was to exploit the theologoumenon of the εἷς θεός in a different fashion for the doctrine of justification (Rom 3.30) – he not only needs no mediator, there is rather no question of his being linked with such a personage.[49] As Lietzmann says: 'the μεσίτης is οὐχ ἑνός, ἀλλὰ πολλῶν· ὁ δὲ θεὸς εἷς ἐστιν: consequently ὁ μεσίτης οὐκ ἔστι θεοῦ, ἀλλὰ πολλῶν, i.e., he represents not God but a plurality, i.e., according to verse 19, the angels.

Of particular importance is J. A. Ziesler's monograph which appeared in 1972, *The Meaning of Righteousness in Paul: A linguistic and theological enquiry*. He distinguishes between the meaning of δικαιοῦν on the one hand, that the *nomos* is a Law negotiated between the *angels* and Israel and *not* between God and Israel. Thus the *emphasis* lies *plainly on God's lack of involvement in the event of the Law-giving* – at least in some sense. That God did not institute the *nomos* is a constitutive element in Paul's proof. He is concerned with this and this alone when the issue is the purpose of the giving of the Law. But this suggests that the view Paul held was that the angels were not only the mediators but also the authors of the Law[50] – and this as we have said is linguistically entirely possible, as διά and ὑπό can be used interchangeably.

However, if the angels are the authors of the Law and if it is their intention to provoke men – and in the context of the argument we must assume that that means all men – to transgress the stipulations of the Law, then the direction of the argument would indicate that this intention is not identical with God's intention. In other words, the angels are now to be understood as demonic beings who in contrast to God do not desire the salvation of mankind. Moses is their 'functionary' (Klein[51]) and this means too that Paul's explanation of the purpose of the Law no longer gives the disastrous impression of being a cynical comment on God.

However, it may be asked whether this interpretation is not radically put in doubt by the temporal clause in Gal 3.19: 'until the offspring comes to whom the promise was made', for this subordinate clause depends on the statement that 'the Law was added because of sin'. Must not the main clause and the subordinate clause be understood as a unit as far as their content is concerned: the Law was added *for the sake of transgressions until* the offspring appears? Is the temporal limit here not also a component of the final statement which is expressed in the main clause, i.e., of the intention of the Law-giving which is expressed there? But of course it is God's intention that is qualified by the temporal clause. But in that case we must ask further whether it is permissible to discern in the main clause a reference to something other than God's intention.

This objection is certainly of sizeable import and so must be taken very seriously. It is however not compelling. Let us look first at the possible senses. It is certainly *possible* that there is an almost seamless transition from a pronouncement on the intention of the angels to a statement about God's intention. At all events we must reckon with the possibility that in certain matters there can be a lack of clarity in Paul's presentation – a lack of definition which also finds expression linguistically and syntactically. Interpretation in such a case means sounding out in relation to each other, within the structure of the clause or sentence, the individual non-overlapping intentions of the various subjects. The danger in such a process is manifest; over-definition can lead to over-interpretation. Since however Paul, as is well known, does at times overload what he says as to content, and as we sometimes find in his statements *an accumulation of perspectives*, we must in this concrete instance allow for various intentions finding their linguistic expression in abrupt juxtaposition to each other. Of course Paul, in dictating, did not consciously wish to switch from one intention or purpose to another, but *we* may – and must – ask what the presuppositions were behind the formulation of individual components of a sentence in any instance. We are therefore concerned with the conceptual presuppositions which are specific to the author, but of whose full range of conceptual relations he may not be fully aware in the actual process of formulating his material. It is this which accounts for the leaps and breaks in his arguments. But if we are to be the ones responsible for showing what determines what the author says in any given instance we have in some measure realised what Wilhelm Dilthey, taking his lead from Friedrich Schleiermacher, demanded: 'the ultimate aim of the hermeneutical process is to understand the author better than he understood himself.'[52]

If in this sense we bear in mind the possibility of a blurring of Paul's actual intentions in verse 19, there is at least no reason initially for excluding the possibility that while the main clause does indeed articulate the intention of the angels – 'it was added for the sake of transgressions' – the subordinate clause expresses God's intention which he pursues alongside that of the angels: 'until...'. This interpretation is suggested if for no other reason than that the immediately following participial phrase 'ordained by angels', as was shown, indicates God's lack of involvement in the act of the giving of the Law.

The main justification for our line of argument is however the question in verse 21a, which may perhaps be paraphrased as follows: if the Law was added to the promises of God to provoke sinful deeds, does not the angelic Law therefore stand opposed to the divine promises? This question[53] at once becomes comprehensible and indeed even necessary[54] if our exegesis so far is correct. If in fact the intention of the angelic Law is to drive men to sinful deeds and so to disaster, does it not therefore stand opposed to God's saving intention which is expressed in his promises? This is a question which occurs fairly spontaneously to an unbiased reader and which too Paul himself expects. Read in this way Gal 3.19-21a presents a consistent line of thought. A sharply phrased assertion, viz., about the non-divine origin of the Law, simply cries out for the question we actually find in verse 21a. Again we ought here to reckon with the various intentions which are well and truly interwoven with each other. Verse 21a indeed may initially even be re-written thus: is the intention of the Law (more precisely, not the intention which is immanent in the Law, but that of the legislator) opposed to the intention of the promises, or in other terms, is the intention of the angels opposed to God's intention? To this Paul replies – perhaps a little surprisingly in view of the previous explanations – 'Certainly not'. But we can again put this more pointedly: the angels' intention of bringing men to perdition is of course directed in the first instance against God's saving intention, but this intention of the angels which is at cross purposes with God's saving intention is nevertheless taken up into God's intention; even if the *nomos* is in the service of *hamartia*, nevertheless in the last resort *hamartia* and *nomos* are in God's service – even if this is against the will of *hamartia* and of the legislators. The evil intent of the angels is overcome and taken up into God's good intention – in the well known dual sense of the German term *aufgehoben* (= 'cancelled out' and 'lifted up'). If not only transgressions but even the terrifying demonic power of sin are incorporated into God's saving plan (verse 22!) then there should be no real difficulty in regarding the demonic angelic powers in the same way. Gal 3.19ff. is thus a development of what we find in Job: Satan, with his capacity to cause disaster, working in the service of the saving activity of Yahweh![55] After all, Paul does refer to the Book of Job (Rom 11.35; 1 Cor 3.19; Phil 1.19; 1 Th 5.22). Is this perhaps where he gets his interpretative paradigm for the Sinai events, the more so as already in the LXX Deut 33.2 he could read of the presence of the angels on Sinai?[56] However it is all one whether Job inspired his understanding of Sinai or not. At all events Job 1 is a pointer to a Jewish interpretation of demons to which Gal 3.19ff. approximates.

The above-mentioned interweaving of various intentions – intentions which Paul however does not distinguish linguistically with sufficient clarity[57] – also provides the key to the interpretation of the subsequent verses. Firstly, it is striking that in verse 21b Paul, in his reply to the question in 21a, emphasises that there is no rivalry between the Law and the promises.[58] And yet the question in 21a was not about rivalry but about contradiction (κατά). It must then be inferred that in denying the rivalry between the Law and the promises Paul establishes that there is no contradiction between the two: the Law is not aimed at creating righteousness as the promises are, as can be seen from the drift of the legislation! To be sure this answer is a little surprising if we look back to verse 12, at least so long as no distinction is made between the immanent intention of the Law and the intention of the legislator. It is naturally of the essence of the Law as such, that he who does the Law shall live. In this sense Paul quotes Lev 18.5 in verse 12, but the angels certainly did not give the *nomos* with this intention. It is then plain that in verse 21b we are not concerned with the primordial intention of the Law. The implication is clear; it is when the *giving* of the Law is under consideration that we find it said that 'righteousness, or justification, was not from the *nomos*'. The line of the argument then becomes complicated by the fact that in verse 22 there is again a clear reference to *God's* intention: the scripture (γραφή), which as an instrument of the promise is already according to verse 8 an expression of the Divine intent, has concluded all men under the power of *hamartia* so that the promise, i.e., that which is promised, will be conveyed to believers on the basis of faith in Jesus Christ. However, with the affirmation in verse 22, following the negation in verse 21, the intention of the law-giver and the intention of God are suddenly bound together in the train of the argument. The solution that both intentions are identical and that therefore the Law of the angels is in the last resort God's Law is of course barred since, as has clearly been shown, God has been argued out of the actual event of legislating in the course of the proofs offered in verses 19ff. To repeat, Paul is concerned to show that the *nomos*, given through a mediator, comes from the angels; but if God were behind the giving of the Law by the angels what would be the point of verse 20?

Once this is seen, the only possible *conclusion* is that God's good intention consisted in taking up the evil intention of the angels and turning it to the purposes of salvation. When in verse 8 we read that scripture had *fore*seen that the Gentiles would be justified by faith, this can be re-worded to say that it was God who foresaw this and who consequently also foresaw the giving of the Law by the angels and the total dominion of *hamartia*.[59]

Scripture – again according to verse 22 – has 'concluded everything under the power of sin' because it was integrating the evil, destructive intention of the angels into the good, saving intention of God. *Thus Paul's entire argument in Gal 3 can be shown to be without inner contradictions by making use of that threefold distinction: God's intention, the immanent or intrinsic intention of the Law and the intention of the Law-givers.* The basis for this interpretation of course remains *a fortiori* our exposition of 3.19ff. It will however appear in the further course of this investigation that this interpretation fits in with other trains of thought in Galatians. Let us, however, first go on to the next verse. Here one function of the *nomos* 'prior to the coming of faith' is mentioned: it is to be the place where we are kept in bondage. This will be discussed in more detail under point 2, but here it is primarily of interest that the same verb συγκλείειν which we came across in verse 22 to describe the activity of scripture is now used in the passive to refer to 'us': we were 'confined' under the *nomos* as those who were 'kept under restraint' (συγκλειόμενοι) with an eye to the coming manifestation of faith. The *nomos*, verse 24 continues, was our tutor (παιδαγωγός), our taskmaster, until the time of Christ '*so that* we might be made righteous by faith'.

But this raises the obvious *question*: does this statement about the Law's purpose mean that God was only too glad to integrate into his plan of salvation the destructive intention of the angelic powers as expressed in the giving of the Law simply because *justification by faith* is of *greater value* than *justification by the Law*, the principle of faith being something more than the principle of 'works'? This is the view one will necessarily arrive at so long as, in the entire argument of Gal 3, one sees only a single intention at work, namely God's. The difficulty of such a view of course lies in the fact that one is compelled not to take entirely seriously the quotation in verse 12 from Lev 18.5 with its 'he will live'; for on a one-dimensional understanding of intention verse 21b with its statement about the incapacity of the Law to ensure life cannot allow the quotation its full force. But would it not be possible to avoid this difficulty by assuming the coexistence and interwovenness of the three intentions? God foresees man's failure in the Law, which, *in itself*, is life-giving. He also foresees the intention of the angels to entice men to destruction through the giving of the Law, and he therefore takes all this into account and creates justification by faith. But then the most important question which was put by Wilfried Joest could be answered for Galatians with a confident affirmative. Joest's question ran: Was Christ, with the justification by faith which he brought, only a 'vicarious emergency solution'? If this is taken much in the sense of the doctrine of the *tertius usus legis* as developed by Joachim Mörlin (d. 1571) then we should have to answer with a simple affirmative.[60] Obviously such an answer is productive of considerable theological discomfiture and it is true that we cannot let the matter rest there. The problem of the relationship of justification by faith and justification by the Law – of faith and action – will therefore have to be brought up again in the course of this investigation, but here in anticipation we may say only this much: the theology of Galatians is not as single-tracked as the pronouncement that Christ is only a vicarious emergency solution suggests. Our assessment will have to allow for more differentiation on this point if we are not to express ourselves misleadingly by means of this half-truth. However, to prevent any misunderstanding arising out of these reservations, what we are adhering to is the exegesis of 3.19ff. given above: the *nomos* is the product of demonic angelic powers.

However, a further objection to this view may be expected. Given that the Law was promulgated by demonic angelic powers in order to drive man to perdition, may this not mean that the stipulations of this Law are themselves bad? And would this not further imply that transgressions of these angelic stipulations are in fact in accordance with God's will, and that such a transgression is therefore not a sinful act – so that transgression, παράβασις, would not be a symptom of being under sin?

But this line of argument is not compelling, for to Paul's way of thinking the angels must have known that men come to grief on the Law (even) if this contains God's commands, which are good. The angels were able to put men in the position of being transgressors of the divine will just because they proclaimed God's holy commandments. This admittedly leaves an unanswered question: what would have happened if not the angels, but God himself, had proclaimed his commandments? Would not men then also have got into this unsalutary situation? It would seem that when Paul composed Galatians he had not yet taken cognisance of this problem. At that time it would indeed certainly have been of no consequence for him; for his thinking started from the fact of the angelic Law and not from reflections on 'what would have happened if...?'

Of course the question remains open how far the angels could count on *all* men coming to grief on the Law. Were the angels aware of the general weakness of men? Did Paul have the story of Paradise and creation in mind when he attributed to the angels knowledge of the future failure of all men? Did the law-giving angels in his view continue that work of temptation which they had previously begun in Paradise?[61] Had they seen that even before the proclamation of the Law on Sinai *all* the thoughts and endeavours of the human heart were only evil (Gen 6.5) and that even the great Flood had changed nothing in this respect (Gen 8.21)? Doubtless these questions are only of speculative force, yet they should be expressed even if they cannot be built into a strict proof.

The question whether the angels could count on the 'success' of their legislation because they were aware of the general weakness of all humanity is linked to the fundamental question whether the failure of all humanity to comply with the Law was only a contingent event which could have been otherwise or whether it was a necessary process because it was rooted in the nature of humanity. I do no more than raise this question here. It will be of fundamental importance in the further course of this investigation – together with the question whether Christ is to be understood according to Galatians as a merely vicarious emergency solution.

It must be clear that Paul's whole argument about the purpose of the Law sounds blasphemous to Jewish ears, that it must inevitably have had a shocking effect on Jews and not merely on the Pharisaic element among them. To suppose for one moment that the Law was intended to provoke sins! By contrast in Ab 1.1 we read: 'make a hedge around the Torah!' Like this demand, the Pharisaic view tended towards further specifying the stipulations of the Torah for the very purpose of ensuring that no transgression of it should take place.[62] Moreover to Jewish ears it was offensive to suggest that the Torah should merely have been '*added* to' ($\pi\rho o\sigma\varepsilon\tau\acute{\varepsilon}\theta\eta$) the promises. This must have had a particularly offensive note about it if as may be supposed there was already in the first century A.D. a belief in the pre-existence of the Torah.[63] But according to Galatians, the Torah is not only later than the promises of God given to Abraham but has also reached its temporal terminus with the coming of the Messiah. The *terminus a quo* and *terminus ad quem* are known. The period of the Law has thus expired; it does not last to all eternity, as Jewish belief held to be certain.[64]

(2) The *nomos* has the function of serving as the sphere of enslavement for man.[65] Man's existence before Christ is a state of *'being under the Law'*. This is expanded in connection with the argument in 3.22ff. to embrace the general state of enslavement which characterises existence in unbelief. He who does not believe can exist in no other way than as someone who is under enslaving powers. Outside the sphere of faith, there is only the domain of oppression. Paul's intention in 3.22ff. focuses precisely on making the Galatians aware of this enslaving dependence to which they wish to commit themselves.

The state of subordination is expressed in many ways: as subordination to sin, ὑπὸ ἁμαρτίαν, 3.22; to the Law, ὑπὸ νόμον, 3.23, 4.4,5; to the 'taskmaster', ὑπὸ παιδαγωγόν, 3.25; to educators and stewards, ὑπὸ ἐπιτρόπους καὶ οἰκονόμους, 4.2; to the elements of the world, ὑπὸ τὰ στοιχεῖα τοῦ κόσμου, 4.3. Here it is noticeable that with these expressions both Jews and Gentiles are in mind. To start with, the multiple proof from scripture in 3.6-18 had been related not only to the Jews to whom the Law was given.[66] In 3.22 we read that scripture had concluded all mankind, τὰ πάντα, under the power of sin. But when we then hear in 3.23 that it was the Law under which 'we' were 'confined' and 'kept under restraint' it is again not only the Jews who are in mind. The parallel between verse 22 and verse 23 is too close to permit of any differentiation: all mankind under sin – the Jews under the Law.[67] But in this way expression is given to the idea that the enslaving power under which Jews and Gentiles stood was in essence the same. There is an erosion here of the distinction between being a Jew and being a Gentile to an extent which would be insupportable for a Jew.[68] Here there is no assertion – as there is in Rom 9.4 – that sonship (cf. Gal 3.26; 4.5), promises and (!) the giving of the Law belong properly to the brethren, i.e., to the Israelites! To be under the Law in the context of the argument in Galatians means being under the hated taskmaster.[69] But now faith has 'come'. As a result 'you are all sons of God' (3.26) and thus are no longer under educators and stewards (4.2), that is no longer minors. Paul again includes himself along with the formerly Gentile Galatians when he writes: 'so we also (οὕτως καὶ ἡμεῖς) were enslaved under the elements of the world (τὰ στοιχεῖα τοῦ κόσμου) when we were still minors' (4.3). A demonic and pagan character of power may be attributed to the elements of the world – despite Delling[70], [71]. For our purposes it is of no great consequence whether the term στοιχεῖα τοῦ κόσμου should, with Dibelius[72], Schlier[73], and others, be related to astral deities or, with Schweizer, to the quasi-divine character of power attaching to the four elements of the world. What matters is only that here, for the Jews, something monstrous is being said: the function of the Torah is identical with that of the pagan deities. Vielhauer, who does not regard the elements of the world as personal entities, even though they were divinely honoured and worshipped,[74] comes to the conclusion: 'he (i.e., Paul) seeks to bring the Gentile and Jewish worlds under the same conceptual denominator by means of this term (i.e., "elements of the world")'.[75] This does not mean that the judgement in verse 23 has been transcended here; for in verse 23 the function of the *nomos* was already equated with that of the most fearsome and cruel power in history, i.e., sin.

Why does Paul place so much emphasis on the function of the Law as the location of enslavement? He does it because for him everything depends on emphasising the freedom which the Galatians have already acquired. You *are* free because you are the sons of God, you *are* free because you believe. This is the concern which he passionately propounds: do not lose your freedom, do not gamble it away, do not let yourselves be enslaved again. Once you served, as slaves, those who are not gods by nature (4.8): why do you want to turn again to the weak and beggarly elements of the world and obey them as slaves (4.9)? Thus he who has faith *is* free but he who lives on the basis of the Law is a slave to the demons (who do exist for Paul! – see 1 Cor 10.20). The *existence of the believer* is *not a state of subordination*. The nerve of his argument lies here. Hence also the proof from scripture (4.21-31), which would not convince any Jew but according to which only the believing Christian is a son of Sarah the freewoman and the Jews are sons of the bondwoman Hagar.[76] They, the Jews, are not the sons of Isaac but the sons of Ishmael and so everything leads up to the great cry, 'Christ has freed you for freedom', from which follows the summons, 'so stand fast...and do not submit again to a yoke of slavery' (5.1).

However, does not Gal 5.13f. relativise what has just been said? Does this passage not correct the view we have so far put forward? Let us postpone exegesis of this passage for a moment and go more deeply into these last few points we have made.

Attention has already been drawn to the Galatians' 'interest in eternal bliss'. They saw themselves as people who were dependent on redemption. This interest must therefore be presupposed if we are to understand why Paul's preaching told and why even his opponents made at least an impression with what they had to say. Perhaps in 1.4, which we may paraphrase as 'Christ has torn us out of this present evil world', there is a suggestion of that motif which had once made the Pauline missionary preaching in Galatia a success, for people who understood their existence as existence in a world that had nothing out of joint would not have been susceptible to the Pauline proclamation. Paul therefore reminds the Galatians that prior to their conversion to Christ they had experienced the dominion of the weak elements of the world. They had themselves experienced the fact that so long as one submits to them they can really dominate and subject men. Even if we do not know precisely what worship of the 'elements' in Galatia was like, it may be supposed that the success of the Pauline missionary preaching was foremost connected with the fact that one could appeal to *the Galatians' fear of the elements of the world*, that in fact they were responsive to the notion, and that they understood the proclamation of Christ as liberation from fear of the elements of the world.[77] If conversion was for Paul a turning away from the Law towards Christ, for the Galatians it was a turning away from the elements of the world to Christ. Thus in both cases the same *conversio* involved a different *aversio* (which however, as has been shown, was interpreted by Paul as being of the same kind). So in designating the actual or supposed turning of the Galatians towards the Law a falling again under the dominion of the world, Paul is hoping to be able to get at them where in fact he had previously already been able to do so. But, if he was aware of the Galatians' old fear of the world-elements, he likewise knew how they had understood their life at that time as in fact a slave's existence in relation to these powers. Thus he appeals to the Galatians' self-understanding. His reproach implies the question, Is your existence again to be determined by fear?

Now it is perfectly clear that the Galatians certainly did not want this. What they wanted was to *make* their freedom from those one-time powers the more *sure*. But ensuring it by means of outward signs and external practices, and by trust in visible entities, is precisely what Paul regards as the essence of unbelief. They are living again on the basis of the works of the Law – on what one establishes in terms of quantitatively determinable deeds – with a magical intention of making the grace of God tangible. Faith is therefore no longer faith. Trust in God's deed in Christ Jesus is replaced by trust in what can be outwardly performed.

Thus the Galatians are seeking to dispel their fear of demonic powers by of all things betraying their freedom, which they do not understand *as* freedom; in other words, the Galatians have not understood their 'interest in eternal bliss' as an *interest in freedom*. Despite their former painful experience of lack of freedom, it has not dawned on them what freedom really is. With their false interest in security they seek by external practices to assure themselves of the grace of God as if it were at their disposal, which in fact it is not. Consequently they lose grace and freedom; in fact they lose grace *as* freedom. Paul, therefore, finds himself confronted with the task of explaining to them that they are 'blessed' if they are free and do not need to assure themselves of their grace, for the free man – and they *are* free – is the man who lives in God's grace. There is no question of their having to assure themselves of it. Everything now depends on the Galatians realising that their 'interest in eternal bliss' can be upheld only as an interest in freedom. If they strive for freedom – even, and indeed particularly, for freedom from the Mosaic Law – then everything else will be given. Perhaps the Galatians would have been able to say – perhaps they did say – 'We are indeed seeking freedom from the elements of the world', but Paul would have countered this by saying, 'You have not however as yet appreciated the depths of what constitutes freedom' – to adapt a saying of Anselm of Canterbury: *nondum considerastis, quanti ponderis sit libertas* (cf. *Cur deus homo*, I 21). If you had understood what is involved in freedom, you would have known that if you have faith, the elements of the world *are* weak and beggarly. But if you seek to assure yourselves of your 'freedom' by works

of the Law, then these are your lords and your gods although by nature (φύσει)
they are not so at all (Gal 4.8f.). The elements of the world are just as weak or as
strong as your faith makes them.[78]

1.4 Fulfilment of the 'Whole' Law

Thus far we have argued that the Mosaic Law in Galatians is seen only in
negative terms. It was given to provoke sinful deeds. It derives from the
demonic angelic powers. It serves as a locus for enslavement, whereas
salvation means precisely freedom. So we have the Law in a functional unity
with the pagan 'elements of the world'. This trend of thought in Paul is, to be
sure, anything but flattering to the Law. Anyone reading Galatians up to and
including 5.12, but without having before him the positive statements in
Romans about the Law, would be unlikely on his own to imagine that the same
author would also write 'the Law is holy and the commandment is holy, just
and good' (Rom 7.12). Of course, if we may again repeat ourselves, we do in
fact read Galatians to a great extent in the light of Romans – with harmonising presuppositions. Thus, precisely because of his familiarity with Romans,
the evangelical theologian when reading Galatians does not even begin to
make the attempt to set on one side everything he has appropriated from that
letter.

But even within the letter does not Gal 5.14 militate against the
understanding of the *nomos* in Galatians which we have elaborated? There we
read that the whole Law is fulfilled in the single saying, 'Thou shalt love thy
neighbour as thyself'; in other words, if you fulfil just the commandment to
love which is written in Lev 19.18 you will have fulfilled the whole Law! But
does Paul really use the expression ὁ πᾶς νόμος in the same sense here in which
he previously used the term *nomos*? The widely held view that the whole of the
Mosaic Law is fulfilled by just complying with the command to love one's
neighbour really produces *a dilemma*. For this view – which we may designate
that of *implication*, since according to it the one command implies the whole
Mosaic Law – is itself not free from ambiguity. Rather it is open to two possible
modes of interpretation, both of which give rise to a dilemma: one must either
interpret it in the sense that the whole Torah, in all its individual commandments, participates in the command to love – in which case we ask ourselves
why commands that are part and parcel of the command to love are no longer
to be obeyed (circumcision, food laws, purity laws) – or else one must say that
the Torah as a whole is in its purport so directed towards the commandment to
love contained in it, that all its other stipulations become superfluous as to
content, i.e., we have a radical reduction in content.[79] In both cases there is a
failure to take seriously the fact that Paul speaks of the *whole nomos*. The

dilemma becomes clearest when we consider that Paul at one point orders the Galatians to refrain from circumcision: for else, according to him, one has to keep the whole Law, ὅλον τὸν νόμον ποιῆσαι (5.3). But then the upshot of this is that one is *not to obey the whole Law!*[80] However, some eleven lines later, he goes on to declare that it is *incumbent on Christians to fulfil the whole Law* through the commandment to love.[81] It is possible to give some consistent sense to these two utterances only if ὁ πᾶς νόμος in 5.14 does not mean the same as ὅλον τὸν νόμον in 5.3. In the essay mentioned in Note 79 I have already argued that with ὁ πᾶς νόμος we have to do with a critical and ironical use of language by Paul. The attributive position of πᾶς does indeed emphasise the totality of the Law as contrasted with the individual pronouncements of the Law.[82] Thus the attributive πᾶς requires a contrasting plural if it is to be meaningfully used. But this effect is lost in Gal 5.14: for the totality consisting of *many* sayings consists in the one single saying![83] Or rather, by means of the linguistic strangeness of using πᾶς in a seemingly meaningless way – that is, by means of this paradox – Paul succeeds in reducing to absurdity the Jewish ideal of keeping the whole Law. By exploiting the linguistic nuance of ὁ πᾶς νόμος as against ὅλος ὁ νόμος Paul is linguistically hitting below the belt in his fight against the Jewish understanding of the Law, or at all events against that understanding of the Law which he presupposes to be the Jewish understanding. (Here we cannot go into the historical question of the extent to which he in fact thereby did justice to the Judaism of the time.) This stylistic nuance is virtually untranslatable in English or German – we would have to put the word 'whole' in quotation marks or speak of the 'so-called' whole Law. It is well enough known that Paul was a master of the Greek language.[84] *Thus the whole Law of Moses simply is not identical with the Law 'as a whole'* which holds good for Christians.[85] When expositors of Gal 5.14 repeatedly speak of a reduction in content of the Mosaic Law, they do so with complete justification in so far as a stipulation of the Torah is quoted, viz., Lev 19.18; but reduction means conscious abrogation of essential elements of the content of the Torah so that we can speak of the 'whole' Law only in the critical and ironical way just described. There can certainly be no question of Paul having intended this in Hillel's sense, according to which the whole Law finds its pregnant expression in a central commandment while everything else is only its exposition (Shab 31a). This idea does not make its first appearance until Rom 13.8-10; which is not to say that Paul there took it over from his pre-Christian period as an allegedly former Hillelite, for if there is one unimaginable notion it is that Paul was a Hillelite before his conversion! Are we to believe that the man who totally rejected his Jewish understanding of the Law (Phil 3.7ff.) would have championed the fundamental approach of his Pharisaic teacher in reference to the Torah?[86]

We must now go more deeply into what has already been briefly outlined in the essay mentioned in Note 82 and in Section 1.1 of the present study. We suggested there that Paul rejects any quantitative reflection in relation to

human existence when he advocates a new ethos by contrast with that
demanded in Deut 27.26 (= Gal 3.10). Let us therefore start by offering more
exact exegesis of the section in Gal 3.10-13 than was made in the initial
approach to the problem of the Law in 1.1. We recall that there all are under
the curse because none has complied with the primarily quantitative demand
of the Law that all – really without exception all—its stipulations be followed
out, so that whoever transgresses against even a single one of these stipulations is accursed. Now, Schlier says that the curse manifestly attaches for Paul
to the action itself in so far as it is related to the works of the Law.[87] He
therefore sees in the quotation of Deut 27.26 an emphasis on the ποιῆσαι and
rejects the current view, which we also support, that Paul was tacitly presupposing that no one wholly fulfils the Law in a quantitative sense.[88] He
concludes that the curse 'is not there only because of the non-fulfilment of the
Law in its entirety in a quantitative fashion, but already because the Law
simply must be "done"....'[89] Of course he does also admit that 'the inner reason
for this state of affairs is not made clear here but can be read off from Rom
7.7ff.'[90] Now our methodological principle is of course precisely that Romans
should not be brought in to interpret Galatians. Nevertheless Schlier's thesis,
that Paul was concerned simply with the necessary interdependence of curse
and deed, must be investigated to see whether it can be justified even if, against
Schlier, we are persuaded by the evidential force of the view that Paul was
tacitly presupposing in Gal 3.10 a general breakdown in the legal principle of
Deut 27.26. For even in the argument in Gal 3 there are individual elements
which might support Schlier's thesis.

It has already been pointed out[91] that Paul appeals to scripture to support
his theological judgement that manifestly no one can be justified before God
by the Law.[92] It is scripture that promises that he who is justified by faith will
live. We can be certain that the Habakkuk quotation is to be understood as a
quotation from scripture[93] because of its substantive link with the
pronouncement on scripture in verse 8 taken together with verse 6. Hab 2.4
cannot be separated from Gen 15.6 and Gen 18.18 in the context of Paul's
argument. Scripture, i.e., God, decrees that justification occurs on the basis of
faith. Even more precisely, justification occurs only on the basis of faith and so
not on the basis of action, 'doing'. God's assent to the principle of δίκαιος ἐκ
πίστεως, it appears, implies his rejection of the principle of δίκαιος ἐκ
ποιήσεως. The nomos is demonstrably not 'of faith', for it itself says: 'he who
does these things (i.e., all the stipulations of the nomos) will live through them'
(Lev 18.5 = Gal 3.12). In fact it appears as if this pronouncement of the nomos
about itself – 'he who does me will live through me' – is then shown to be false
by the authoritative pronouncement of scripture and thus by God's authority
itself. Does this mean, then, that a scriptural quotation is opposed to
quotation from the Law – where the scriptural quotation is thus seen as the
expression of Divine truth and the quotation from the Law as the expression of
falsehood and deception, running counter to God? If from this contrast

between the two quotations, with their promise of life motivated in each case in opposite ways, we look back to the quotation from Deut 27.26 in verse 10, we can appreciate the attractiveness of Schlier's thesis that the curse attaches to the deed as such.

Yet however compelling the argument may at first sight appear, it is not conclusive. For in this attempt to interpret the passage, one thing has been overlooked: the curse pronounced by the Law in Deut 27.26 is completely effective, and it is completely effective precisely because it is *God's* curse, though of course pronounced by the Law![94] So effective is it, that God himself then appears on the scene and makes it ineffective for man by the death of his Messiah on the cross, the Christ of God subjecting himself in this to a further stipulation of the curse of this Law (Deut 21.23 = Gal 3.13).[95] Thus it will be necessary to speak not just of the authority of scripture and thus of God's authority in the course of the argument of Gal 3 but also in exactly the same sense of the authority of the Law. But if this is so and if the pronouncements of the *nomos* in regard to Deut 27.26 and Deut 21.23 are so effective, because of the power of the Law, that (to overstate the point somewhat) even God's plan for salvation cannot circumvent them but is indeed bound to them, then neither is it possible to see the promise of life in the *nomos* at Lev 18.5 as falsehood and deception. *If the Law says* that he who fulfils all its stipulations will *live* then *this pronouncement is also true* (as an expression of the immanent intention of the Law!). He who does everything, but of course everything without remainder, will live, and will live in exactly the way the man justified by faith will live![96]

If this too is true, then it obviously raises the question how the Habakkuk quotation could be brought into the argument by Paul at all as evidence of the negation of the promise of life given by the *nomos*. For the interpretation of verses 11ff. made it clear that God's will is justification on the basis of faith and only on the basis of faith. For this reason – and thus not on the basis of an empirically assessed discernment – it is 'manifest' (δῆλον) that no one is justified by the Law! Accordingly both the following elements seem to have been introduced by Paul into his presentation of the evidence:

(1) *the authority of scripture*, which in the last resort is the *authority of God* himself, puts the Law in the wrong with its justification on the basis of quantitatively complete fulfilment of all the stipulations of the Law;

(2) *the authority of the Law* is so great that it is capable not only of putting all men under the curse and promising real life but in addition of moving God himself to react to the stipulations of the Law.

These two lines of thought intersect in Gal 3 without really being reconciled intellectually. The direction of the argument in the two parts of the proof is simply different in each case. We will therefore hardly be able to say, with Luz, that it possibly escaped Paul that the quotation from Lev 18.5 was just as valid as that from Hab 2.4.[97] What we have rather is two valid life principles set in opposition to each other in such a way as to make it clear that the *nomos*, if indeed its principle is wholly adhered to, does guarantee life fully and completely; but Luz is right to the extent that *Paul's starting point is the faith which now justifies.* [98] From this standpoint certainly the *nomos* principle has lost its validity: so he is talking about a validity *which has been lost.* The intention of bringing life which is inherent in the *nomos* as such (to use once again terms which have earlier proved helpful) is valid where the *nomos* alone is or could be the effective tribunal. God's intention, however, has as its focus justification by faith; but what then is the relationship of the intention inherent in the Law to God's intention looked at in both instances from the standpoint of the life which is to be attained for men? (In Section 1.3, it may be remembered, the relation of the Law-givers' purpose to God's purpose was discussed.) Here again it is apposite to note that the relation of the two intentions is not explicitly dealt with as such by Paul, and thus can be arrived at only by means of inferences on our part. Here our starting-point must be the fact that in the first place the two intentions are contradictory; but we must also start from the fact that Paul's reflections, as Luz has correctly noted, start from the basis of faith which now justifies. The question why he who fulfils the Law in all its parts is *not* to live *now*, is consequently disqualified as being one which has an unreal starting-point. Paul therefore can also produce two divergent items of evidence in his argument because *in the last resort* they are not divergent at all. And this is why they do not contradict each other: *each is valid in a different sphere of existence.* Thus too it is only on a superficial level that we can really say that for Galatians Christ is only a 'vicarious emergency solution' – as Joest formulates the problem (see Section 1.3). If one wanted to see the chronological element as the really supporting structure of Gal 3 and therefore saw the individual parts of the argument as objectivising in this sense, then Christ and justification by faith really would have been devalued into a stopgap, albeit one which was unfortunately necessary. This objectivising of 'salvation history' however is not possible, as Paul speaks of the existence of the believer *on the basis of* the believer's existence, i.e., *only* in the field of justification by faith does justification by faith hold good. This statement can be seen as a tautology only if we overlook the level on which Paul is arguing, i.e., that of faith. On this new level, however, action, 'doing', is not abrogated (see Schlier's view, rejected above); it is *given a new quality.* Here we have to take into account, at the same time, everything Paul says after he introduces the notion of the fulfilment of the 'whole' Law by love of one's neighbour: anyone who is 'driven' by the *pneuma* no longer stands under the *nomos* as an enslaving power (in 5.17 *nomos* again means the Torah and so is not identical with ὁ πᾶς νόμος in 5.14!) with its quantitative claims. Even before 5.14 it is said that in the person who lives by faith, this faith of his takes effect as love; for faith is the energy of love (5.6: πίστις δι᾽ ἀγάπης ἐνεργουμένη). Did Paul perhaps consciously choose the expression ἐν-εργ-ουμένη to contrast it with the ἔργα νόμου? We do not know, but neither should we exclude it as impossible: the 'whole' *nomos* as the energy of faith contrasted with the whole *nomos* with its quantitatively defined works. This energy is the fruit of the *pneuma*, of which the primary and supreme specific is love, ἀγάπη (5.22), and as love amounts to the 'whole' Law, i.e., the one and only Law, other expressions such as joy, peace, etc., are only modes of ἀγάπη (5.22f.).[99] The works of the flesh (5.19ff.) – again we have the term ἔργα: Paul had some understanding in fact of 'linguistics'! – are not done by the person who is driven by the *pneuma*. Paul of course does not mean to say that these works of the flesh are identical with the works of the Law. That should be clear enough from what we have already said. But it should also be clear that the person who does not live on the basis of faith and who consequently is not led by the Spirit is simply not in a position to achieve what is called in 5.22f. the fruits of the Spirit. Thus *it is only at the level of argument involving faith that there is demonstrated the impossibility for those outside the bounds of faith of 'doing' the love which is required by the Law (Lev 19.18)*. It is the carnal man, the man of σάρξ, who is here meant by 'men'. Once we have seen this, it then becomes clear that the non-fulfilment, presupposed in Gal 3.10, of the quantitative requirements of the Law by all men implies their carnal nature. *Quantitative fulfilment is not possible because the Torah contains stipulations which must be 'qualitatively fulfilled.'* After all, even the 'whole' Law, which makes demands on the Christian, is a demand of the Torah. The man presupposed in Gal 3.10 vainly imagines in his flesh, his σάρξ, that he can 'do' the Law and in his illusion loses himself in the quantity he has to produce, and because he does not know that true fulfilment of the Law is possible and real only as a fruit of the Spirit, he deceives himself in seeking to obey a quantitative standard. He understands the fulfilment of this standard as solely *his* work but does not know that his activity, because love is something which belongs to God, can take place only as an outcome of the activity of the Spirit of God in man.

A further brief note on Schoeps's interpretation of Gal 3.10ff.[100] Schoeps sees here the application of the thirteenth hermeneutical rule of Rabbi Ishmael, according to which, when there is a contradiction between two verses of scripture, a third is to be sought which will eliminate the contradiction. Here, Schoeps thinks, a passage in the Torah and a passage in the prophets are at odds with each other, and the resolution of the problem is given by a further passage in the Torah, namely, the sentence in Gen 15.6 which has already been quoted. Against this, Mussner objects that in reality no third passage is quoted to resolve the contradiction so that Rabbi Ishmael's thirteenth *Midda* cannot be involved. Consequently, he conceives Hab 2.4 as the scriptural opposition to the principle of the Law which is given expression in Lev 18.5.[101] But Mussner's argument against Schoeps operates too much on one level only. The dialectics which Paul intends and the seriousness with which he takes Lev 18.5 are thus not given full value. Schoeps is right in that the matter cannot be left as a contradiction, but in Paul's mind there is not as he supposes a conflict between a passage in the Torah and one in the prophets, but between a passage of Torah and one in scripture – understanding 'scripture' here, not as the corpus of the Law, the prophets and the Writings but as the statement of God's promise which finds its written expression in the books of the Old Testament. For Gen 15.16, i.e., a Pentateuchal passage – yet *not* a passage of Torah in the proper sense, but like Hab 2.4 a passage of scripture! – bestows upon the Habakkuk quotation, as has already been shown, the quality of being a statement of scriptural promise, on the basis of its link with Gen 18.18 in verse 8. Hab 2.4 in fact is in substance extremely closely connected with Gen 15.6. Thus if in Gal 3.10ff. Torah and scripture[102] confront each other with their conflicting pronouncements then we have to make this contrast transparent within the framework of those considerations which were outlined in 1.4. We then discover that a mere 'no' to the principle in Lev 18.5 simplifies the theological point in Gal 3.

Notes

1. Jewett, 'The Agitators and the Galatian Congregation', *NTS* 17, 208, attenuates this point when he makes Paul's opponents say in their 'cunningly devised tactic': 'In his (sc., Paul's) work as the representative of the "pillars" to the Gentiles (1.12, 15-19) he simply began a work which we have come to complete (3.3). But in order not to offend you when you were still pagans (1.10), Paul softened some of the harder and more advanced features of the faith.' There is no support in the text for the view that Paul's opponents did make use of this tactic. Recourse to the ἐπιτελεῖσθε in Gal 3.3 (ibid., 207) cannot support such a construction.

2. This is almost universally the opinion: e.g., Burton, *Gal.*, 153-159; Oepke, *Gal.*, 69; Foerster, 'Abfassungszeit und Ziel des Gal' = *Apophoreta*, 139; Luz, *Geschichtsverständnis*, 280, n. 56; Eckert, *Verkündigung*, 75f.; Jewett, 'The Agitators and the Galatian Congregation', *NTS* 17, 200; Mussner, *Gal.*, 221, n. 46, but ibid., 216!; Schlier is uncertain in *Gal.*, 127; as against this, Schmithals, *ThLZ* 98, 749 (Eckert review, *Verkündigung*): 'but the text itself however really only (?) allows an exegesis which sees Gal 3-4 as determined by the tradition, and, by contrast, Gal 5-6 as directed to the then situation.'

3. But if the preachers in Galatia brought the theme of Abraham into play, this too would provide further corroboration for the view that Christian Judaisers as opposed to Christian Gnostics were involved. On this question see n. 36 of Section 2.2 of the present enquiry.

4. Eckert, *Verkündigung*, 100; Holsten, *Das Evangelium des Paulus*, I.1.93.

5. On Gen 15.6 in Paul see F. Hahn, 'Gen 15.6 im Neuen Testament' = *Probleme biblischer Theologie*, 90-107, esp. 97-100; but see also previously von Rad, 'Die Anrechnung des Glaubens zur Gerechtigkeit' = *Ges. Stud.*, 130-135; ibid., 133, E.T.: 'The process of "reckoning" is now transferred to the sphere of a free and wholly personal relationship between God and Abraham'; ibid., 134, E.T. 'On the contrary he says that only faith, which is wholehearted acceptance of Yahweh's promise, brings men into a right relationship – that Yahweh "reckons" it to him.' On this view Paul has not misunderstood Gen 15.6 so very seriously!

6. Mussner, *Gal.*, 222f.

7. On *bᵉrit* in the Old Testament, see Weinfeld, art., *bᵉrit*, *ThWAT* I, 781-808; perhaps even more important Kutsch, art., *bᵉrit*, Verpflichtung, *ThHAT* I, 339-352; and on the

understanding of διαθήκη see also Lang, 'Gesetz und Bund bei Paulus' = *Rechtfertigung*, 305-320, esp. 312ff.

8. Is Paul referring here only to Gen 15 but not to Gen 17? Though this cannot be proved, the argument just presented is in its favour.

9. Cf. Burton, *Gal.*, 159: 'Circumcision, which was the chief point of contention, he does not mention, perhaps because the argument of his opponents on this point *could not be directly answered.*' (My italics.) When further to this pronouncement Burton declares that *instead* of this Paul was discussing the basic question of the nature of the divine demand on men, i.e., faith, he could hardly regard it as avoiding action on Paul's part but as the expression of his mode of argument: everything is seen from the standpoint of *matters of principle*. (Von Rad's explanation of Gen 15.6 – see n. 5 – shows that he is actually right on target here.) It is of course true that 'How he would have dealt with one who admitting this central position should still have asked, "But is not circumcision nevertheless required by God?", these chapters do not show' (ibid., 159). But we have to reckon with Paul's being asked this question, even if not in Galatia, then in other places where note was taken of Galatians! On this see Section 2.1 of this enquiry.

10. On Gal 3.26-28 see also Betz, 'Geist, Freiheit und Gesetz', *ZThK* 71, 78-93 and especially 80-83.

11. Cf. Burton, *Gal.*, 155: 'Here (viz., Gal 3.7) appears for the first time the expression "sons of Abraham", which with its synonym, "seeds of Abraham", is...the centre of the argument in cc. 3 and 4.'

12. Schlier, *Gal.*, 128.

12a. Thus e.g., Lietzmann, *Gal.*, 19; Schoeps, *Paulus*, 183f. (E.T. 176f.); Oepke, *Gal.*, 72; Burton, *Gal.*, 164; Eckert, *Verkündigung*, 77; Hübner, 'Herkunft des Paulus', *KuD* 19, 215; Mussner, *Gal.*, 226 (though there appealing to Rom!); for a different view, Schlier, *Gal.*, 132ff.; Herold, *Zorn*, 176f. (over-interpreting).

13. The Pauline quotation shows only slight differences from the LXX and these are of no import for our argument.

14. Noth, in 'Die mit des Gesetzes Werken umgehen...' = *Ges. Stud.*, 156, draws attention to the fact that Paul, as well as adding πᾶς and πᾶσιν, has also altered the LXX text (he has 'book of the law' instead of 'this Torah'). Of more importance than this point is his view that even according to Deut 'transgression of the law – *even though it be in only one particular* – implies a forsaking of covenant-loyalty, and consequently covenant-breaking and defection' (ibid., 167f., E.T. 128 – my italics). Further: 'What we could conclude about *Deut* XXVIII from the historical situation at the time of composition – that the curse was not merely a possibility but an actual reality – is given direct expression in *Lev* XXVI' (ibid., 170, E.T. 130). The conclusion of the essay is that 'On the basis of this Law there is only the possibility for man having his own independent activity: that is transgression, defection, followed by curse and judgement. And so, indeed, "All those who rely on the works of the law are under a curse" ' (ibid., 171, E.T. 131). This approximation of the intentionality of the Torah to Gal 3.10 does not seem to me to be entirely unobjectionable. To be sure there are statements in Deut according to which individual transgressions of the Law do involve the curse (Noth refers among other passages to Deut 13.6; ibid., 167, n. 35, E.T. 128, n. 35). But is this really the same idea as the presupposition behind Gal 3.10, that *all* are under the curse because *nobody* fulfils the law *in every detail*? In Noth there are two overlapping statements: (1) the curse for the *individual* who has transgressed even a single stipulation of the Law, and (2) the curse which has befallen Israel as a whole at a historic moment. Noth's essay does not arrive at any real reconciliation of these two points.

15. The phrase ἐκ πίστεως qualifies the term ὁ δίκαιος and so is not to be taken with ζήσεται, cf. Lipsius, *Gal*, 32; Schweitzer, *Mystik*, 204 (E.T. 208); Nygren, *Röm*, 69 (referrring admittedly to Rom 1.17); Hahn, 'Gen 15.6 im Neuen Testament' = *Probleme biblischer*

Theologie, 98, n. 41. To different effect we have Mussner, *Gal*, 227, n. 71: 'But then the article ὁ would have to be repeated after the subject...'; cf. previously Michel, *Röm*, 47, to similar effect: 'If he wished to cut through Old Testament tradition, he would have had to rearrange the sentence: ὁ δὲ ἐκ πίστεως δίκαιος ζήσεται.' But is it possible to give so much weight to these stylistic arguments – quite apart from the fact that an Old Testament quotation is involved? Ellis, *Use*, 118 writes polemically against Nygren: 'But not only the grammar is against Nygren; for Paul there is no "law-righteousness" or "work-righteousness".' The progress of our enquiry will show that specifically this argument of Ellis is unconvincing.

16. On the origin of this view see Hübner, 'Herkunft des Paulus', *KuD* 19, 215-231: the interpretation of Deut 27.26 in Gal 3.10 can be most easily traced historically if we assume that Paul carried on his missionary activities along the lines of the School of Shammai. This of course can be said merely as a conjecture, but if we do not share this view, then it becomes hard to understand Paul's exegesis in the light of his once having been a Pharisee. This much at least seems certain to me: J. Jeremias's view in 'Paulus als Hillelit' = *Neotestamentica et Semitica*, 88-94, to the effect that Paul came from the School of Hillel, is in my opinion untenable. According to Shab. 31a Hillel regarded the negative form of the 'Golden Rule' as the Torah *in nuce*. According to J. Jeremias the theologoumenon produced by Paul in Gal 5.14 is Hillelite. (But see in this present work pp. 36f. It is only when we come to Rom 13.8-10 that Paul argues in Hillelite fashion.) But would Paul – despite Phil 3.7f. – have continued to think as the Hillelite he allegedly once was at such a central point in the understanding of the Torah? To my mind the question already implies a negative answer. For the rest, I would repeat what I have said already in *KuD* 21, 252, n. 45 as a supplement to the essay mentioned first: I am not absolutely concerned to show that Paul was a Shammaite, but rather that he was not a Hillelite, i.e., that he did not belong to the conciliatory wing of the Pharisees. With J. Maier, *Die Geschichte der jüdischen Religion*, 74f., I assume that the familiar division into the two Schools of Hillel and Shammai merely pinpoints two main tendencies and conceals a picture which is really much more varied. Against J. Jeremias see also Haacker, 'War Paulus Hillelit?' = *Institutum Judaicum Tübingen 1971-1972*, 106-120, and also his 'Die Berufung des Verfolgers und die Rechtfertigung des Gottlosen', *ThBeitr* 6.10.

17. The question will be raised later whether in Paul's sense no one *can* match up to this demand.

18. See Schoeps to different effect in *Paulus*, 184, (E.T. 176): 'the assertion is made as an implication of common experience'.

19. H.-W. Kuhn, 'Jesus als Gekreuzigter', *ZThK* 72,1-46 tries to demonstrate a distinction between the specific statements about the *cross* in the New Testament and the other statements about the *Passion*. At least as regards Paul it cannot be denied that his methodology is heuristically most valuable. To this effect he rightly says of Gal 3.13 that 'from the standpoint of the idea of representation the cross now conversely appears as what deprives the Law of its power' (ibid., 35).

20. Schmithals, 'Die Häretiker in Galatien' = *Paulus und die Gnostiker*, 23, E.T. 39.

21. On the connection between the life of Paul and his theology see Haacker, 'Die Berufung des Verfolgers', *ThBeitr* 6,1-19.

22. See also Eckert, *Verkündigung*, 189 and the authors mentioned there (ibid., 189, n. 5).

22a. But see Gal 2.16bc!

23. To different effect see Suhl, *Briefe*, 57ff.

24. On the discussion of κατασκοπῆσαι see Mussner, *Gal*, 108 and 108, n. 44. Note also the double κατα-: κατασκοπῆσαι and καταδουλώσουσιν.

25. So Mussner, *Gal*, 111 and most other exegetes of Gal.

26. On the παρεισάκτους ψευδαδέλφους see Mussner, *Gal*, 108ff.; ibid., 109, n. 50 against Schmithals, *Paulus und Jakobus*, 89f. (E.T. 107f.), who understands them as referring to Jews, not to Jewish Christians. Mussner considers this to be 'as improbable as one can imagine'.

26a. See also Georgi, *Kollekte*, 16: 'In the person of the uncircumcised Titus, uncircumcised Gentile Christianity had appeared on the scene in Jerusalem.'

27. This is in no way to contest Vielhauer's correct recognition, in 'Gesetzesdienst und Stoicheiadienst im Gal' = *Rechtfertigung*, 545, that we simply cannot deduce from Gal 5.3 that Paul was imparting something new to his readers in the link he makes between Law and circumcision; and that the emphasis is on the ὅλον. To be sure Paul's opponents also made *some* legal demands in connection with circumcision – most probably of a cultic nature.

28. Cf. R. Meyer, art. περιτέμνω, *TWNT* VI.83.11ff. (E.T. *TDNT* VI.83.25ff.): 'Gl.2:7 shows us, of course, that fundamentally freedom from 'Ιουδαισμός was simply noted in Jerusalem; in fact, for all the mutual loyalty, the two fronts remained.'

29. K.G. Kuhn, art. προσήλυτος, *TWNT* VI.731.29ff. (E.T. *TDNT* VI.730.12ff.). Cf. Bornkamm, *Paulus*, 33; Lohse, art. Mission II Jüdische Mission, *RGG*, 3rd ed., IV.972.

30. Wilckens does not go quite so far ('Aus Werken des Gesetzes...' = *Rechtfertigung als Freiheit*, 87; 'Abfassungszweck des Römerbriefs' = ibid., 131) with the supposition that the Galatian agitators but not the Jewish Christian leaders had regarded the Pauline Gentile Christian congregations as 'godfearers' and had now energetically demanded proselyte status; likewise again in 'Christologie und Anthropologie', *ZNW* 67,68.

31. See also Eckert, *Verkündigung*, 24f.; also Bruce, *Paul*, 181: 'Paul's position on the circumcision question was clear-cut because he had thought it through; the Jerusalem leaders had not as yet had any occasion to think it through, and so their position was not so clear-cut.'

32. Schrage, *Die konkreten Einzelgebote*, 238; see also 232.

33. Hübner, 'Herkunft des Paulus', *KuD* 19, 222ff.: Even if Paul was a diaspora Jew by birth and even if as such he was also a 'Septuagintal Jew' (Deissmann, *Paulus*, 71, E.T. 92), nevertheless his attitude to the Jewish mission may not have been in agreement with the liberal position taken among the diaspora Jews. H.-W. Kuhn in 'Jesus als Gekreuzigter', *ZThK* 72, 32, n. 140, referring to K. G. Kuhn/H. Stegemann, art. Proselyten, *PW* Suppl. IX, 1259f., rightly draws attention to the point that Hellenistic diaspora Judaism did not set such a decided value on the full incorporation of Gentiles into Judaism by circumcision (against Kasting, *Die Anfänge der christlichen Mission*, 22ff.). But if Paul – perhaps even as a missionary to the Jews – had originally championed the strict position, i.e., of demanding circumcision as a matter of principle, in the Jewish mission, as a sign of one's obligation to obey the Torah totally, then we might suppose that he owed his formerly so rigorous basic Jewish attitude (Gal 1.14!) not to his being a diaspora Jew, but to his attachment to the strict Pharisaic tendency of the School of Shammai; see n. 16.

34. Despite Munck, *Paulus und die Heilsgeschichte*, 103ff. (E.T. *Paul and the Salvation of Mankind*, 111ff.) James could have been a champion of strict Torah observance. Munck is certainly right in not regarding as 'sources of historical value' the report by Hegesippus on the death of James (Eusebius, *Hist. Eccl.* II.23,4-18). Munck's reason is the legendary nature of this item (ibid., 110, E.T. 117). On the other hand his view depends on the very uncertain equation 'certain men from James' (Gal 2.12) = 'certain Jewish Christians of Jerusalem' (ibid., 94, E.T. 102).

35. This could be the element of truth in Munck's position outlined in the previous note.

36. In my view this is the point at which Schmithals's first argument against Eckert's 'Erneuerung der traditionellen Judaisten-Hypothese' (i.e., 'Revival of the traditional "Judaising" hypothesis') comes unstuck (review of Eckert's book, *Die urchristliche Verkündigung...*, *ThLZ* 98, 747-749): it leaves unexplained why Paul is then so concerned at the start of his letter to demonstrate specifically his independence from those at Jerusalem (ibid., 747). Yet the demonstration becomes meaningful if the reproach against Paul was that *although* he was dependent on the Jerusalem authorities he had taught differently from them! Thus *dependence on Jerusalem was not in itself a matter for reproach*, but it was mentioned as a presupposition *in the framework of conditions relative to a reproach*; cf. Bruce, *Paul*, 180: 'they

(scil., the Galatians) would be told that the authority of Jerusalem was superior to Barnabas and Paul's' – i.e., they were kindly to keep to what Jerusalem said!

37. Against Schmithals cf. among others Wilson, 'Gnostics – in Galatia?', *StEv* IV/1, 358-367; and Vielhauer, 'Gesetzesdienst und Stoicheiadienst im Gal' = *Rechtfertigung*, 552: 'Paul mentions these festival periods...not as an example of superficial and magical practices, but as part of the law'; Drane, *Paul*, passim and particularly 89-94; Schenke, *Einleitung*, 87f.

38. Vielhauer continues the sentence partly quoted in the last note as follows: '...his choice of specifically this "harmless" part introduces – probably deliberately – a discordant element into the remarks in vv. 8-11; their theological weight is derived from his taking it as *pars pro toto*.'

39. Hengel, *Judentum und Hellenismus*, 427ff. (E.T. 217ff.); Limbeck, *Die Ordnung des Heils*, *passim*.

40. Thus among others Lipsius, *Gal*, 37; Schlier, *Gal*, 152; Oepke, *Gal*, 81. Eckert's exposition is too dependent on Romans; cf.Eckert, *Verkündigung*, 82: 'not a function which protects from sin, but one which increases it...(cf. Rom 5.20; 7.7ff.).'

41. Schlier, *Gal*, 152: likewise too earlier Sieffert, *Gal*, 199: to be understood in this way, Paul would have had to write: τῆς ἐπιγνώσεως τῶν παραβάσεων χάριν. However Mussner, *Gal*, 245 again explains the passage in a cognitive sense, but by appealing to Romans! Burton, *Gal*, 188 stands between Sieffert, etc., and Mussner: 'Nor can it be justly said that this interpretation (viz., παράβασις = violation of explicit law) involves the supplying of the phrase "knowledge of"..., but only the discovery in the expression τῶν παραβάσεων of its implicate, τῆς ἐπιγνώσεως τῆς ἁμαρτίας. For the evidence (!) that the latter was in Paul's thought a function of the law...see Rom 3.20 (!)...' So we again have the typical proof from Romans: 'evidence' for an interpretation of Galatians by means of statements in Romans!

42. Lipsius, *Gal*, 37; see also the translation in the *New English Bible*: 'It was added to make wrongdoing a legal offence.' The note gives as an alternative translation, '...added because of offences.'

43. Sieffert, *Gal*, 198.

44. To different effect we have Bring, *Christus und das Gesetz*, 82ff. Cranfield, 'St. Paul and the Law', *SJT* 17,62 tones down the 'depreciatory purpose' – which he regards as probable: '... it is probably simply to suggest a certain (!) superiority of the promise...' He speaks of a 'certain depreciatory flavour'.

45. Thus among others Lipsius, *Gal*, 38; Sieffert, *Gal*, 201; Burton, *Gal*, 189; Mussner, *Gal*, 247; MacGorman, 'Problem Passages in Galatians', *SouthWestJTh* 15, 44.

46. Schlier, *Gal*, 155f.; Oepke, art. διά, *TWNT* II.65.30; ibid. 66.6ff. – but ibid., 66.27! (E.T. II. 66.30; ibid. 67.13 but cf. 67.31); Menge, Langenscheidt's *Großwörterbuch*, 166.

47. Schlier, *Gal*, 157; my italics.

48. Sieffert, *Gal*, 209; Oepke, *Gal*, 82; but see Schlier, *Gal*, 161, n. 2: 'Yet such data rest more on rumours than on careful enquiry.'

49. Cf. among others Lietzmann, *Gal*, 22f.; Schweitzer, *Mystik*, 71 (E.T. 70); Oepke, art. μεσίτης, *TWNT* IV. 622.17ff. (E.T. IV. 618.16ff.); Oepke, *Gal*, 84; Schlier, *Gal*, 161: 'The simplest solution'; Luz, *Geschichtsverständnis*, 190 and 190, n. 204; Eckert, *Verkündigung*,83; Klein, 'Individualgeschichte und Weltgeschichte' = *Rekonstruktion und Interpretation*, 209, n. 105; Mussner, *Gal*, 248f. Otherwise Sieffert, *Gal*, 208: 'By contrast with ἑνός the duality...of the parties to be reconciled has to be considered.... This means that in the historical use of the statement as a contrast to unity we may have in mind only the duality of God and the people of Israel and not the plurality of the people...nor that of the angels...'; similarly Lipsius, *Gal*, 37f.

50. Schweitzer, *Mystik*, 71 (E.T. 70); Schoeps, *Paulus*, 190f. (E.T. 182f.); Bornkamm, 'Die Häresie des Kolosserbriefes' = *Ges. Aufs.* I.148: 'In Gal 3.19f. Paul himself draws on this Gnosis (i.e., "gnosticising Judaism") for the idea that the Law is not the gift and revelation of

a gracious God but comes from the angels and has been mediated by a μεσίτης.' Klein 'Individualgeschichte und Weltgeschichte' = *Rekonstruktion und Interpretation*, 209, n. 105: 'In my view the further reference to the mediator compellingly shows that he (i.e., Moses) nevertheless does not see the angels in our passage merely as a mediating authority. Are we to suppose that Paul was reflecting on *two* acts of "mediation" of the Law?' Klein can therefore speak of Moses as a 'functionary of powers opposed to God'; and he describes the sphere of history committed to Moses as 'frankly demonised'. 'This is *in nuce* Israel's history disqualified' (ibid. 210); Luz, *Geschichtsverständnis*, 190 and 190, n. 204; see also Eckert, *Verkündigung*, 82f. H.-W. Kuhn, too, in 'Jesus als Gekreuzigter', *ZThK* 72, 36, n. 155, seems to defend the view that the Law comes from the angels. I do admittedly find that his related claim that Gal 3.13 has to do with the curse of the Law but not with the curse of God carries little conviction. Oepke in *Gal*, 84 is undecided: 'Thus the Law does not come from God, at least(!) not directly...'; ibid. 98: '...rather (!) do we get in Gal a picture of God's temporarily leaving the field to hostile powers...'; according to Lietzmann, *Gal*, 23, the Law does not stem from *one* personality, i.e., God, and 'therefore' (!) is 'not absolutely' (!) divine. Lietzmann's conclusion remains lacking in definition. His 'therefore' is not meant entirely strictly. Drane, in his extremely noteworthy essay, 'Tradition, Law and Ethics in Pauline Theology', *NovTest* 16 (1976), 167-178, cf. esp. 169, has indicated that the statement in Gal 3.19 about the origin of the Law should, 'in the light of other Pauline passages' be evaluated as an over-reaction due to his opponents' own exaggeration. However, 'if we confine ourselves to Gal' we can hardly reach any other conclusion than that of Schoeps.

51. See n. 50 above.

52. Dilthey, 'Die Entstehung der Hermeneutik' = *Ges. Schriften*, V.331.

53. On the assumption that with Sin, A et al. (as against p⁴⁶, B) we should read τοῦ θεοῦ this argument gains further force: Does the *nomos*, which is expressly not described as the *nomos* of God, stand opposed to the promises, which are explicitly described as the promises of God? Our line of argument is not of course dependent on this variant reading, because in any case the promises are understood by Paul as promises of God but the Law has been disqualified *immediately* beforehand as διαταγεὶς δι' ἀγγέλων.

54. Lietzmann, *Gal*, 23: 'Thus the Law appears in a position of direct contrast to God's intention, so that the question in verse 21 presses itself involuntarily upon us...' However, Lietzmann's view differs from ours in that, as he sees it, it is not the intention of the angels to impede God's promises; see also Oepke, *Gal*, 84f.

55. The theological problems in Job 1 need not concern us here; on this, see Horst, *BK* XVI, on the passage. The only thing of significance here is the history of the subsequent influence of the book of Job.

56. See Schlier, *Gal*, 156f. and the other passages from Jewish exegesis of the Sinai theme given there.

57. Once again: that the intentions merge so far as the language used is concerned is a presupposition or hypothesis of exegesis. It is indeed the starting-point for interpretation, which has the obligation to read between the lines (and in so doing must be aware of the hypothetical element in its exegesis!). Thus it will not be admissible to marshal against the exegesis attempted here the details of the intentions, which Paul does not clearly distinguish from each other – unless the right is disputed of bringing out in sharp definition in one's exegesis ideas of an author which in linguistic terms flow into each other. Any possible objection would need thus to show from the overall trend of the argument in Gal that the drift of argument here 'purported' to be Paul's is inappropriate.

58. Schlier, *Gal*, 163; Mussner, *Gal*, 251.

59. Naturally the question cannot be asked how it could come about at all that God did not prevent *hamartia* and law-giving of this kind. Even the substantially more considered theology of Romans contents itself with the 'actual' appearing of *hamartia* (Rom 5.12). Paul

(and the entire New Testament with him) simply *does not explain* how evil arose. Evil is simply not rationally explicable – and this itself is also a theological pronouncement. An evil which can be explained, i.e., which can be traced back to a *cause*, is no longer evil.

60. Joest, *Gesetz und Freiheit*, 52, 139.

61. See the Jewish interpretations of the snake in Gen 3, e.g., Apocalypse of Moses 16; *VitAd*, 16; on which see Foerster, art. ὄφις, *TWNT* V.577.7ff. (E.T. V.577f., para.2c).

62. Cf. Ab 1.1. Even if the chain of tradition in Ab 1 is a late construction (see on this J. Neusner, *The Rabbinic Traditions about the Pharisees before 70*, 3 Parts, Leiden 1971, *passim*) the expression 'a hedge around the Law' could already have been a fixed *terminus technicus*. As early as Rabbi Aqiba this expression is used to formulate further pronouncements which were based on it: Ab 3.14.

63. On Sir 24 see Wilckens, art. σοφία, *TWNT* VII.504, n. 257 (E.T. VII.503, n. 257); ibid. 509 (E.T. VII.509.2ff.); cf. also Bill. III.256f.; IV/1.435ff.; Davies, *Paul and Rabbinic Judaism*, 170; Hengel, *Judentum und Hellenismus*, 309ff. (E.T. *Judaism and Hellenism*, 168ff.).

64. Davies, *Torah in the Messianic Age, passim*; Bill. I.244f.; Mussner, *Gal*, 246f.; Schäfer, 'Die Torah der messianischen Zeit', *ZNW* 65, 27-42; to different effect Schoeps, *Paulus*, 178ff. (E.T. 171ff.) – but his reference to Nidda 61b is not convincing; see also Hengel, *Judentum und Hellenismus*, 311, n. 411 (E.T. 170, n. 411)! Mussner, *Gal*, 247: 'There are early Jewish items of evidence which even speak of a "new Torah" which the Messiah will bring, but how we are to understand "new" here is controversial.' It is a pity that Mussner has not adopted a specific attitude to this controversy.

65. Mussner, *Gal*, 255: not ὑπὸ νόμου, but ὑπὸ νόμον; thus what is meant is the sphere of dominion.

66. Among others Schlier, *Gal*, 136f.; Klein, 'Individualgeschichte und Weltgeschichte' = *Rekonstruktion und Interpretation*, 206f.

67. Oepke, *Gal*, 85; Schlier, *Gal*, 166; Mussner, *Gal*, 256, n. 61 draws attention to the inclusion of the addressees (i.e., former Gentiles!) in the ἐφρουρούμεθα; Klein, 'Individualgeschichte und Weltgeschichte' = *Rekonstruktion und Interpretation*, 212 and 212 n. 118.

68. If however it is possible to talk of such a levelling out of being a Jew and being a Gentile, i.e., if being under the Law and being under the elements of the world correspond, then it is no longer possible to say with M. Barth, 'Die Einheit des Galater- und Epheserbriefs' (= review of Mussner, *Gal*) in *ThZ* 32 that '...the curse (viz., of Deut 27.26 = Gal 3.10) is a threat only to the Covenant People – and to them only when they break the Covenant and transgress the laws; the giving of the Law and the threat of the curse appertain to the conclusion of the Covenant.' But the theological quality of the curse of Deut 27.26 is explained in the course of the argument in Gal in relation to the misery of Gentile existence! M. Barth misunderstands the drift of Paul's argument.

69. Schlier, *Gal*, 168ff.; Mussner, *Gal*, 256ff., describes the παιδαγωγός too positively, but rightly sees that Paul is not cognisant of an 'educative function' of the Law in the positive sense.

70. Delling, art. στοιχεῖον, *TWNT* VII.685.15: 'that whereon the existence of this world rests' (E.T. VII.684.17); strong sympathy for Delling's view is shown by MacGorman, 'Problem Passages in Galatians', *SouthWestJTh*, 15.487ff., but in the end he leaves the question unresolved. We cannot enter into discussion here with Bandstra, *The Law and the Elements of the World*. I cannot share his view that 'the law and the flesh constitute the fundamental cosmic forces (v. 3, στοιχεῖα τοῦ κόσμου)' (ibid. 67).

71. *Inter alios* Schweizer, 'Die "Elemente der Welt" ' = *Verborum veritas*, 254, 258f.; other literature there.

72. Dibelius, *Die Geisterwelt im Glauben des Paulus*, Excursus III.

73. Schlier, *Gal*, 191ff.

74. Vielhauer, 'Gesetzesdienst und Stoicheiadienst im Gal' = *Rechtfertigung*, 550.

75. Ibid., 553; see also Klein, 'Individualgeschichte und Weltgeschichte' = *Rekonstruktion und Interpretation*, 216: 'In this way the profanisation of Judaism has acquired its radicality.'

76. On Gal 4.21-31 see the commentaries; I cannot here go into the study of this section by Barrett, 'The Allegory of Abraham, Sarah, and Hagar in the Arguments of Galatians' = *Rechtfertigung*, 1-16. On the relation of Gal 4.21ff. to Gal 3.6ff. see Dietzfelbinger, *Heilsgeschichte bei Paulus?*, 14ff.

77. In my view it is improbable that Paul first introduced this idea, as Vielhauer, 'Gesetzesdienst und Stoicheiadienst im Gal' = *Rechtfertigung*, 552f., supposes.

78. See further on the theme of 'freedom' the excellent explanations in Niederwimmer, *Der Begriff der Freiheit im NT*.

79. For more detailed support and reference to individual authors advancing this exegesis, see Hübner, 'Das ganze und das eine Gesetz', *KuD* 21, 240ff., where there are also reflections on the relation between Paul and Stoicism in regard to Gal 5.14. We shall not enter into this complex of questions here.

80. Cf. Bultmann, *Theologie*, 342 (E.T. I. 341): 'Paul's struggle in Galatia against the Law as the way to salvation is simultaneously a struggle against the ritual and cultic rules, particularly against circumcision and the Jewish festivals (Gal 4:10).' Not, therefore, "the whole Law"!

81. πληρῶσαι should be interpreted, with Schlier, *Gal*, 245, as 'has been done'.

82. See Hübner, 'Das ganze und das eine Gesetz', *KuD*, 21, 241, n. 11 for relevant literature, especially Kühner-Gerth, *Grammatik* II/1, 632.

83. Of course it is a saying of the *Torah*! (To different effect Ulonska, *Funktion*, 73, with the formal justification that the Lev 19.18 allusion is not identified as a quotation.) We cannot here discuss further the content of this Torah saying in Lev 19.18. Let the following comment suffice: Paul, stressing immediately beforehand (in v. 13) that freedom is freedom *limited* by the 'other' – and doing so with the emphasis he has previously used in speaking of freedom – shows how he regards the one imperative logos of loving one's neighbour as pertaining to the core of Christian existence. Is freedom, then, not after all Paul's last word? Does he understand the demand which becomes concrete for me *in each encounter* with my neighbour as what I am freed *for*? Does what Greeven has so finely said of the 'neighbour' in the story of the Good Samaritan also hold good for Paul? 'The story of the Good Samaritan shows that one cannot say in advance who the neighbour is but that the course of life will make this plain enough.... One cannot define one's neighbour; one can only be a neighbour.' (Greeven, art. πλησίον, *TWNT* VI.316.4ff., E.T. VI 317.23f.) This we could supplement for Paul by saying '...and it can only be learned afresh on each occasion when one encounters his "neighbour".' However this much at least is certain: for Paul freedom is never something defined by the individual in the sense of subjectivism. *Freedom is constituted by one's encounter with one's neighbour*. However, in misusing freedom as an 'operational basis for the *sarx*' (Gal 5.13) – the *sarx* being in each instance the individual *locus* for *hamartia*, which is 'supra-individual' – we find that *freedom for the sarx* means a new *enslavement by hamartia*. Thus for Paul *agape* is on the side of freedom; paradoxically in Paul's sense, *slavery vis-à-vis one's 'neighbour'* is *freedom from sarx and hamartia*.

84. See the quotation from U. v. Wilamowitz-Moellendorf in Bornkamm, *Paulus*, 33, not reproduced in the English edition but running as follows: 'At last, at long last, somebody is speaking in Greek too about a fresh, inward experience of life.'

85. Maurer, who sees in 5.14 a statement about the Torah (*Gesetzeslehre*, 30), then has to take refuge in the view that the solution to the problem of how the Law could thus have two different sides can only be seen in full clarity in Rom. 'The right answer is there in Gal, but it cannot be straightforwardly found, as on this problem Paul still expresses himself extremely unclearly' (ibid., 31). Maurer has at all events clearly seen where in Gal the decisive question is

asked.

86. Cf. Hübner, 'Herkunft des Paulus', *KuD* 19, 215-231; 'Das ganze und das eine Gesetz', *KuD* 21, 250f.

87. Schlier, *Gal.*, 134.

88. Ibid., 132f.

89. Ibid., 134.

90. Ibid., 134. Ulonska, *Funktion*, 57 also criticises this in Schlier.

91. See p. 22 of this investigation.

92. ἐν νόμῳ is most likely instrumental. But should Lipsius for instance be nevertheless right (*Gal*, 33) in saying that ἐν νόμῳ means 'in the sphere of the Law' that would change little; for the interpretation would then have to be 'in the sphere where the Law holds sway' i.e., where it has the means to hand.

93. To different effect we have Ulonska, *Funktion*, 55, n. 50: 'In contrast to what we find in Rom 1.17 Hab 2.4 is not identified as a quotation; thus we must have in mind the thought that Paul is not concerned about the answer to a text of scripture: contrariwise (!) his emphasis is particularly on the content.' This contrast between text and content fails to convince. In connection with this thesis Ulonska also argues against the notion that behind Gal 3.10 there is the implicit presupposition that no one 'has' the Law entirely (ibid., 50).

94. In my view we have an attenuation or indeed domestication of the idea which is not true to Paul when Burton, *Gal*, 264, says 'The curse of which the verse speaks is not the curse of God, but, as Paul expressly calls it in v. 13, the curse of the law.' Similarly we have in H.-W. Kuhn, 'Jesus als Gekreuzigter', *ZThK* 72, 36, n. 155, the idea that this is supported by the extreme statement that the Law was only given by angels. Kuhn attacks G. Jeremias, *Der Lehrer der Gerechtigkeit*, 133, who supposes that we must attribute ὑπὸ θεοῦ to his reservations about speaking expressly of the curse of God. Now for its part this attribution has nothing to justify it. The rabbinical exegesis of Deut 21.23 which he adduces cannot serve as an expedient.

95. On Gal 3.13 see G. Jeremias, *Der Lehrer der Gerechtigkeit*, 134, on which see Hübner, 'Herkunft des Paulus', *KuD* 19, 218. By way of filling this out it may be added that my interpretation of Gal 3.10 in that essay, against the background of Paul's Pharisaic-Shammaite past, does not exclude the possibility that G. Jeremias is correct in his view that the description of Christ as someone accursed arose from (Jewish) polemics about Christ which appealed to Deut 21.23. Should this in fact be right, the question does of course remain how Paul – as an ex-Pharisee! – was able to understand Deut 27.26 in terms of Gal 3.10f.

96. Thus Ulonska, *Funktion*, 57, is right, against Schlier, when he says, 'Thus the curse lies not on what is done but on what is left undone.'

97. Luz, *Geschichtsverständnis*, 150f.

98. Ibid., 151.

99. In writing in 5.23 κατὰ τῶν τοιούτων οὐκ ἔστιν νόμος did Paul have in mind Aristotle, *Pol.*. III 13p 1284a 13f.: κατὰ τῶν τοιούτων οὐκ ἔστιν νόμος. αὐτοὶ γάρ εἰσι νόμος? To make such an assumption is naturally not the same as presupposing that Paul actually read this work of Aristotle's.

100. Schoeps, *Paulus*, 185f. (E.T. 177f.).

101. Mussner, *Gal*, 228, n. 79; where there is agreement with Dahl, 'Widersprüche in der Bibel, ein altes hermeneutisches Problem' in *StTh* 25, 12 (1971): 'The entire trend of thought in Gal 3.1-12 rests on the presupposition that the two scriptural texts in Hab 2.4 and Lev 18.5 are mutually contradictory, and that the corresponding principles, "by faith" and "by the Law" are mutually exclusive as the presupposition for justification and life.'

102. 3.22 shows that 'scripture' in Gal is not always 'scripture of promise'. But at least promise is in that passage the context of scripture, because of the final clause! We cannot look for the ultimate in consistency within Galatians.

2 NOMOS IN ROMANS

2.1 Abraham and circumcision in Rom 4

We noted earlier that Paul in Gal 3 did not take up the link between covenant or testament (διαθήκη) and circumcision, which is characteristic of Gen 17 – and this even though he brings in the Abrahamic διαθήκη as evidence for his message of justification. This would be all the more remarkable if we were right in our supposition that Paul's opponents were in fact arguing from Gen 17: 'if you Galatians, in order to be Christians, wish to be sons of Abraham, that is, if for the sake of being Christians, you wish to participate in the covenant of Abraham, you must get yourselves circumcised.' We may further recall that in Galatians Paul immediately sees the demand for circumcision from the perspective of the Law. He warns the Galatians, 'If you wish to be circumcised, then you have also bound yourselves to keep the entire Law of Moses.' But the obligation to keep the entire Law leads one into a dilemma, subjects one to the curse because nobody keeps the entire Law. Thus circumcision is radically rejected because it necessarily leads to a devastating slavery. Standing as *pars pro toto* of the Law, it is precisely this – circumcision – that has entirely lost its theological entitlement because of the Abrahamic διαθήκη which rests on faith. Indeed it has not merely lost its entitlement but has also been theologically condemned: it may no longer be practised! And anyone who does nevertheless practise it has fallen from grace.

If we have this trend in the argument of Galatians in mind as we read Rom 4 then at first sight we are struck by a notable shift in the way the question is put. Let us proceed initially in comparing Rom 4 with Gal 3 by setting out the following: (1) in what points do Gal 3 and Rom 4 agree? (2) what elements in the arguments of Gal 3 has Paul not taken up again in Rom 4? (3) what elements in the argument are new in Rom 4 as against Gal 3? (4) what elements in the arguments from Gal 3 have been modified in Rom 4? The answers to these four questions may then enable us to answer the major question: in what sense do we find in Rom 4 a modification of the entire drift of the argument in Gal 3?

(1) As in Gal 3.6 Paul in Rom 4.3 also takes Gen 15.6 as his starting point. In both passages there is a verbatim quotation from the Septuagint.[1] Paul further emphasises in both letters that the faith of the uncircumcised Gentile Christian

is of a kind with the faith of Abraham (Gal 3.8f. and frequently; Rom 4.11 and frequently). In the course of the discussion of Abraham in both letters the connection between Law and transgression, παράβασις, is established (Gal 3.19; Rom 4.15). In both letters the promise(s) made to Abraham – ἐπαγγελία(ι) – are emphasised as characteristic of him (Gal 3.16ff.; Rom 4.13ff.). The assertion of the temporal priority of the promise over the Law or over circumcision (Gal 3.15f.; Rom 4.10f.) is common to both letters.[2]

There is consequently a series of extremely important points from Gal 3 which Paul takes up again in Rom 4. A fairly extensive continuum thus exists between the two letters.

(2) However, there are also naturally essential elements of Gal 3 which no longer appear in Rom 4. Above all we miss in Rom 4 the linking of the theme of Abraham with the argument that the *nomos* is to be obeyed without remainder and that anyone who does not, in accordance with the ordinance of legal righteousness, match up to the *nomos* in even just a single stipulation is under the curse. Equally, the idea, which is linked in Galatians to this theologoumenon, of the representative acceptance of this curse by Christ is also missing. In addition there is astonishingly no mention of the notion of the covenant or testament, the διαθήκη which was basic to the argument in Gal 3.[3] In consequence neither is there any further talk of the διαθήκη's having been given force four hundred and thirty years before the *nomos*, so that this *nomos*, added so much later, could not annul the διαθήκη. The four hundred and thirty years are, as it were, reduced to the short period between Gen 15.6 and Gen 17. If we are to suppose that Paul knew the synagogue chronology, then the 430 years would have shrunk to 29 years.[4] Also missing from Rom 4 is the connection of the Abraham theme with the reception of the Holy Spirit (Gal 3.14; see 3.2).

(3) New themes and ideas not found in Galatians are the reference to God as the one who makes alive and who is the Creator (Rom 4.17), the understanding of faith as hoping against hope (4.18), which is connected with this, and the Sarah theme (4.19ff.) which again is connected with it. Attention may also be drawn to the hermeneutical principle in 4.23f., linked with the kerygmatic formula in 4.25 which is taken over from the tradition.[5]

Of greater importance, however, is the fact that Paul finally makes explicit the reference to Gen 17 which we had missed in Gal 3, and in which circumcision is understood as a sign, σημεῖον – of course in an unusual modification: in Gen 17.11 circumcision is called a 'sign of the διαθήκη', whereas in Rom 4.11 we hear of 'the sign of circumcision'. As already mentioned under point 2, the term διαθήκη is taken out of the argument. Gen 17.10ff. is thereby subordinated to Gen 15.6, since the sign of circumcision is interpreted as a seal of the justification by faith which had already been attained in the uncircumcised state. This now makes it possible for Paul to introduce a further determinative idea: for the circumcised Jewish Christians, Abraham is the father of circumcision in so far as they are not only circumcised but also believe (4.12). *Thus circumcision has force only when conjoined with faith.* However – and this is what is radically new in contrast to Galatians – in this correlation it does indeed have force![6]

(4) The recognition of this new function of circumcision brings us to point 4; for the addition of this new element in the argument already involves clear changes. This is even more true of the broader perspective from which Paul discusses the question of Abraham. If here we may follow Käsemann we would say that Rom 3.31 with its striking assertion, 'we uphold the Law', is not the conclusion of the section 3.27-30 but the transition to Chapter 4.[7] Whereas in Gal 3, in the course of the argument on the necessity of rejecting circumcision in every circumstance, Abraham functions as the epitome of justification by faith – which, by definition, is not justification by works of the Law – we find that – initially at least, with the appearance of a paradox – in Rom 4 Abraham is again introduced as indeed the epitome of a justification by faith which excludes justification by works, but nevertheless with here the specific purpose of upholding the Law.[8] To put it summarily, Paul upholds the Law by using Abraham to show that justification before God is the very thing which does not come from the *nomos*.

A further important modification is the new use of the term 'seed of Abraham'. In Gal 3.16 Paul relates this to Christ in a piece of bold and arbitrary exegesis – because it is singular – and describes Christians as the seed of Abraham (3.29) only in a roundabout way by means of the theologoumenon that all are one in Christ Jesus (3.28). By contrast, in Rom 4 this term is used in verse 13 first of all in its proper sense of physical descendants and then in verses 16 and 18 in an extended sense as embracing spiritual fatherhood also.

Let us now try to draw out the sense of the findings which we have detailed under our four separate heads. In Rom 4 the decisive difference from the pronouncements in Galatians is surely the no longer wholly negative assessment of circumcision which has now ceased to be the object of a fiercely polemical attack. In Galatians the entire discussion of Abraham occurred *solely* by way of support for the view that circumcision leads to an existence on the basis of the works of the Law, and that it therefore effects a falling from grace (Gal 5.3f. takes up Gal 3.10; but this verse is an essential part of the Abraham argument). Now, however, Paul is more discriminating in his judgements. Being a child of Abraham is now no longer regarded as a mere opposite of circumcision. Someone who has previously read only Galatians is astonished to note that Paul is now suddenly in a position to integrate the idea of circumcision into that of being a child of Abraham.[9]

Of course we must first ask whether this difference may not perhaps be only of a very superficial nature and whether it could not be adequately explained by the different audiences addressed in the two letters, to the effect, say, that in Galatians Gentile Christians had to be protected from the danger of confusing the Christian faith with the Jewish legalistic religion, while in Romans, among other things, theological reflection on the nature of Jewish Christianity was involved. And in fact it is methodologically imperative to ask, particularly when interpreting a difficult text, how far the situation of the addressees may help to clarify the text. But quite apart from the basic hermeneutical consideration that we have to infer who the addressees were from the text, and are thus moving within the inevitable hermeneutical circle, might it not be more reasonable to suppose that Paul had given thought to certain inconsistencies in his arguments in Galatians which we have already noted, and had abandoned them? We noticed earlier in Section 1.2 that there was a break in his argument: if in Gal 5.4 Paul condemned as a fundamental *falling from grace*, and a fundamental *separation from Christ*, the intention of the Galatians to have themselves circumcised and therefore – even if not perhaps fully consciously – to take upon themselves the obligation to keep the whole Torah, there is an inescapable further question as to how he could still regard himself as in ecclesiastical unity with the Jewish Christians in Jerusalem, who doubtless had abandoned neither circumcision nor obedience to the Torah and who were not only proud of their circumcision but were also continuing to subject their new-born sons to this rite. Might we not suppose that this inconsistency in his argument at that time had meanwhile become clear to Paul? Did he re-think the relationship of Gentile Christianity to Jewish Christianity? Was he perhaps even asked how he could reconcile the denigration of circumcision in his communities as a separation from Christ with at the same time addressing Jewish Christians as brothers in Christ? Of course we know nothing about discussions of this kind – and unfortunately where Paul is concerned we do not have the possibility of following the indispensable rule that the other party should be heard (*audiatur et altera pars*) – but we may best assume that between the time when Galatians was written and the writing of Romans, there lies a far from trivial process of reflection and development in Paul the theologian – a process which would be understandable even as a response to Jewish-Christian objections to his understanding of the *nomos*. To ascribe the sharp formulations in Galatians merely to momentary excitement and annoyance – that is, to an uncontrolled torrent of words from Paul – so that we would not need to affirm any real break between Galatians and Romans, comes to grief in my view because of the basic message of the crucial passages in Galatians. This view would gain further weight should H. D. Betz be right in saying that Galatians is to be regarded as a 'highly skilful composition'.[10] Someone who has conducted the kind of crucial negotiations on circumcision which were conducted at the Synod on the Gentile mission, and who is as familiar with the material as Paul is, will hardly declare without any reflection – as it were, just in the heat of his polemics – that anyone who has himself circumcised has fallen from grace and separated himself from Christ. And even if he did not make the point *thus* at the Synod[11] such a formulation would still have to be considered as the actual conviction of Paul at the time when Galatians was composed. At most, one could say that Paul had finally shown his true colours, and in the excitement of the moment had ultimately 'let the cat out of the bag'. At all events, however, we should not relativise the crucial theological pronouncements in Galatians on circumcision and Law because of less radical statements in other Pauline letters, nor seek to take them in less than their full sense, but should rather evaluate them as expressing the fundamental theological conviction of the apostle at that very time. Rather than supposing the verdicts on circumcision and the Torah in Galatians, which are so sharp, to be explicable from the situation of the Galatians and that of the author of the letter, it is then clear that in fact Paul had not at that time as yet given thought to the inconsistencies of which we spoke above, and that it was perhaps the very fact of Galatians becoming known in Jerusalem that occasioned the posing of critical questions to the author[12] – which the latter then also, contrary to all expectations, began to ask himself![13] It is always very easy to say in retrospect that Paul must immediately have become aware of those inconsistencies, but do we not have ample knowledge from history of how often historical tragedies on the greatest scale have been needed before whole peoples finally realise, as if scales were falling from their eyes, that they have not in fact perceived what was obvious? How often is historical discernment and understanding of what is actually perfectly transparent a product only of historical detachment? Is Paul therefore to forfeit some of his ecclesiastical and theological stature only because for a period there were in some respects scales before his eyes too? Only those who do not think historically and who apply the yardstick of pettifogging logic to men who are great in the unique moment will consider this impossible. To my mind, the difference between Galatians and Romans is best explained if we assume that there was a far from trivial theological development on the part of Paul between the two letters. Our further reflections in this monograph are intended to proffer the *tesserae* for such a mosaic.

Rom 2.25ff. and 3.1ff. also show that Paul could speak or write quite differently in Romans from Galatians. It would of course be possible to take 2.25 as applying solely to the past ('circumcision is indeed of use if you obey the Law, but if you break the Law, your circumcision has become uncircumcision'), in so far as all, and that is to say, even all Jews, are, according to 3.9, under the power of sin. This would then correspond to the statement in Galatians according to which the man who keeps wholly to the Law will live (Gal 3.12b). But the usefulness of circumcision is not regarded in Romans only from the standpoint of the keeping of the Law. It is true that according to Rom 2.26 even the Gentile who follows the legal stipulations of the Law is regarded as one to whom circumcision can be accredited (λογισθήσεται) just as what is entailed in being a Jew is straightforwardly spiritualised in 2.29 (περιτομὴ καρδίας ἐν πνεύματι!). It is therefore surprising when Paul concedes a certain usefulness to circumcision (and thereby to Judaism as an ethnic quantum![14]) in that the promises of God[15] are entrusted to the 'Circumcision'. It is a reasonable assumption that among these promises we are to understand also, and indeed specifically, the promise to Abraham. This is of course also true if with many exegetes we were to take τὰ λόγια τοῦ θεοῦ in the wider sense.[16] However, it is inconceivable that Paul in Galatians should have seen himself as able to speak of the usefulness of circumcision in such a way as to suggest that God's promises were specifically entrusted to that circumcision. It was in fact the promise to Abraham which induced Paul to make his sharpest attacks on circumcision.

However, to bring out even more plainly the difference from Galatians, we need a further definition of the relationship between circumcision and Law in Romans. As the first part of this investigation has shown, the facts can be reduced so far as Galatians is concerned to the brief formula that circumcision means *total* obligation to the Law. In Romans, on the other hand, the idea of an obligation which is total drops out;[17] at the least it is, noticeably, not expressly stated. What is retained from Galatians is the notion of circumcision as an obligation to obey the Torah (2.25). In this context, Paul harks back to the Old Testament idea of the circumcision of the heart (Jer 9.24f.)[18] and in doing so radicalises it in a peculiar way: physical circumcision is superseded by the circumcision of the heart (2.29). 3.1, however, shows us that this superseding does not mean the complete negation of physical circumcision. Paul is speaking *dialectically* here: physical circumcision means something only if the Law is fulfilled, that is, if the heart too has been circumcised. Doing the Law can in itself even be regarded as circumcision. Nonetheless, it would be wrong to say that Paul here is spiritualising, for it is precisely to the physical circumcision that the promises of God have been entrusted. What constitutes the specific element in the theological thought in Romans is however the notion that physical and spiritual circumcision can in any particular circumstance be assessed only in their inter-relationship, that is to say, that each without the other loses its substance, a substance which however has to be redefined for each set of circumstances. Because physical circumcision thus has in the theology of Romans as a whole an indispensable status, Abraham can then also – *contra* Galatians – be reckoned as the father of the truly circumcised, i.e., of those Jewish Christians who like him have been circumcised and at the same time believe. In view of the extent to which Paul, in emphasising the theological value of physical circumcision, bestows theological relevance on the 'history of Israel', we will need to treat with caution pronouncements in a single dimension, such as Michel's, that 'Abraham is first of all the father of the Gentile Christians and only then father of the Jewish Christians'.[19] This is not entirely false, but Paul's remarks in Romans are too multi-layered to permit us to make a pronouncement of this kind in such an unqualified fashion. The problem which here raises its head is that of the theological significance of the history of that people which exists as the physical 'Circumcision' – and consequently as a people under obligation to obey the Torah. In this respect too there is a prior expectation that Paul will not have been understood where what has been attempted is simply to render his thought into handy formulae which are the product of a one-dimensional survey. This much however must already have become clear: the theme of circumcision which, as we find it in Romans, exhibits a serious modification of what we find in Galatians, points to the close connection between the theme of 'Law' and that of the 'history of Israel'.

2.1.1 The 'history of Israel' and Law

If in Romans Paul is no longer giving only a negative evaluation of circumcision, but has rather won through to a more discriminating perspective on this point, then this must also have consequences for his understanding of Israel's history and, concomitantly, for his understanding of the Mosaic Law; for when he says that it is specifically to the Circumcision that the promises of God are entrusted, this probably does in fact mean that these promises are entrusted *to the people of Israel*, considered also as an ethnic group.

In regard to Gal 3, Klein says: 'To overstate the case, we may say that for Paul the Old Testament is not an element in the history of Israel, but rather the history of Israel is an element in the Old Testament, and as such is thereby relegated to a subordinate position in advance.'[20] To the extent that the Law, which essentially co-determines the history of Israel, is disqualified in Gal 3, we have few objections to this presentation of the case, which is explicitly said to be an 'overstatement' – *so long, of course, as it refers only to Gal 3!* But as soon as we apply it to Romans it is wrong, for Rom 9-11 forms an essential part of the overall argument of this letter of the apostle's, which was probably his last.[21] Rom 9.4f. lists as co-ordinate terms, among others, the following: υἱοθεσία (Gal 4.5 – as a synonym for ἐλευθερία – specifically in the sense of freedom from the *nomos*!), διαθῆκαι (plural!), νομοθεσία (i.e., the giving of the Law by Moses which here is specifically not contrasted with the promises!) and ἐπαγγελίαι (among which promises the promise to Abraham must assuredly have been numbered!). All in all, Rom 9.4f. is at least initially a positive evaluation of the 'history of Israel', but – and this is immediately to qualify again what has just been said – this passage must not be seen in isolation. What immediately follows itself indicates that Paul does not have in mind a one-dimensional view of Israel's history such as might initially be suggested by the co-ordinated listing of legislation, promises, etc., in 9.4f. It is in fact broken up dialectically. The presupposition of the argument from verse 6 onwards is of course Israel's manifest failure as she emerges from her history. The 'history of Israel' is actually a history that has miscarried in that it has not reached its goal. It is in fact a history directed towards the coming of the Messiah – but Israel's failure is specifically a failure in relation to that objective. In sum, *the 'history of Israel' which was directed towards the coming*

of the Messiah has failed because Israel failed when confronted with the Messiah.
And once again the positive implications of this negative statement must be
seen if we are not to miss the overall picture. Just as the positive statement
about the history of Israel in 9.4f. was qualified by the negative statement in
9.6ff.,[22] i.e., by being set in relation to the failure mentioned in 9.6, and was
thus placed in a wider context, so too a similar process must now take place in a
reverse direction: the statements regarding Israel's failure in its history as it is
confronted with its history have theological relevance only if and when the
divine component[23] in this history does not lose its force. This is the really
decisive factor for Paul. He clearly sees that the failure of the people of Israel in
its history could prompt a thoughtful person to reflect that God's word and
God's promise have therefore also lost their force (see also Rom 3.3!). In other
words, Israel's failure is the failure of the divine promise and therefore God's
own failure. The answer Paul gives is surprising: it is not the promise that is
problematic but rather what is meant by 'Israel'. For since the 'history of
Israel' cannot fail – being something which stands under the promise of God –
but the historical Israel has failed, the entity 'Israel' must be taken in a new
sense so that the divine promise may remain valid.

   This is effected first of all by means of the paradox in verse 6b in which Paul
plays with the idea of 'Israel' in a way which is typical of him: not all who are of
Israel are Israel.[24] In the first instance Israel means the historical entity which
was the people of Israel, but in the second instance it means those of the Jewish
people who believe in Christ. The second Israel is thus a very small part of the
first Israel. It would of course be wrong to see here a contrast between an ethnic
idea of 'Israel' and a theological one,[25] for without question even Israel in the
sense of the Jewish people is given theological qualification, as is clear from
verses 4f.[26] Israel as a historical ethnic entity does indeed constitute those Paul
has in mind when he uses the honorific title 'Israelites'.[27] To this extent then the
history of Israel also has theological relevance even if the predicate 'salvation
history' applies to it only in an admittedly somewhat odd sense. What we have
said about verse 6b holds good correspondingly for verse 7. The biological fact
of descent from Abraham does not necessarily entail a prerogative, for not all
those who can call themselves 'the seed of Israel' are also his 'children'. Here
too the history of Israel is again taken seriously from a theological standpoint,
in that the 'children' constitute a selection, albeit a small one, of the 'seed of
Abraham'. In the context of the argument presented in Rom 9.1-13 it is in fact
not the relationship of Jews and Christians but of Jews and Jewish Christians
that matters. In *this* context Paul substantiates his thesis that the word of God,
or, more precisely, the promises of God have not fallen by the wayside (verse
6a).[28]

   Paul's argument is of course not entirely self-consistent. Initially (verses 6b,
7a) Paul has simply argued quantitatively with his repeated assertion 'not all',
and thus, with regard to the people of Israel, has upheld the continued validity
of the divine promises reductively, i.e., for precisely *this* people. That is to say,

initially the apostle does not make a contradictory contrast between the people of Israel and the new Israel, or, in even sharper terms, between the false Israel and the *true* Israel, but at most a contrary relationship. However in what follows he does indeed make, by his exegesis of Gen 21.12, an exclusive contrast: the children of the flesh are precisely not the children of God. The only ones who can properly be regarded as the children of God are those to whom as children of the promise (verse 8) descent from Abraham has been specifically ascribed (λογίζεται). In this context we now have a straight separation of the promise from the historical entity which was the 'people of Israel'.

The fact that in the course of his argument Paul moves from a standpoint which theologically *qualifies* the history of Israel to one which *negates* that history theologically, and that he therefore does not remain consistent in his overall argument,[29] must not be misjudged. We should not suppose that the qualifications previously expressed have been abandoned because of the subsequent negation; for then indeed the starting-point of Paul's exegesis in verses 4f. would have been abandoned, as indeed should be clear from our discussion so far. Nevertheless the very abrupt contrast in verse 8 does put the emphasis very clearly on the promise. On the one hand it has been made within the field of Israel's history, but at the same time it transcends this field in so far as it is realised outwith the ethnic entity of Israel, and indeed against that entity, as the subsequent comments on the Gentile Christians show (see, for example, the Hosea quotation in verses 25f.).

Käsemann is right to see in Rom 9-11 these dialectical jumps from the affirmative to the negative and again from the negative to the affirmative as connected with the doctrine of justification: 'Paul's doctrine of salvation history is a variation on his doctrine of the justification of the ungodly.'[30] We shall therefore have to keep to the notion that the 'history of Israel' has not been cancelled out by Paul in Romans. Israel – including her Law! – remains a positive theological entity; positive because, to follow Luz, God has given Israel its character *as* Israel.[31] If, in addition, the promises are made without reservation even to unbelieving Israel, and if therefore Law and promise, which in Galatians are contrasted to each other as mutually exclusive principles of salvation, are in Romans together regarded from the standpoint of a gracious deed of God done to his people,[32] then it is simply not plausible to suppose that Paul, as Luz thinks, had not reflected on the relationship of Rom 9.4 to Gal 3.[33]

If we take Romans as being a writing which has a very well thought-out theology, then into the reflections that lie behind it there might well also have flowed what Paul had previously thought about the questions involved – even if this was by way of a deliberate rejection of what had once been said on a previous occasion. For Paul to remain true to himself in the preaching of his gospel does not mean that he remains constant in the theological expressions of his thoughts. For his self-consistent identity does not lie there at all. His very faithfulness to his commission is what commits him to constantly renewed reflection and to ever new approaches in his theology. The gospel cannot be superseded, but a particular stage of theological reflection may very well be superseded, and theological reflection to a great extent also means departing from theological ideas which at one time have gained favour. Paul well understood that theology takes place again and again in a field of tension between continuity and discontinuity. The church still derives its life from this today.

2.2 The Synod on the
Gentile Mission – a misunderstanding corrected?

We noticed an inconsistency in Paul's argument in Galatians:[34] those who have themselves circumcised and therefore take upon themselves the obligation of fulfilling the whole Law (5.3) have fallen from grace (5.4); but despite this conviction, Paul concluded his agreement with the Jerusalem Jewish Christians – that is, with those who after all continued to circumcise their new-born sons in loyal obedience to the Torah, and who were proud of their own circumcision. From Gal 2 there is no mistaking that Paul negotiated freedom from the Law *only* for the Gentile mission. We may well therefore go on to ask whether the theological judgement of Gal 5.4 held good only for the Gentile Christians.

In our discussions in 1.2 the question also remained unsettled whether Paul had understood the agreement differently from his Jewish Christian partners in the agreement. History shows us often enough that arrangements and agreements are understood differently by the various parties to the agreement as they are subsequently differently interpreted by them; but then agreements frequently owe their existence to the fact that those involved had 'come to terms' on formulae which were not unambiguous! To be specific in the case of the Synod: had future controversies not already perhaps been built into the agreement, by the very fact that whereas Paul understood it to involve freedom from the Law as a matter of principle the 'other side' saw in it only a concession, a release from circumcision and the laws on purity, perhaps even only as a temporary concession – quite apart from the fact that seemingly no one as yet had the problem of mixed congregations in mind at all?[34a] In view of the one-sided nature of the sources, it is unlikely that it will ever be possible to provide a definitively unambiguous answer to the question whether the agreement was taken in different senses by the various parties. It is therefore all the more necessary at least to formulate the question with complete clarity. At all events we should note that in Gal 2 we have only an *interpretation* of the Synod. It is of course the authentic interpretation from the one side, but by that very fact it is only *one* of the two authentic interpretations. How much further on we would be if only we also had the authentic interpretation of the Jerusalemites – quite apart from the fact that, most importantly, the tradition contains nothing of the formulation of the agreement *in so far* as it relates to the difficult subject of circumcision or the Law (though by 'formulation' we can hardly mean an official 'text'; for a communiqué with a fixed text is surely an anachronism!).[35]

Let us assume that Paul's Galatian opponents[36] were the so-called Judaisers who had some kind of contact with Jerusalem even if in their legal strictness they went further than the official attitude of James and his people. (As was suggested earlier in 1.1, the appeal Paul's opponents made to the idea of being children of Abraham, in the context of a circumcision which was regarded as indispensable, tends to favour Judaisers and consequently not Gnostics – even if this was only offered as a convenient reason.) *But we must then suppose that James and the Jerusalem church leaders were familiar with Paul's argument in Galatians at least in outline.* It is possible that even the exact text of this letter was known in Jerusalem; but this would mean that the Pauline interpretation of the Synod on the Gentile Mission would have been available in Jerusalem as the authentic utterance of the man who gave himself out as the apostle called for the Gentile mission.

However, let us initially suppose simply that Paul in chapter 2 correctly reproduced the arrangement made at that time. Let us therefore assume that Paul at the Synod had actually come to the conclusion that liberation from circumcision *meant* freedom from the Law. But in that case the *theological consequences* which Paul had drawn from this in Gal 3ff. must not merely have filled James and those close to him in Jerusalem with consternation, but must also have incensed them to the utmost. Even if they could not agree with what Paul's opponents in Galatians were doing – for this in fact contravened the arrangement – yet with the best will in the world they could not, from their standpoint, accept Paul's verdict on the Torah in Galatians, for to do so would have been to abandon all that they stood for. The antinomian passages in Galatians *must* have embittered all Jewish Christians who attached great importance to the Torah. Furthermore what Paul wrote there was simply grist to the mill of those radical legalists who, in their extremism, perhaps made life difficult at times even for a man like James; and perhaps he was now given to understand by them that he was finally 'reaping the reward' for having been too conciliatory at that time towards Paul.

However the supposition just made, viz., that Paul interpreted the arrangement in exactly the same sense as the Jerusalem authorities, is subject to the greatest of reservations. Are we to suppose that the Jerusalemites had really so far transcended their own position that they accepted a total freedom from the Law – as a matter of principle – for the Gentile mission, although to all appearances they considered themselves to be the true *Israel*? Let us therefore for the next stage in our reflections assume as a hypothesis that Paul had wrongly interpreted the Synod in taking it in the way we have suggested. We would then of course expect that the Jerusalem church authorities would do everything in their power to make it clear to Paul, now on his missionary travels, how wrong his interpretation was. It must have been of the utmost importance to the Jerusalem church to make it absolutely clear to Paul that that church would never have countenanced arrangements which were in this way free from the Law in principle, and that he, Paul, now had the responsibility of putting things to rights again! We must therefore surmise that Paul was given to understand that he must in no circumstances continue to interpret the agreement at the Synod in such a way as he had done in his letter to the Galatian congregations. And we can reckon with the fact that James himself will have taken the opportunity of setting the record straight in Galatia – most likely by advocating a middle position between Paul and his opponents. Wilckens complains that the commentaries and monographs have 'remarkably' not in general handled the outcome of the Galatian conflict.[37] He sees as an essential reason for the writing of Romans the total failure of Paul in Galatia: 'the disaster in Galatia, however, equally caused his position in relation to Jerusalem to deteriorate greatly.'[38] For this reason Paul, before taking his collection up to Jerusalem, writes to the Roman congregation to secure their solidarity and intercession on his behalf, i.e., their help in regard to Jerusalem.[38a] However, Wilckens does not consider the possibility that James or one of his close associates in the Jerusalem church leadership may have previously entered into contact with Paul to make clear to him the faulty interpretation of the agreement – doing so out of the same concern that motivated Paul, viz., that the Christian church should not be permitted to disintegrate (in the sense of Gal 2.2?).

To many people such considerations may seem too much like speculation, but in interpreting texts and in the associated reconstruction of historical situations, we cannot entirely dispense with a certain element of speculation, of piecing together the various indicators we may have. All attempts since Ferdinand Christian Baur[39] to clarify the situation from which and to which Romans was written[40] have in this sense been speculation – speculation which has admittedly fitted the hard facts together differently in each case. These hard facts are well known: the theological comments of the letter, understood as *'doctrinae christianae compendium'* – a compendium of Christian doctrine – (Melanchthon, *Loci Communes, Introductio*); the admonitions arising from the conflict between the 'strong' and the 'weak' in chapters 14f.; the discrepancy between Paul's strong expression of his desire to preach the gospel in Rome (at the very beginning of the letter!) and the 'ominous non-intervention clause'[41] (Rom 15.20); the explicit characterisation of the Christians in Rome as Gentile Christians (1.5; 11.13), and the address 'you who are a Jew' (2.17), coupled with the effort to prove plainly to Gentile Christians that justification does not come from the Jewish Law. Obviously we cannot here deal with all the introductory questions of Romans *in extenso*, but doubtless Schmithals is right in this: we must not go back to the days before Ferdinand Christian Baur; we must explain Romans *historically*, i.e., on the basis of the concrete circumstances of its composition,[42] and in so far as it is necessary for our enquiry to grasp the historical circumstances as a necessary horizon of understanding, these problems must also be dealt with.

I agree with Wilckens that the developing history of the Pauline congregations is what provokes Paul to his theological endeavours.[43] I further agree with him to a great extent when he writes: 'now (i.e., in Romans) he is no longer conducting *polemics* as in Galatians, *but wants to enter into dialogue*; he takes seriously those objections which prevent his opponents agreeing with him; he thinks them out for himself anew in order to convince them. This distinguishes Romans from Galatians, although the train of thought in Galatians is at the back of Romans. Romans is a repetition of Galatians on which there has been reflection, and this reflection serves the purposes of dialogue and of possible agreement.'[44] I am of course not, like Wilckens, of the opinion that Galatians was written shortly before Romans.[45]

Let us therefore assume that James had knowledge of Galatians and thus of Paul's interpretation of the Synod on the Gentile Mission. Let us further assume that Paul had seriously misunderstood the agreement made at this Synod. He now therefore learns that of all people James, to whom he had appealed in Galatians, is contradicting his account of the results obtained at the Synod. Perhaps he learns that James has gone further and intervened among the Galatians to this effect. It would be easy to see how under such circumstances Paul would have been prepared to see unity with Jerusalem disintegrate rather than to go back on his own view by a single iota. But the fact of the argument in Romans which was already adumbrated in Section 1 of this chapter, and will be still more plainly exhibited in the further course of our investigation, suggests that such was not his reaction. Paul *was* rather persuaded to reconsider what had been said in Galatians once again. There must have been compelling arguments which led him to do so, and there must have been one or more among the Jewish Christians whose opposition did not lead him to make his own position even more rigid but rather to conciliate. And this not simply as a concession which he might have been ready to make solely for tactical reasons. *No, there must have been one (or more) from whom he would really accept advice!* Are we wrong to suppose that this was James? For Paul must above all have been concerned to reach agreement with this man who was so important for Jerusalem. Total disagreement with Jerusalem meant failure for Paul (Gal 2.2!). And is it sheer imagination to consider further whether James himself might not have raised a questioning objection to Gal 5.4 (he who allows himself to be circumcised has fallen from grace),[46] asking how Paul could then make an agreement at all with such as continued to circumcise their sons and remained proud of their circumcision, if as he saw it only freedom from the Law was to be regarded as taking seriously the saving work of Christ? How can one possibly practise church unity with Jewish

Christians who continue to practise circumcision, which the Torah demanded and which required obedience to the Torah, if Christ was being preached as a total negation of the Torah? It would indeed be difficult to deny that Paul may well have also spoken in terms of Gal 2.2 at the Synod, that is, championing the need for Christian unity. But did James then let him know that he should ask himself how seriously the apostle to the Gentiles was really taking the unity of Jewish and Gentile Christians if he was condemning circumcision as a falling from grace?

We are not in a position simply to draw cogent conclusions here as to the nature of details which have not been handed down to us. But should our presupposition be correct, according to which James knew the argument in Galatians and according to which James and Paul were in one decisive point at odds with each other in their interpretation of the agreement made at the Synod, then we might at any rate have to consider the notion that Paul was led to a further reappraisal of his position by being confronted with James's reaction[47] – and this would be a reappraisal involving reflection on James's objections, and so their reassessment, at the same time as he remained faithful to his own original concern.

Thus it no longer appears so very odd that Paul should fear that his collection might not be accepted in Jerusalem (Rom 15.31). It is widely acknowledged that for Paul the collection meant something more than a merely charitable undertaking. Its point was to demonstrate the unity of the church which was composed of Jewish Christians and Gentile Christians.[48] As we have seen, Paul had earlier been concerned with this unity at the Synod, and now as he contemplated at last returning to Jerusalem with the very collection promised the last time he stayed there, he could not but fear that his earlier statements about Torah in Galatians would have inflicted such damage both on his position *and* on James's that James – or, if not James, other Jewish Christians in Jerusalem – might well feel unable to accept a collection from the hands of Paul, the opponent of the Law. For Paul the situation has a real element of tragedy. He can see why it may be that the collection – the very sign of church unity – will be rejected, and rejected as the gift of someone who, by his antinomian utterances in Galatians, had broken the bonds of this same unity.[49] Consequently, we now find him making intensive theological efforts at *mediation* between his position, viz., justification by faith with its universal aspect, and the Jewish Christian standpoint.

We would now have to go on to consider whether what some scholars have said about Jerusalem being the covert destination of Romans[50] may not after all contain an element of truth. This would not be in the sense of the letter sent to Rome being intended to achieve *as such* something in Jerusalem. But – always on the assumption that Paul was concerned to still the waves of indignation that had been whipped up in Jerusalem by Galatians – we should perhaps consider whether it was not Paul's concern to let his 'theology of mediation', preserved for us in Romans, become known even *prior to* his arrival in Jerusalem. Given the particular situation, is it really so perverse to consider the possibility that there may even have gone to Jerusalem a letter identical to a great extent with Romans – a letter, of course, which (for transparent reasons) has not been preserved? If we are right in assuming that once Paul had been told how far the Jerusalem interpretation of the Synod on the Gentile Mission differed from his, he had worked hard to find an honourable compromise, then it would indeed be surprising had he not staked everything, prior to his arriving once again in the Jewish metropolis, on making known his 'new' theology of the relationship of Jewish and Gentile Christians, and on making it known in such a way that it would be as clear as possible – that it would pick up and reply to everything he knew of in the way of objections to his theology.[51] Of course, at the point when he writes his letter to the congregation at Rome, he still does not know how his 'U-turn' has been viewed in Jerusalem.[51a]

It is reasonable to suppose that Paul did not think he was being untrue to himself in this new theological endeavour. Nothing has in fact changed in what really matters to him, which is justification by faith in that gospel which reveals Jesus Christ. He has re-thought his theology of justification solely in respect of its implications for Israel – such at least is surely a correct interpretation of his intentions. The price he had to pay for this was, of course, a completely new view of the Torah. Thus the question finally remains: how does Paul now regard the agreement at the Synod? Does he now suppose that at that time what was conceded to him was only freedom from circumcision for the Gentile Christian congregations but that no freedom from the Law in principle had been decreed? Perhaps what has been said in 2.1 already constitutes some kind of answer to this question. The fact that in Romans he gives a virtuoso treatment of the theme 'Law' in the context of justification by faith, and does so in a dialectic which is carried on with great systematic force, does in my view exhibit an endeavour to see Christ as indeed the end of the Law (Rom 10.4), but at the same time to see the Law as the epitome of God's holy will. The reflections which follow are intended to provide fuller evidence for this and to elucidate it, but first of all I should like to give in a brief excursus some further reflections on Schmithals's thesis that the integrity of Romans should be questioned!

2.2.1 Excursus: The question of the integrity of Romans

The hypothesis put forward by Walter Schmithals in his monograph, *Der Römerbrief als historisches Problem* (1975), basically boils down to the question of how the letter is divided. The main argument runs as follows. In 14.1 – 15.6, Paul has in mind a group of 'strong' people, who constitute the majority of the congregation, but nothing is said of such a group in chapters 1-11.[52] In chapters 1-11, Gentile Christians have indeed clearly been addressed, but the argument consists in the refutation specifically of the Jewish standpoint. The striking fact is therefore that 'Paul argues both with the Roman Gentile Christians and with Jews'.[53] From this Schmithals infers that Paul had written a first letter to the congregation at Rome (say in 1.1-11.36 and 15.8-13), in which he expressed his intention to preach his gospel also in Rome as an apostle called to the Gentiles. He then later wrote a second letter (perhaps found in the remainder of Romans without 13.1-7 and chapter 16) in which he arrogates to himself the right to deal with the congregation as if it had been founded by him, and to intervene with plain speaking in a dispute within the congregation.

This hypothesis does indeed have its attractions. Apart from the illuminating explanation which it offers of a series of difficulties,[54] it is above all capable of resolving the apparent discrepancy between the advance notice of his preaching of the gospel, given in chapter 1, and the clause in 15.20 about non-intervention.[55] The attractions are not lessened by the fact that Günter Klein's attempt to explain this difficulty has not won support. What he suggested was that Paul, by his preaching, wanted to lay the foundation mentioned in 15.20 but which was still lacking in Rome, viz., to establish the apostolicity of the Roman group of Christians and thus to erect it into a church.[56]

We shall therefore have to come to terms with Schmithals's attempted solution as one which is an interesting and serious endeavour to grapple with the riddle of Romans. The fact that specifically Romans is the subject of doubt as to its integrity should actually not be discountenanced as the killing of a sacred cow, as Schmithals himself fears.[57] If, as I hold, 2 Corinthians and Philippians at least are each demonstrably compilations of letters,[58] then such analogous considerations cannot *a priori* be dismissed out of hand for Romans. We shall therefore not find it possible to ignore the attempted solution which Schmithals has put forward.

However, in my view, there is a series of grave objections that can be raised against this hypothesis. Let us begin with a consequence which arises from the hypothesis itself. It should not be necessary to refute the idea that substantial sections of Galatians and Romans, for all their theological differences – the unravelling of which has been made a methodological principle in our investigation – do none the less have their counterparts in the two letters.[59] Thus, *inter alia*, even Gal 5.14 has its counterpart in Rom 13.8-10.[60] However, if Rom 13.8-10 belongs, as Schmithals suggests, to Letter B, then there is specifically no counterpart to Gal 5.14 in the anti-Jewish argument of Letter A, and therefore no counterpart to that passage which occupies a key position in Galatians. We would then have to suppose that Paul produced this counterpart in his second letter by chance even though, when the first was written down, he certainly had no thoughts as yet of the second. It is perhaps clear enough that this seems somewhat illogical – or to put it very cautiously, it *may* seem to be such. Schmithals's exposition, too, compellingly suggests that Rom 13.8-10 occupies a central position in the course of the argument beginning at 12.1, the more so if he is correct in his supposition that 13.1-7 does not belong to this context.[61] Thus on the basis of his own conclusions themselves, he cannot detach 13.8-10 from Letter B and locate it in Letter A.

There is a further point closely connected with the problem we have mentioned. Gal 5.14 and Rom 13.8-10 are in each case the central point on which Paul's ethical injunctions hinge. Schmithals of course rejects the view that Rom 12-15 is to be understood as the paraenetic part of the whole letter and says that this view rests on a false conception of Romans as a kind of compendium of Pauline doctrine.[62] But here too it needs to be pointed out that detachment of the paraenesis from Rom 1-11 means understanding the whole structure of Letter A in such a way that there is no element in it corresponding to the paraenesis in Galatians. Even on the assumption – for which H. D. Betz has at least offered very weighty reasons[63] – that Galatians is to be taken as far as its composition is concerned as an 'example of the "apologetic letter" *genre*',[64] and that *for this reason* paraenesis does have its place in *this* letter[65] while the reasons therefore which led Paul to introduce the paraenetic section into Galatians no longer were appropriate for Romans A, the remarkable fact would however remain that despite extensive correspondence in substantial – even if modified – elements of the arguments in the two letters, Galatians and Romans A, there would be no paraenesis in Romans A.

Now the arguments adduced by us – (1) the correspondence of Gal 5.14 and Rom 13.8-10 and (2) the higher-order correspondence of the paraenetic sections in Galatians and Romans with this correspondence – certainly could not in the last resort be held to be compelling, but their force should not be underestimated.

Schmithals creates a further difficulty for himself. He first shows that the formation found in Rom 12.1 (παρακαλῶ followed by διά + Genitive and clause of purpose) does not occur within a Pauline letter where a new topic is being broached. Consequently we have here the beginning of the body of the letter.[66] But then he operates specifically with Rom 15.30, suggesting that there, in Romans B, this formulation is to be found at the beginning of the concluding (!) paraenesis.[67] Thus the very turn of phrase which was previously supposed to prove the beginning of the *body* of the letter is now seen as the 'deliberate conclusion to the argument of the letter'! Schmithals has thus again undermined his own argument.

These objections to Schmithals's thesis do of course leave unanswered his basic question: how is it that Paul in chapters 1-11 is able to treat Gentile Christians as if they were Jews? How is it that in chapter 1 he can boldly introduce his preaching as the preaching of the missionary to the Gentiles, but then crudely introduce his formula of non-intervention in 15.20? How can he, in chapter 1, make such cautious, downright diplomatic statements despite the boldness with which he announces his preaching of the gospel, and yet quite plainly read the riot act to the Romans in chapters 14f. (15.15: τολμηροτέρως)? Does not all this point to two very different situations in which the apostle is writing? And of course we must also note that Schmithals is not the first to offer hypotheses for the division of Romans.[68]

Almost simultaneously with Schmithals's investigation (1975) there appeared Alfred Suhl's monograph – *Paulus und seine Briefe. Ein Beitrag zur paulinischen Chronologie*. We cannot here undertake a full evaluation of this work, the conclusions of which to a great extent differ from those put forward here, but one of his reflections does seem to me to be worth considering for the problem we are at present dealing with, and indeed to be very helpful. Schmithals's starting-point is that in each case a very specific point of view is being countered in the two Roman letters; in Letter A we have a Gentile Christianity which thinks Judaistically and in Letter B a congregation which has a Pauline understanding of itself and which is in process of acting out its Paulinism unlovingly. On both occasions Paul sees himself obliged to intervene on his own initiative in the particular situation. But might it not also be that Paul was approached for support – that, as Suhl thinks, the contact with Rome goes back to the initiative of *one* group within the Roman congregation?[69] This of course would be the Pauline group. Paul then declared his readiness to help: πρόθυμον (1.15)![70] But if *one* group asked him to intervene, then it may be supposed that Paul's argument is directed towards the source of the attack on the Pauline Romans. But equally we can also see why the apostle would also tell his own people a few unpleasant home truths – see chapters 14f.!

Consequently, it is easy enough to see why Paul introduces himself in Romans as an apostle to the Gentiles and why initially the polemical thrust of his argument is directed against those Jewish Christians who were making life difficult for the Pauline Gentile Christians. As yet this tells us nothing whatever of the relative size of the two groups. Even the description of the two groups as 'strong' and 'weak' in the hortatory part of the letter does not allow us to draw any further conclusions in this respect. Paul is simply adopting here the terminology which he had earlier found useful in Corinth (1 Cor 8.1ff.). There is thus no difficulty at all in conceiving that Jewish Christians, expelled from Rome because of the edict of Claudius in 49 A.D., were returning and were now taking offence at the freedom of the Gentile Christians.[71] Yet this hypothesis, though it seems to me very much the most likely one, is not compelling. Suhl's suggestion that the conflict could also have arisen between Gentile Christians and proselyte Christians[72] should not be dismissed. In this case Paul would have seen himself particularly obliged, as the apostle to the Gentiles, to intervene in the conflict, since he certainly did not allow his competence in respect to proselyte Christians to be disputed. For what, after the coming of Christ, would be the point of conversion to Judaism? And – last but not least – there could be no question of his being interested at all in conversions to Christianity via Judaism! (even if he was not disposed to think or speak and argue so rigorously and apodeictically in Romans as he had formerly done in Galatians.) But if, as supposed above, the opponents of the Pauline party were Jewish Christians, then Paul might well have considered even in that case that he had some entitlement to intervene. Nothing had been agreed at the earlier Synod on the Gentile Mission about mixed congregations; indeed the problem had not been envisaged.[72a] But since, in this situation – which was new in relation to the Synod – Paul could hardly have regarded such congregations as a missionary sphere for the Jewish Christians, he will have considered those places where, alongside Jews and Jewish Christians, there were also Gentiles and Gentile Christians as his mission field, or at least as *his* mission field *too*.

A plausible explanation for Paul's writing as if to Jews to a congregation which is (also!) Gentile Christian is therefore possible on other presuppositions than those of Schmithals alone. The Gentile Christians may in fact have besought him to do so! Of course this does not answer the problem about the discrepancy between chapter 1 and the non-intervention clause. Indeed, Paul first intimates his intention to preach the gospel at Rome (1.15) and then he declares it to be his ambition not to proclaim the gospel (again we have the verb εὐαγγελίζεσθαι as in 1.15!) – where Christ is already being spoken of, so that he may not build on someone else's foundation (15.20). But it is very much an open question whether Rom 15.20 really refers to Rome! It is *because* Paul does not wish to proclaim a gospel where 'the name of Christ' has been 'proclaimed' by others before him[73] that he goes to Rome *in order to* reach Spain from there. But as for Rome itself, Paul does not jib at preaching the gospel there, for even if he did not found the Roman congregation himself, he nevertheless sees it as his mission field, as his Paulinist followers live there.[74]

2.3 The new function of the *nomos*

By way of conclusion to his argument in 1.18-3.20, Paul writes that knowledge of sin 'ἐπίγνωσις ἁμαρτίας' arises through the Law (3.20b). As the immediate context 3.20a itself indicates, this theological judgement can be more closely defined as follows: it is *only* knowledge of sin that arises through the Law. It is presently undisputed that this exclusive sense alone corresponds to what Paul wanted to say. However, it is still not a wholly unambiguous statement of the content of this pronouncement, which is so important for Paul. For we can still ask, *for whom* does the Law afford knowledge of sin? Can the Jew know his sin through the Law, the more so as it is valid specifically for him? Or can sin as *hamartia* be recognised in Paul's view only by the believer, because the Jew who still exists outwith faith in Christ can recognise his sinfulness only to a limited extent? At all events, Paul presupposes in his polemics against 'the' Jew (2.27ff.) that the latter is at least in a position to see his sinful *deeds* as guilt before God, for he does indeed know God's will – he is in fact brought up in the Law (2.18). Just for this reason he is inexcusable (2.1).[75] However, the question remains whether *as* a Jew his progress is not limited to the knowledge of individual deeds of sin, that is, to the knowledge of παραβάσεις or παραπτώματα. However, this must at least be certain: the ἐπίγνωσις παραβάσεων is clearly possible for him, in some sense, for otherwise the argument in Rom 2.1-3.20 would become pointless.

According to Ulrich Wilckens the judgement that 'no flesh is justified before God from the works of the Law' is introduced expressly as a judgement of *the Law*. Wilckens argues that Paul is certainly not claiming that this judgement could only really be understood from the perspective of faith, for it is indeed through the *Law* that knowledge of sin is arrived at.[76] Käsemann contradicts this: according to him the reply in verse 20b being short is oracular in its effect, and cannot be recognised as a general truth before Christ. Knowledge of sin has its place not in the course of a progressive development but only at the end of the road.[77] One could now ask, of course, whether the truth does not lie in between these two views, in so far as 3.20a is indeed a judgement that can be pronounced, in Paul's sense, only in faith (anyone who has discerned the incapacity of the Law to justify is no longer a Jew!), while 3.20b is nevertheless clear and acceptable to the Jew – because of 2.27ff.! – so long as it is not said that it is *only* recognition or knowledge of sin that occurs through the Law.

But what does 'sin' mean here? This much is clear to start with: the argument leading up to Rom 3.9 is intended to show that even the Jew – indeed precisely the Jew – should at least attain to the knowledge that *hamartia* somehow or other has the character of power. This can already be seen from the expression 'to be under *hamartia*' which we find in 3.9. This formulation gives linguistic expression to the dimension of the catastrophe as a cosmic event. Sin (in the singular!) cannot therefore be fully defined on the basis of the individual deeds of each person, i.e., on the basis of the παραβάσεις or παραπτώματα. Thus although in 1.18-3.20 the nature of *hamartia* is established only in fragmentary fashion – Schmithals rightly says that nowhere in this section is there a dogmatic development of the concept of sin[78] – nevertheless the contours of something essential pertaining to this *hamartia* are delineated.

The character of sin as a power is trenchantly stated among other places in Rom 5.12ff.: quasi-personification and the verb βασιλεύω as a predicate for sin and death. As a clarification of 3.20b however, the section 7.7ff. is even more important. Let us look first of all at section 7.7-13. It is true that in this 'apology for the Law'[79] sin is not the main subject of reflection. But the relationship of Law and sin is raised here[80] in connection with the question – which Paul energetically negates – whether the *nomos* is *hamartia*, i.e., whether one may assert that *nomos* and *hamartia* are the same in substance.[81] Even if the *nomos* is in no sense *hamartia*, nevertheless a relationship to it[82] cannot be denied.[83] The relation between *nomos* and *hamartia* is initially expressed as a *relation of knowledge*: a γνῶναι ἁμαρτίαν exists only because of the Law. We should note that *the exclusive thrust of the statement has been inverted, as against 3.20*. There we had: 'we arrive *only* at knowledge of sin through the Law'. Here we have: '*only* through the Law do we arrive at knowledge of sin'. Thus despite a 'material' agreement in both theological judgements the perspective is different.[84] What the sin amounts to which is experienced[85] concretely through the Law is shown in one's own *epithumia* (covetousness/desire) which has become conscious because of the Law (cf. the γάρ which is used to offer a reason!). [As this Pauline concept cannot be precisely reproduced by the word 'longing' or 'desire' (German 'Begierde') the German text leaves it mostly untranslated in what follows – as with *hamartia*. We have conformed to this in the English. (Translator)] Here Paul is following a Jewish tradition which understands sin on the basis of *epithumia* (see below).[86] In this tradition *epithumia* is radicalised. As in 4 Maccabees 2.6, so too in Rom 7.7 the command οὐκ ἐπιθυμήσεις (a quotation from Ex 20.17/Deut 5.21) is introduced without an object. This radicalising is then given expression by Paul in Rom 7.8 by his speaking of 'every' *epithumia* which *hamartia* caused through the commandment. Here clearly we have *a transition from the noetic to the ontic* (see Note 84). While according to verse 7 *hamartia* and *epithumia* are together referred to as objects of knowledge – both *are* already there and because of the *nomos* also *become* such objects – according to verse 8 'every *epithumia*' is the object, or more precisely, the product of *hamartia*. Accordingly the term '*epithumia*' is not used in precisely the same sense in the two verses.

Paul's concern may then be set out as follows: because the *nomos* is misused by *hamartia* as its operational base, no guilt can be attached to it. Rather it was, in its basic imperative, concerned with life: ἡ ἐντολὴ ἡ εἰς ζωήν. It is *hamartia* that was guilty of the perversion of the εἰς ζωήν into an εἰς θάνατον (7.10). The two prepositions εἰς are however in no sense completely identical as to content. The first is intended to express the primordial intention of the Law (or of its author) – what it was really out for; but the second seeks merely to show the direction in which *hamartia* has perverted the *nomos*. Αὕτη εἰς θάνατον is accordingly not intended in the similarly actual and direct sense as is ἡ ἐντολὴ ἡ εἰς ζωήν. Αὕτη εἰς θάνατον is a sheerly paradoxical turn of phrase. It is used to express the reason for the command being misused contrary to its proper εἶναι εἰς. Thus here the command or Law is not the active but the passive element. Even to speak of the *nomos* working with sin is possible only in what is an improper sense of the term. In *this* sense we can agree with Niederwimmer[87] and Käsemann[88] in speaking of a distinction between the original intention and the actual functioning of the Law. But even the expression 'actual functioning' is still a little too strong. Functioning in the proper sense of the word is indeed solely the concern of *hamartia*. In its functioning, *hamartia* makes use of the 'function' of the Law, but uses the command as an operational base (7.8,11: ἀφορμὴν λαβοῦσα against the intentions of either the Law or the commandment.

Thus with perfect clarity Paul can state that it was not what was good which brought death 'to me', i.e., not the Law, which is holy, and its commands, which are holy, just and good (7.12) – but *hamartia* which by the very fact that it abused and exploited the good showed itself to be beyond all measure sinful and heinous (7.13).

Up to this point Paul's train of thought might appear to be still somewhat simple – *hamartia* is so frightful and so depraved that it distorts the intention of the holy *nomos* of God into its opposite; but the Law, despite being abused, remains holy. However, the interpretation of Rom 7.7-13 is complicated as soon as (1) we ask who the 'I' is to whom Paul refers here, and (2) the question is posed whether any further sense may attach to *epithumia*. Both questions, however, are closely interconnected.

According to Günther Bornkamm among others, the term *'epithumia'* has a *double sense*, viz., both a desire for what the *nomos* forbids one to desire (its *antinomian* aspect) and the desire to fulfil the Law and thus to establish one's own righteousness before God (cf. Rom 10.3; its *nomistic* aspect).[89] If this is right, then there is one interpretation which can immediately be reconciled with Paul's argument up to and including verse 10: when sin awoke through the coming of the commandment, it seduced the 'I' – whoever that 'I' may have been or is – into transgressing the commandment and likewise into its *nomistic* abuse in the sense of self-justification before God. However, difficulties arise if verse 11 is supposed to refer, in the context of the preceding verses, to the temptation in paradise.[90] For sin – understood on such an interpretation as an oblique reference to or interpretation of the serpent – did not intend to deceive man by seducing him into a nomistic misuse of the commandment! Nor according to the Biblical story did Adam in any sense want to 'establish his righteousness' (Rom 10.3) by fulfilling the commandment given by God! Thus initially the following alternative interpretations suggest themselves:

(1) Rom 7.11 and consequently 7.8b-11 (with the explanatory γάρ in verse 11) tell by way of explanation the 'story'[91] of Gen 3. In this case however the intention cannot be that the *epithumia* in verses 7, 8a is also to be understood nomistically.

(2) Paul understands the *epithumia* in its dual character of desiring what is forbidden by the *nomos* and of desiring to establish one's own righteousness before God. In this case Paul cannot have Gen 3.13 in mind at Rom 7.11.

It will be hard to contest that, from the standpoint of the overall design of Romans, the assumption of the dual character of *epithumia* is the most immediately obvious. On the other hand, however, there is something attractive about the interpretation which sees in Rom 7.8b-11 an allusion to Gen 3 – an interpretation already championed by a succession of Church Fathers (Methodius, Theodore of Mopsuestia, Theodoret[92]): 'there is nothing in the passage which does not fit Adam, and everything fits Adam alone'

(Käsemann).[93] Let us therefore first of all examine the arguments against an allusion to Gen 3.

Kümmel regards the interrelation of *nomos* and *entole* in the section Rom 7.7-13 as completely incomprehensible on the supposition that *entole* refers to the command in Gen 2.16f.[94] However, if we take the *entole* as the prohibition of the *nomos* which forbids basic evil (see above), then the respective uses of *nomos* and *entole* in Rom 7.7-13 become completely transparent and meaningful. This also answers the objection which argues that in the interpretation in question the *entole*, 'thou shalt not covet', would have to express the content of the prohibition in Gen 2.17; but there, it is argued, while the prohibition to eat is referred to, there is nothing about that of coveting.[95] Of course, it is incontestable that Rom 7.14ff. cannot be explained on the basis of Gen 2 and 3,[96] only there a new idea is already involved, as the change of tense indicates.

According to Bornkamm Paul's statement that without the Law *hamartia* is dead (Rom 7.8b) cannot refer to man's primal state; for 7.8f. speaks of man's being in a world where sin has already found an entry.[97] However, this objection stands only if Rom 5.12[98] is taken very narrowly to mean that sin is *present* among men, i.e., in history, only once the individual Adam has sinned: in other words, that there was a period for Adam without sin. But does Paul intend to be understood in such an objectifying way? Does Paul really want to separate in this way the first man, Adam, and the successors of Adam who exist historically in history? Kierkegaard saw clearly the dilemma which such an interpretation poses: if Adam's sin conditioned the sinfulness of every man who lives historically, but this sinfulness caused such a man's initial sin in each case, then Adam would stand outside the human race. 'With the first sin came sin into the world. Exactly in the same way is this true of every subsequent first sin of man, that with it sin comes into the world.'[99] This view of Kierkegaard's corresponds entirely to the purport of what is said in Rom 5.12: sin came into the world through Adam and *therefore* death – death came to all men *because* all sinned. Thus on both occasions sin, or sinning, is seen as the historical presupposition of death. If we do not wish to attribute an objective theory of sin to Paul, then we must start from the fact that he does not intend to explain the source of sin in the form of an aetiology, but understands Adam in such a way that every man existing historically is bound up in the fate of the protoplast who also lived historically.[100] In other words, sin comes into the world through every man *because* every man sins (Rom 5.12 would be expressed in concentrated fashion by this statement). Thus it is true of every man that we may call his sinning, in quasi-mythological fashion, a 'coming of *hamartia*'. It is true of every man 'that *sin presupposes itself*, that it so comes into the world that by the fact that it is, it is presupposed'(Kierkegaard),[101] but in that case the assumption of Adam's being in a world into which *hamartia* has not as yet found entry is a mythological objectivisation which we can no longer entertain. To quote Kierkegaard once again: we would then be localising Adam's sin as sin in a 'fantastic beginning' outside 'the history of the human race' and making an 'assumption' which is a 'dialectic-fantastic one'.[102] Thus one might even say that Paul too in his time offered an 'existential interpretation', i.e., as regards sin he saw Adam and also men living 'after' Adam, within their own individual histories and historicity, and was thus able to see both historical beings in their interrelatedness.[103] Paul might well have assumed the 'historicity' of what is related in Gen 3 but yet not – unlike the Jahwist![104] – in such a way that he would have presented an historically datable (in his chronological scheme) and historically completed event from the past as an explanation in terms of cause and effect.

Thus there are good reasons for supposing that in Rom 7.8b-11 Paul is referring to Gen 3. But there is still the unresolved difficulty that Gen 3 cannot serve as the justification for an *epithumia* which is nomistically understood. And there is a further difficulty. Since it is most reasonable to take Rom 7.8a as an explanation and development of the idea in 7.7, we shall not expect to see the start of the appeal to Gen 3 until 7.8b – this part of the verse is connected antithetically by νεκρά with 7.9 (ἔζων). But in that case the phrase ἀφορμὴν λαβοῦσα διὰ τῆς ἐντολῆς in verses 8 and 11 has a different sense in each instance. In verse 8 it provides the immediate context for the thesis that recognition of *hamartia* and *epithumia* occurs as a result of the *nomos*. We have indeed seen how as it were in the bygoing the statement about something noetic is transformed into one about something ontic. The term *epithumia* is not always used in the same sense: in verse 7 it is that desire which already 'exists' prior to the act of recognition, and which becomes conscious because of this particular act; in verse 8, on the other hand, it is produced only as a result of the *hamartia* which is already there as the desire each particular man himself exhibits. Behind this vacillation in the use of the term there is, to be sure, a latent theological concern: *epithumia* is both prior to man and at the same time specific to each man as his desire (ἐν ἐμοί). What is said here about man in relation to *epithumia* is similar to what Rom 5.12 says about his being given over to sin (fate) *and* being a sinner who is responsible for his actions (the responsible act in history). Despite the interlocking of the noetic and ontic aspects, it is nevertheless still the noetic aspect which is uppermost in verse 8a in that the phrase 'all kinds of covetousness' is intended to bring out even more clearly the radicalisation which omission of the accusative object in the command quoted in verse 7 had already intimated. What determines the sense of 7.7, 8a is this: *when* 'I' am told 'thou shalt not covet' *I become* someone who does covet both in antinomian and in nomistic terms. In *this* way, according to verse 8, *hamartia* uses the commandment as the operational base for its shameful activity. By contrast, the command is understood differently as the operational base in verse 11: sin – represented by the serpent, which is not expressly mentioned here – slanderously misrepresented the command which God had given in paradise – a command, moreover, of which the purpose was life – by describing it as hypocritical, thus itself hypocritically seeking to produce death by an 'anti-promise' of life. Sin deceived (Gen 3.13: ἠπάτησεν Rom 7.11: ἐξηπάτησεν cf. 2 Cor 11.3) by opposing to the life-bringing command of God the allegedly life-bringing demand which was however death-bringing in its purpose. Thus, according to Rom 7.11, *hamartia* used the command only *indirectly* as an operative basis, but according to 7.8 it used it *directly*.

However, we may again ask whether Paul here is not deliberately embracing two aspects of the effect of *hamartia* within a *single* linguistic usage. In fact he does not, as was already shown, introduce Gen 3 to register a past actuality. To follow Käsemann once again: we are all implicated in the history of Adam.[105] But if every man is implicated in the story of Adam's fall, then in every sin something of what we find in Gen 3 also becomes acute. But then we have an analogy between Adam's being seduced by *hamartia* and each new seduction of man. We again discover that what Paul intends is only really disclosed when we are prepared to take into account his consciously vague use of crucial terms – if we are to extract from them a maximum of meaningful possibilities. Thus his use of the verbs 'live' and 'die' and of those words which are semantically related to them in Rom 7.8-11 is symptomatic of how in a certain sense he levels out the difference between the sin of Adam (and Eve! cf. 2 Cor 11.3), concretely described in Gen 3, and every other sinful deed. Although Kümmel decidedly rejects the idea of discerning a connection with Gen 3 in Rom 7.8ff. (see above: even in ἐξηπάτησεν in Rom 7.11 he sees no allusion to the serpent[106]) his very careful exegesis can take us further on this point: in Rom 7.8 νεκρά means that sin though it is present is not imputed[107] – as Lagrange puts it, sin is 'sans force',[108] and ἔζων in Rom 7.9 means, as B. Weiss says, being alive 'in the full meaning of the word', while ἀνέζησεν in Rom 7.9 means to be fully effective,[109] and ἀπέθανον in Rom 7.9 means the cessation of life in the full religious sense of the phrase.[110] In brief: ζῆν and ἀποθανεῖν do not simply mean physical life and physical death.[111]

If then, it is also true of Rom 7.7ff. to say that Paul does not, in accordance with some modern ideal, use language as a system of non-ambivalent signs, this reinforces the view that *in* telling the story of Gen 3 he interprets it in such a way that men 'after' Adam, or rather men *as* Adam are *also* referred to in it. But that is to say that Paul 'reports' how sin (the Serpent) deviously used an 'anti-promise' against the paradisal command which promised life and thus *at that time* misused the command of God as an operational base for its loathsome activity. In this way however, Paul at the same time has *already in mind* how man through hearing the Law experiences confrontation with the sin that dwells within him – or, in concrete terms, how man experiences confrontation with the *epithumia* which continues to characterise him and of which he has only now become conscious. So Paul does not think and argue on just a single level.[112]

Karl Prümm speaks very finely in this way of Paul as the *'Mann der Zusammenschau'*, the man who takes a synoptic view.[113] Thus the apostle sees

the death of Adam and the 'death' (and dying!) of the sinner synoptically, and
he has a similarly synoptic view of how under the power of *epithumia* man in
different ways becomes sinfully covetous . And even if it is incontestable that
Adam did not wish to establish his own righteousness before God by following
the divine command, yet Adam's sin mentioned in Gen 3 and Israel's sin
referred to in Rom 10.3 do find their *tertium comparationis* in one point: *Adam
wanted to be like God.* Unconsciously (ἀγνοοῦντες) however, Israel too
presumes to *want to be like God*; for those who seek to justify themselves do
presume on what is God's prerogative.

To resume: the train of argument in Rom 7.7-13 suggests the following
analysis, if, that is, we are willing to assume for this section the dual sense of
epithumia.

Rom 7.7: the Law is not sin but *in being* promulgated to man it makes him
aware of sin or, concretely, *epithumia.*

Rom 7.8a: intensification of the idea that by making use – *in principle* – of
the divine command, sin causes all kinds of *epithumia*, antinomian and
nomistic.

Noetic and *ontic* standpoints merge into each other in Rom 7.7f.: in that he
becomes conscious of his covetousness as a forbidden covetousness, the
covetous man *sins* as a result of precisely this covetousness-which-has-
become-conscious. (We are just coming to the discussion of how far *epithumia*
understood nomistically can become conscious as a result of the *nomos.*)

Rom 7.8b-11: Paul appeals to Gen 3 to justify his attitude. However, Gen 3 is
used in *such* a way that it illuminates every man's situation under the Law. Thus
Paul adduces reasons for the 'fundamental' pronouncement in verse 8a in the
shape of an event which initially refers only to a single point in time but which is
capable of being extended to embrace the fundamental views enunciated in
verse 8a. But this argument takes place on a dual level not so much in the
interests of the man who has been deceived by *hamartia* but rather primarily to
champion the *nomos*: it is true that there is a cognitive relation between *nomos*
and *hamartia* – but only *hamartia* is to blame.

Rom 7.12f.: Thus the *nomos* is good and holy and *hamartia* has for this very
reason shown itself to be all the more sinful.

The basic question at the start of this chapter was whether according to Rom
3.20 the Jew is able to recognise the *hamartia* which determines him. This
question was made more specific: does the Jew recognise *hamartia* as such, or
only its symptoms, i.e., individual deeds of sin and individual transgressions of
the Law?

In what respect can Rom 7.7-13 advance the enquiry? Let us first of all
dismiss the possible objection that the question has been wrongly put. The
point can be made thus. Because this section is organically linked with 7.14-25,
in which section however we have to do with a description of man under the

Law from the perspective of faith, therefore 7.7-13 too can be interpreted only as conceived from this point of view. Thus it is said that we cannot here expect any answer to the question of the kind of discernment the Jew could attain to from *his* perspective. Now, however, Kümmel, to whom we owe the final breakthrough to the recognition that Rom 7 involves a Christian interpretation of the fact that man necessarily fails when confronted with the Law,[114] has shown that in 7.7-13 we have a description of how man falls prey to death as a result of sin. But he has also shown how this event is explained in 7.14-24 by introducing for that purpose a consideration of the nature of the Law and of man.[115] But in that case we have a methodological reason for not excluding in advance at least the possibility of finding the answer to the question that faces us in 7.7-13. For the specifically Christian 'explanation' of the state of affairs described in these verses is not in fact provided till 7.14ff.! With Ernst Käsemann, it is correct to say of 7.14ff. that 'what sin really is, and the nature of its dominion, escape the category of what may be experienced even in standing under the law...They are brought to light only by the Gospel. The pneumatic alone can perceive them.'[116] In fact: 'Paul's theology as a whole stands or falls with this statement, since the justification of the ungodly is its centre. For it the moral man is the very one who is most deeply engulfed in the power of sin without being able to recognise it according to 9.31 or 10.3.'[117] The perspective adopted by man under the Law is thus too narrow for him to have been able to understand himself in terms of the criteria in 7.14ff. *As a man under the Law*, he is in fact *defined by the fact* that he *cannot recognise the direction in which hamartia has seduced him* and continues to seduce him. As someone who misjudges the nature of his own existence to such a degree he can in no way discern the profundity of the dimension of sin. *He misjudges himself because he misjudges hamartia.* He does not discern that even should he have such power over himself as no longer to covet in the antinomian sense, he would still be *totally* determined by *hamartia* and *epithumia*, precisely in his striving for righteousness before God. The tragedy of man under the Law is expressed in precise terms in Rom 7.15: 'What I do, I know not (οὐ γινώσκω).' And because this statement is made from the perspective of the believer, it can be rephrased in the third person: he does not know that he does not know what he does.[118] The 'knowledge of sin' which is expressed in 7.14ff. is thus not a possibility for a Jew. Accordingly, in 3.20b we read of the 'knowledge of *hamartia*'; moreover 3.20a makes clear that this judgement, intended specifically as an exclusive judgement (...only through the Law), is clearly a judgement of faith. Paul thus cannot mean at the end of the chain of proof in 1.18-3.20 that the deep dimension of sin in the sense of 7.14ff. dawns on the Jew as a Jew through the Law. Anyone who has made as much progress in his knowledge as the 'I' in Rom 7.14ff. has left the status of being a 'Jew' far behind.[118a]

In Rom 7.7-13 on the other hand, the argument is, as we have seen, conducted on at least two levels. As regards *epithumia* understood in an antinomian way, it must, however, be plainly said that even the man under the Law knows when he is offending against the command (or prohibition), 'thou shalt not covet'. And if we bear in mind that the radicalisation of *epithumia* achieved in Rom 7.7, and thus the interpretation of *hamartia* (not of sinful *deeds*!) by this same *epithumia*, is neither specifically Pauline nor specifically Christian – if we bear in mind that Paul is following a Jewish tradition 'in understanding the commandment against covetousness as the core and sum of the Law',[119] when he – with Käsemann (and Lagrange) – sees in *epithumia* 'the beginning of all sin',[120] he can certainly never have meant that the recognition or knowledge of this 'beginning of all sin' was restricted to the Christian. In Rom 7.7 – once again quietly setting aside verse 8a – it is in fact specifically knowledge of the *parabasis* of the *epithumia* prohibition that is evaluated as knowledge of *hamartia*. In other words, *in becoming aware of the sinful deeds of this or that moment, man already becomes conscious of something of the essential power of hamartia.*[121] But then in my view it is no longer possible to see sin, as Bultmann did, as 'not something that is discernible in the empirical man', and as not identical with man's moral lapses (understood by Bultmann as total divergence of sin and moral lapses) as he did in 1924 in his essay 'Das Problem der Ethik bei Paulus'.[122] If our argument above is valid, then sin is not discernible 'only in the moment...when it is forgiven, only to the Christian view'.[123] We must, of course, agree with Bultmann that according to Rom 7.14ff. the intention of the unjustified man and the purpose of the Law are directed towards life, but that this man simply does not recognise that the consequence of his activity is in reality death; this is necessarily not clear to him simply because he lives apart from Christ. 'Everything that is done is from the beginning directed against its own real intention.'[124] Hans Jonas formulates the philosophical expression of this idea in his brilliant, even if not entirely unproblematic, meditation on Rom 7. He speaks of the existential antinomy of the ethical dimension in itself: 'with the utmost brevity it says that, given human ambivalence, the endeavour to achieve holiness of will condemns itself to becoming an unholy will'.[125]

Let us turn our attention once again to *Galatians*! We saw earlier that the idea expressed in Rom 3.20, 7.7 regarding the recognition of sin through the Law is not as yet found there. Gal 3.19 is rather to be taken in the sense that it is a function of the Law to call forth sinful deeds. Thus while in Romans Paul endeavours with great energy to avoid making the *nomos*, as the *nomos* of God (and thus God himself!), appear to be in any way an element causing sin, and while therefore the relation between the Law and sin (at least primarily) is emphatically defined as a relation of knowledge or recognition, in Galatians Paul writes without hesitation that 'the Law was added because of sins' (i.e., to provoke sin). It is possible to read out of Galatians the notion of the task of making sinful deeds known (where sinful deeds are still understood as far as possible as a symptomatic expression of *hamartia*), only if one has previously read this idea into Galatians from Rom 3.20, 7.7. Correspondingly, in Galatians Paul denigrates the Law as an angelic Law while in Romans he sets the greatest store on its being holy, just and good (7.12) – that it is spiritual (7.14: πνευματικός), i.e., on God's side but not on that of hamartia, God's opponent (6.22).

If we keep this in mind, then we may assume a distinction which is not merely peripheral between the nomos conception in Galatians and that in Romans. For in each of the two letters the function of the nomos is set forth too divergently, not to say incompatibly, to suppose anything else.

However, this observation, so obvious provided the exegesis of Gal 3.19 and Rom 3.20 and 7.7ff. here set forth is accepted, is again put in question if attention is drawn to the existence in Romans also of statements which appear to stand close in content to Gal 3.19 (now taking 'because of transgressions' as referring to God's intention): viz., Rom 4.15 'where there is no law there is no transgression' (parabasis), 5.20 'law came in, παρεισῆλθεν' to increase the trespass' (paraptoma), and above all 11.32 'God has consigned all men to disobedience, in order that he may have mercy on all'. Are these passages not plainly fatal to our hypothesis? Lipsius, for instance, expressly says that according to Rom 5.20 the point of the Law would be to multiply Adam's paraptoma and the multiplication of hamartia thereby occasioned occurs 'in that it became manifest in a multiplicity of transgressions of the Law (not: 'in that man became subjectively aware of it')'.[126]

Let us turn first of all to Rom 4.15. In 4.15a nomos is mentioned as an instrument of God. It is the occasion for the wrath of God – doubtless a reference back to 1.18. According to Michel, there is a lack in verse 15 of an intermediate link such as: the Law occasions transgression but transgression occasions the wrath of God.[127] We may then ask how we are to understand the idea of transgression's being occasioned by the Law? There is already a difference between Rom 4.15a and Gal 3.19 in that the wrath[128] caused by the Law is not occasioned by an angelic Law. Moreover it is not a final, i.e., purposive, relation that is here expressed. In other words, we are not told that the nomos was specifically promulgated for the purpose of provoking sins. Rather we have here a consecutive relation, negatively formulated: where there is no nomos, none can be transgressed. However, if we follow the laws of logic, the positive statement implied in this negation should be, simply, that where (a?) nomos[129] is promulgated, it can also be transgressed. But there is no question here of saying that transgressions are a necessary concomitant of the promulgation of the Torah. The Law, in fact, is only the necessary presupposition (in the sense of the conditio, but not the causa), for the possibility of transgressions. If more is read out of 4.15b than this, then we are presupposing from the start that the sentence, which is not formulated as a final clause, was intended by Paul to be final in its purport. But this would be to assert as necessary those transgressions of the Law which are stated in this sentence to be simply a possibility. The train of the argument thus implies

(transposing the sequence of the arguments adduced and conceived in order to arrive at it with some clarity):
1. Where there *is* no *nomos*, it cannot be transgressed;
2. Where a/the *nomos* is promulgated, it can be transgressed;
3. But where transgression occurs, it occasions the wrath of God.

From this it must be inferred that the promulgation of the *nomos* is a necessary link in the articulation of the conditions for the occurrence of the wrath of God.

Accordingly to say that the *nomos* 'occasions' the wrath of God is in no way to make a 'monocausal' statement. Paul does, of course, presuppose that the Law has in fact exercised *this* function for all. But here too, analogously to Rom 7.7ff., we can speak of 'function' only figuratively. In a sense, therefore, the expositions of 4.15 and 7.7ff. support each other. And it is Michel, interpreting 4.15 as 'the Law works transgression', who sees in 7.7-25 the climax of the development through 3.20; 4.15; 5.13; 7.7ff.[130]

But what are we to say of 5.20: 'law came in, *to* increase the trespass'? Our first question is what is meant here by *paraptoma*: is it sin in the sense of *hamartia*, or transgression that is a sinful deed in the sense of *parabasis*? Certainly the individual sinful deed of Adam and the individual sinful deeds of the many are understood by the term in 5.15f. 5.17 repeats 5.15. However, in 5.20 this term is significantly not in the plural; it is not *paraptomata* which are to multiply or increase but the single *paraptoma*![131] And Paul continues – once again significantly – by saying, 'where *hamartia* increased grace abounded all the more'. In this respect we can assume that *paraptoma* here is synonymous with *hamartia*. But if that be so, then this much is at least clear: the final clause in 5.20a, which cannot be denied, cannot mean: so that sinful deeds may increase; *thus there is no direct parallel to Gal 3.19 in Rom 5.20*.[132]

As yet, however, the decisive point has not been mentioned at all. If Paul speaks of sin increasing, that means it was there already! But in Gal 3.19 it was said that the *nomos* was given to provoke transgressions in the first place. In Rom 4.15 it is still only presupposed that there can be no transgression without *nomos*. But here what is being said is that sin is to increase as a result of the 'intervention' of the *nomos*. So here we have a further increase in the power of the already powerful and trans-subjective *hamartia*. The individual sinner is not being discussed here at all. In the universal perspective of 5.12-21, the individual is not primarily under consideration; not that of course we wish in the least to contest the idea that for Paul in the last resort a 'world history', detached from the individual, is inconceivable.[133] What is being said here is that in 'world history' (πάντες οἱ πολλοί) there is to be an increase in sin – certainly, in the context of Romans, as a result of sinful deeds becoming a conscious matter as a deliberate transgression of the Law – *so that* God's gracious act (χάρις) may become superabundantly great and may rule royally.[134] In this way the final clause subserves the higher order final clause in 5.21. Thus whilst in Gal 3.19ff. the drift of the argument moves from the transgressions of the Law which are provoked to the all-embracing power of sin (verse 22), we find in Rom 5.20f. the reverse perspective: the *nomos* is there to increase sin, and the corollary that sin finds expression in sinful deeds is argued out only in the subsequent drawing out of the implications of these claims.

In parenthesis: we may note a certain imbalance in Paul's argument. According to Rom 5.13 there was a period in history, viz., between Adam and Moses, when *parabaseis* were not possible as – see 4.15! – the *nomos* had not yet been given. On the other hand, the Gentiles are a law unto themselves (2.14) and they therefore sin as such without the *Mosaic* Law (2.12). But what then is the position of the Jews up to the time of Moses? Were they not a law unto themselves? It is of course true that this imbalance is manifested only if we regard 5.12-21 as being in the last resort an objectifying statement. Paul can 'contradict himself' uninhibitedly in regard to 'salvation history' because it is not his intention to write history. In no way does he reduce history to human existence, but neither does he reduce existence to history.

Rom 11.32 – the climax of Paul's whole argument on justification – may seem to present the most serious difficulties for the thesis we are trying to develop,[135] for do we not have here the 'final' statement, the lack of which in 4.15 made it possible to differentiate this passage from Gal 3? 'God has consigned all men to disobedience *in order that* he may have mercy upon all.' And do we not find here the very cynicism in regard to God's action which could be combated in Gal 3 only by differentiating the various individual intentions (of God, the Law and the angels)? Now, of course, the exegesis of Gal 3.22 itself showed that συνέκλεισεν as a statement about scripture should be regarded as being on the side of God: God has subsumed in his saving activity the perdition wrought by others. But we should not then assume in Rom 11.33 that Paul falls short of what was said in Gal 3, the more so since in chapter 7 he stood out energetically against the endeavour to make the Law of God coincide in substance with sin. We must therefore ask what verse 32a is saying. How are we to understand the claim that God has consigned all men *to disobedience*? Undoubtedly this verse does stand in the context of predestinarian pronouncements so that disobedience which, in the last resort, is unbelief[136] could appear to be the work of God. If, however, we reflect that, as Käsemann has rightly emphasised, predestination in Paul cannot be grasped using the categories of determinism or indeterminism,[137] and that it is precisely man's disobedience that is regarded as the act for which he is responsible (Rom 11.30f.), then we will have to ask whether the idiom 'to consign to disobedience' should not be explained along the lines of 'afflict with disobedience': God has firmly bound the disobedient to *their* disobedience – has locked them up in it. God has shut them up in the prison of their own disobedience. This idea is given a specific stamp because of the basic forensic features of Romans: being afflicted with one's own disobedience means that God has given them up and abandoned them to their disobedience[138] by counting it against them as disobedience.[139] Karl Barth in his *Church Dogmatics* expressed this in his own particular way. 'We can now continue our answer to the question of the corruption of man in a third proposition which we take from the comprehensive saying of Paul in Rom 11.32. The fact that God willed to have mercy and did have mercy on all men in the sacrifice of Jesus Christ, means that "He hath concluded them all in disobedience". "Concluded" means that he has placed them under an authoritative verdict and sentence which cannot be questioned or disputed, let alone resisted, with all the questions which that involves.'[140]

If we look back on Section 2.3, we may now be able to perceive a theological development from Galatians to Romans, in which the Law of Moses gains in theological force. But this is not an invitation to 'throw the baby out with the bath-water'. There can be no question of obscuring our basic thesis by simply contrasting Galatians and Romans with each other. The two letters are linked in relation to the problems here discussed, at least by the thought that sin is the transgression of God's holy will, as this (so far as Galatians is concerned) gains expression even in the law given by angels – for otherwise this law, as was shown, could not bring into effect the fearful curse. Furthermore, it is also characteristic of Galatians that Paul – from the perspective, of course, of the new order of salvation – does not permit the validity of an existence on the basis of the works of the Law because otherwise man grasps at what is God's: existence is not something which can be produced from the works of the Law understood quantitatively, that is to say, it is not something which is at man's disposal! Even if, in Romans, the quantitative angle is no longer discernible (see below, Section 2.4), we nevertheless in Galatians find in this very category of the quantitative a sort of prelude to a thought which is a key one for this letter. Justification is God's affair alone because it is not something which man can achieve. Yet more: even if Paul was in Galatians plainly arguing in an antinomian fashion, this was done, paradoxical though at first it may appear – in the last resort – because of a basic conviction not so very far removed from what the Law, properly understood in the Old Testament sense, had intended. At all events, Paul's *intention* is also fully an Old Testament one, for – and this can probably be said despite all the problems involved in talking about *the* Torah – the Torah was not concerned with a nomistic attitude and nomistic behaviour. Thus in this way it is possible to see the very work which, within the New Testament, has the most antinomian look about it, as upholding the Torah, rightly understood.[141] But this is just the point: in Galatians, Paul did not as yet see in the proclamation of the angelic law the purpose of a divine law rightly understood. The idea which occurs in both letters, that God integrates *nomos* and *hamartia* in his saving purpose, is to be found differently worked out in each case. In Galatians, the apostle made use of the highly mythological idea of the angelic law. In Romans, he no longer needs this myth. Now, in order to sustain his theological concern which could already be clearly seen in Galatians, he is able to integrate the *nomos* as the *nomos* of God with his theology of justification. Now we no longer have the angelic law provoking sinful deeds, *parabaseis*, but rather we have the divine Law making the sinner conscious of sin, *hamartia*.

2.4 The Fulfilment of the Torah

In Pauline studies, Rom 13.8-10 is repeatedly adduced as a material parallel to Gal 5.14 in the fullest sense. Our discussion so far however suggests that the two passages are significantly divergent. We do not of course expect this divergence to be total: rather we will have to reckon with Rom 13.8-10 being a further development of the thought expressed in Galatians, in such a way that there is no longer a contrast between the Torah and the Law which is valid for the Christian.

In the first place, it is manifest that Romans no longer contains a statement of the idea, which dominates in Galatians, and which contrasts the Law understood quantitatively and requiring complete numerical fulfilment with the Law qualitatively defined in terms of its content and requiring a new kind of 'wholeness'. The argument which Gal 5.3 represents when read in the light of Gal 3.10 is no longer discernible at all in Romans. The category of 'wholeness' no longer has any part to play in Romans in this regard. To be sure, in Rom 13.8-10 we do still hear of 'fulfilling'; the verb πληρόω is just as constitutive for this passage as for Gal 5.14. Moreover the Levitical command to love, Lev 19.18, is referred to both here and in Galatians as λόγος. But the decisive point is that Paul no longer makes use of the phrase 'the "whole" Law'. So we note that *there is no contrasting of 'the whole Law (of Moses)' and 'the "whole" Law (for the Christian)' in Romans*. Such a contrast would indeed run counter to the whole train of argument in this Pauline document. It would have no place in the thought-structure of the letter; it would be pointless in the letter's framework of meaning, and thus would be lacking in sense and incomprehensible.

Of the triad in Gal 5.14 – the whole Law, fulfilling, and the command to love one's neighbour – it is thus indisputable that the element ὁ πᾶς νόμος has been replaced by νόμος, and this in the sense of Torah. *Now we really are concerned with the fulfilment of the Mosaic Torah!* 'He who loves his neighbour has fulfilled the Torah.'[142] Käsemann is correct in saying that 'it should never have been contested that the reference really is to the Torah (*contra* Spicq, *Agape*, II.56; Sanday and Headlam...)'.[143] According to Käsemann the real problem lies in the fact that there is no sort of polemic against the *nomos*.[144] The *fact* of the absence of such a polemic is clear. However, if our reflections so far are right, there should be no real problem in this. On the contrary, the clear lack here of a polemic against the Torah was to be expected, but the text is not entirely as unproblematic as may at first sight appear.

In Rom 2.17ff., the Jews' violation of the Torah is seen as the infringement of the Torah regarded as the expression of the moral will of God. It is entirely in line with this that now the content of the Law is actually no longer reduced to a single prescription and that Paul is rather concerned to show that the *logos* of loving one's neighbour 'sums up' the other commands (ἀνακεφαλαιοῦται). But this is precisely where the problem lies. However much it may appear as if in Rom 13.8-10 the idea of reduction so essential for Galatians has been relinquished because we no longer have, as we had there, a single command emphasised in contrast to a plethora of commands, it is nevertheless now solely the so-called moral commands which are summed up in the command to love one's neighbour. Above all, the corpus of Levitical regulations on purity which is so fundamental to the priestly document is ignored.[145] Correspondingly in the very next chapter we find the double programmatic statement that 'nothing is unclean of itself' and 'everything is clean' (Rom 14.14,20) – standing extremely close to the revolutionary pronouncement by Jesus in Mk 7.15.[146] Scholars are divided over whether Paul knew this saying as a pronouncement of the pre-Easter Jesus. In my view this is certainly something to be considered seriously. But however we may decide about this, the only thing that matters is *the fact that* Paul agrees with Mk 7.15 as to content and says this 'being persuaded in the Lord Jesus' (Rom 14.14).[147] With regard to Mk 7.15 Käsemann has made the well-known statement which has since become classic: 'But the man who denies that impurity from external sources can penetrate into man's essential being is striking at the presuppositions and plain verbal sense of the Torah and at the authority of Moses himself...he is removing the distinction (which is fundamental to the whole of ancient thought) between the *temenos*, the realm of the sacred, and the secular, and it is for this reason that he is able to consort with sinners.'[148] On Rom 14.14 he now says: 'The lasting dogmatic significance of verse 14a lies in the fact that it does not just answer the question of clean and unclean foods but that it removes for Christians the basic distinction of all antiquity, which is still influential today, between the cultic sphere and the profane.'[149] Thus Käsemann can use almost the same words about Paul as about Jesus!

The question which then presses in upon us is how it is that Paul is able to speak so consistently about the Torah as an expression of the will of God, how in this connection he nowhere draws distinctions in Romans with respect to the content of the prescriptions of the Torah, yet can then suddenly contest the most important of the Torah's stipulations (admittedly in a context which is not concerned with Torah) and so at the same time reject a basic implication of its spirit. The sentences quoted in Rom 14.14,20 are certainly not uttered as a criticism of pronouncements of the Torah! Thus in Rom 13.8-10, despite the idea – new in relation to Galatians – of summing up the many commandments in a single one, we have, even if not explicitly stated, *reduction* within the Mosaic Law, just as we find in Galatians, though nothing is said about abrogation; but then in chapter 14 we do have *abrogation* of the commandments of the Mosaic Law which rest on a cultic approach, without express mention of *reduction*, i.e., without explicit criticism of the commandments of the *Torah*.

Though in the last resort reduction and abrogation do amount to the same thing, i.e., the validity merely of the 'ethical' commandments (here more precisely defined as those regulating men's relations with each other) and the invalidity of the cultic commandments – that is, though reduction and abrogation represent solely the two complementary aspects of the same thing – Paul has not attempted to clarify their relationship in Romans. The two ideas are not so interlinked that they deal with the single subject of the Torah in mutual co-ordination – quite apart from the fact that the eschatological word of admonition in Rom 13.11-14 separates the two sections from each other. In fact we should probably see the verses on the fulfilment of the Law and the word of admonition which provides their eschatological justification as marking the conclusion of the general paraenetical part in 12.1ff,[150] so that Paul can now go on to draw the necessary consequences for the situation in the Roman congregation. What Paul then urges is that despite the abrogation of the cultic prescriptions these must still be heeded if the brother who thinks of himself as being bound to them takes offence at their not being observed. Such an attitude demands *love*,[150a] i.e., that commandment which constitutes the fulfilment of the *Torah*. But the matter of fact way in which Paul writes in 14.14,20 – when addressing those who do know the Law (7.1)! – leads one to suppose that what he is concerned about in 13.8-10 is not a *concentration* of the entire Torah *but* in fact its *reduction*. For love, precisely as the sum of the *Law*, does in fact in the concrete instance demand obedience to legal stipulations which have been *cancelled*! More briefly (and paradoxically!): for the sake of fulfilment of the Law, no less, they should renounce the abrogation of the stipulations of the Law which is already in force (!) though only, of course, in individual cases when it is requisite for the sake of one's neighbour. But if this is right one can hardly say that in his discussions in chapters 12 and 13 Paul did not have in mind the question of the relationship of reduction and abrogation. But he did not express the implications which press themselves upon *us* as questions – something which repeatedly strikes us in the exegesis of the Pauline writings. To take just one of many possible examples: in Gal 3.10 Paul simply presupposes that everybody sins; but he does not specifically say so (see above).

When Paul in chapter 14 clearly intimates the repeal of the cultic stipulations of the Torah, he transcends – like Jesus – the idea of the 'concentration' of the Torah, which was expressed in contemporary Judaism. There is in fact nothing specifically Christian about this 'concentration' as it is expressed e.g., in Mt 22.34-40 (though there it is of course in the form of the *dual* command of love), i.e., as it is also found in the New Testament. Despite Neusner's objection to the authenticity of Hillel's *logion*, according to which the golden rule in its negative formulation constitutes the *whole of the Torah* in a nutshell, whereas all other commands are only explanatory thereof (Shab 31a), in my view it is still true that this idea had been clearly expressed before Jesus.[151] Similarly there should be no real doubt but that in the basic text or *Grundschrift* of the Test Patr the command to love is seen as the central command of the Law, so that here too this 'concentration' has taken place – no matter how we may in detail assess Jürgen Becker's literary critical findings.[152] On the other hand, however, in Jewish writings of the period we do not find the idea that the ethical commands are being played off against the cultic commands as Klaus Berger for instance tries to show.[153]

Ben Sira is typical. Johannes Marböck draws attention to the point that it is specifically in summary formulae (Sir 17.14, 28.6) that one's behaviour towards one's neighbour is mentioned, while typically Israelite laws such as the stipulations regarding the Sabbath and foods and purity, and also polemics against idolatry, are not found there.[154] Nevertheless Ben Sira's particularly special concern – so Marböck – is the continued existence and maintenance of the Zadokite priesthood or the priestly theocracy.[155] However anyone who has so unmistakably championed the cause of the priesthood will never deliberately or consciously make a move against the cultic stipulations, no matter how much he may see in the ethical commands an essential element of the Law.

Thus Hengel's criticism of Berger's position must be sustained: 'We do not find within the pre-Christian Judaism of the diaspora, let alone in Palestine, a real and *fundamental* criticism of the Law, that is, one with a religious motivation, which, say, rejected the whole of the ritual law and concentrated only on the moral commandments.'[156] If this is right, then it is true to say that Jesus and Paul put forward an idea which was *new* in the history of the religious traditions of their Jewish world. This assessment of Jesus and Paul does not mean that we are ignoring such Hellenistic tendencies in pre-Maccabean Jerusalem as prepared the ground for the Syrian king Antiochus IV – with their opposition to circumcision, the ritual law, etc.[157] For these circles, in contrast to Jesus and Paul, did not take God seriously in the matter of the demands of his holiness – they were not concerned with the God of Israel. Contrary to this, Jesus and Paul were in no sense interested in advancing the cause of an enlightened and cynical religion.

Might it not, however, be possible to discern in the Pauline judgement in Rom 14.14 that 'nothing is unclean in itself' an attenuation of Jesus' unambiguous pronouncement? We could in fact lay the emphasis on the δι' ἑαυτοῦ: if something is unclean it is not so intrinsically. This would mean the exclusion only of that condition of uncleanness which is in fact intrinsic – this as distinct from the other condition of uncleanness which is given articulation in the famous sentence of Rabban Johanan ben Zakkai: 'By your life a dead person does not make you unclean and water does not make you clean, but there is an ordinance of the king of all kings; God has said: I have laid down a

Law and established an ordinance; no man is entitled to transgress my ordinance; for we read: this is an ordinance of the Torah which the Lord has given' (Pesiqta 40b).[158] But the distinction between uncleanness or cleanness which is intrinsic and uncleanness or cleanness which is the result of God's ordinance is anachronistic. For the priestly legislation of the Old Testament such a question is inappropriate because it lies outside the orbit of that kind of thinking, and as for Paul, we must recognise that he too cannot perceive *this* alternative at all. The very fact that in verse 20 the phrase 'everything is indeed clean' occurs without the 'qualification' we have in verse 14 should give food for thought. Paul's real concern is with a completely different distinction, that between intrinsic uncleanness and uncleanness *for someone* and in this respect Paul does in fact make a qualification. Otto Michel rightly says: 'Despite this fundamental agreement (viz., with Mk 7.15) the apostle limits the scope of this thesis. In itself no food is unclean but it may well become so because of the person who considers it to be unclean.'[159] However this limitation is not intended to reverse the fundamental repeal of cultic legislation. Paul's real interest is in his *theological reflection which starts from the human being concerned.* That is to say, his starting point is not 'objective' dogma. Thus, as is well known, in Rom 3.25 he incorporates in a traditional dogmatic formula the obtrusive phrase 'by faith' – which for him is in no sense obtrusive but rather urgently necessary. Similarly the elements of the world are in themselves weak and beggarly elements and in reality are not gods at all (Gal 4.8f.). But *for that person* who puts himself under the power of the Torah they are nevertheless enslaving powers. If one believes in them, or in the Law which is functionally a unity with them, they *become* a cruel and fearful power. Here we can see Paul's *existential* mode of thought in action: his theological pronouncements are fundamentally made within the system of co-ordinates represented by 'for the believer/for the unbeliever'. However different the individual letters may be, even in regard to content, the existential structure of Paul's theological thought remains. To revert once more to Johanan ben Zakkai: once the idea of 'intrinsic uncleanness' has been expressed by Christian theology, and specifically by Paul's theology, a rabbinic reaction is conceivable in the terms mentioned above. However, the alternative element, 'intrinsic cleanness', is now incorporated in a new distinction, viz., between 'clean/unclean intrinsically – clean/unclean by the ordinance of God', and this distinction can best be understood as a polemical formula or as a polemical disclaimer.

Notes

1. A simple καθώς introduces Gal 3.6 whereas Rom 4.3 has the question, τί γὰρ ἡ γραφὴ λέγει; the LXX initially has the sequence καὶ ἐπίστευσεν Ἀβραμ (not Ἀβραάμ), Gal 3.6 has Ἀβραάμ ἐπίστευσεν and Rom 4.3 has ἐπίστευσεν δὲ Ἀβραάμ.

2. Dietzfelbinger, *Heilsgeschichte bei Paulus?*, 12: In Rom 4 Paul does not deal with the Sinai event explicitly. 'But the subject-matter of Gal 3.17, the temporal priority of the promise

to the Law, is trenchantly introduced in Rom 4.13...'

3. διαθήκη occurs in Romans in the singular only at 11.27 and there, significantly, in an Old Testament quotation. In 9.4 the term is used in the plural. There it means the covenant agreements of God with his people which have taken place during the 'history of Israel' (on which we shall have more to say as these reflections proceed). We must clearly accept that the sense of 'testament' or 'will' for διαθήκη, as we find it in Gal 3, is no longer to be found in Romans, nor at all, after Galatians. διαθήκη does to be sure appear in Galatians in the Sarah-Hagar allegory of 4.21ff., as distinct from its use in 3.15ff., in a peculiarly modified way. Here the term is, in the view of many exegetes, still used in the sense of 'the two (mutually exclusive) testaments' (see e.g., Schlier, *Gal*, 219; Mussner, *Gal*, 321, n. 26; but contrast Lang, 'Gesetz und Bund bei Paulus' = *Rechtfertigung*, 314). At all events it is difficult after what we have said up to now to see the Hagar διαθήκη, as Schlier and Kähler do, in terms of a 'divinely established order'. Thus διαθήκη in Gal 4.21ff. will rather be interpreted as a neutral quantity in the sense of 'order' (cf. Behm, art. διαθήκη, *TWNT* II.133.24 – E.T. II 130.29), given a theological dimension only because of Sarah and Hagar. To an extent it is possible to draw a line from Gal. 4.21ff. to 2 Cor 3, but then we must also assume for Paul, with reference to the term διαθήκη, an element of theological history – i.e., a theological process of development: in 2 Cor 3 old and new διαθήκη are contrasted in the sense of Old and New Covenant (Bultmann, *2 Kor*, 79ff.). The two covenant agreements do not stand merely in a relation of discontinuity to each other (3.6 letter/spirit; death/life). The ministry of Moses like that of the Spirit now took place in divine glory, in *doxa* (3.7f.). From this, continuity can also be asserted by means of the category of *a fortiori* (3.11: πολλῷ μᾶλλον). If as often as Moses is read a veil lies over the hearts of the Jews, the implication is that Christians, who have the Spirit, can hear from Moses God's word of promise (cf. Bultmann, *2 Kor*, 90ff.) (3.15 and 4.13).

4. Bill. III.203.

5. Thus most exegetes – among others Käsemann, *Römerbrief* 120 (E.T. 127). [Note: the English translation is based on the fourth German edition and consequently cross-references therein to the German text do not match ours. (Translator)]

6. Dietzfelbinger, *Paulus und das Alte Testament*, 13, n. 27: 'And in Romans 4 we have the only passage where Paul attributes a certain relevance in terms of salvation-history to circumcision, but only to Abraham's circumcision...' Thus Dietzfelbinger sees how Romans differs from Galatians, but soft-pedals the significance of circumcision in Romans too much (see Rom 3.1f.!). However it is not correct to say that in Rom 4 only Abraham's circumcision is involved! It is therefore also an over-statement when in *Heilsgeschichte bei Paulus?*, 42 this author, appealing to Gal 3 and (!) Rom 4, says that Paul excluded the Jewish people as such from the descendants of Abraham. In the course of our exposition it will become apparent that Paul's dialectical mode of argument can only be expressed in rather more carefully distinguished statements. It is not enough for Dietzfelbinger, ibid. 42, to say that Paul did not block the path of the Jews to faith.

7. Käsemann, *Röm*, 97 (E.T. 104f.).

8. For more detailed exegesis of Rom 3.31 see Section 3.3 of the present study.

9. Goppelt, *Theologie* II, 383, in continuity with his previous publications (*Typos*, 164ff., 279), understands Abraham as a type: in Rom 4 the justification of Abraham and that of Christians are '*not linked by the continuity of history*' (Goppelt's italics). We are not going to discuss here how far there is a typology in Rom 4 (according to Bultmann, 'Ursprung und Sinn der Typologie als hermeneutischer Methode' = *Exegetica*, 377, there is no typology in Rom 4). We would simply point out that Goppelt's opposition to a historical continuity is not sufficiently subtle. In *Theologie*, 383 he does indeed refer only to Rom 4. But in *Typos*, 164ff. there is an undifferentiated exegesis of Gal 3 and Rom 4. Might it still be possible for this to find expression in the quotation produced above? For the rest the question of typological

thinking in Paul does not seem to me to be very productive for our enquiry.

10. Betz, 'The Literary Composition and Function of Paul's Letter to the Galatians', *NTS* 21, 356. We should then of course have to reconsider the relation of 'highly skilled composition' to the Pauline letter as a product of dictation by word of mouth.

11. See Section 2.2 of this study.

12. See Section 2.2 of this study.

13. Or perhaps when all is said not so entirely unexpectedly if we take Gal 2.2 completely seriously. D. E. H. Whiteley in *Theology*, 300 has a very concrete way of referring to a possible *Jewish* objection to the argument from scripture in Gal 3: 'At this point a Jewish objector would have gasped with rage and surprise and would have said: "The brazen impertinence of the man! Has he forgotten that the διαθήκη with Abraham was in fact sealed with the blood of circumcision?" We may speculate that someone did make this supremely obvious point and that this led Paul to make the reply expounded in Rom. iv. that it is recorded that Abraham put his faith (Hebrew 'aman) in God (Gen. xv. 6, and here only), while his circumcision was not recorded until Gen. xvii.' Thus Whiteley also considers that Paul's attitude to circumcision in Rom 4, which seeks to cope with Gen 17 too, could be traced back to an objection to Gal 3. However, the expression, 'a Jewish objector', suggests that the 'someone' objecting on the strength of Gen 17 was in fact a Jew. But why may he not equally well have been a *Jewish Christian*? Even a Jewish Christian well-disposed to Paul's Gentile mission with its freedom from the Law must nevertheless have reacted 'with rage and surprise' to the argument in Gal 3. There could in fact be really but *one* reaction from the most or from the least tolerant Jewish Christian: 'This is a deliberate and diabolical perversion of the Torah! It is the intransigent work of a renegade! It is treason against Israel!' On the supposition which most recent Pauline research has increasingly substantiated – viz., that Paul's opponents in Galatia were Judaisers – it is in my view inconceivable that the Jewish Christian Church in Jerusalem would not have heard of the antinomian pronouncements in Gal, and if it did hear of them, then we may very reasonably suppose that it reacted in one way or another (see also Section 2.2 of this investigation)! On the relationship between the Galatian opponents of Paul and Jerusalem Schenke writes as follows: '1. The success of the agitators in Galatia can only be understood if they came on the scene with a clear claim to authority, i.e., if they appealed to Jerusalem. 2. The people in Galatia who were pressing for the circumcision of the Christians must somehow or other be in a relationship with those who had already made this demand before the apostolic council in Syria and at the apostolic council in Jerusalem' (Introduction I, 82.). So is it pure imagination to suppose that Paul's Galatian opponents were intimating to Jerusalem that Paul was perverting the Law in Gal because he was betraying what was written in Gen 17?

14. In Rom 3.1 τὸ περισσὸν τοῦ Ἰουδαίου and ἡ ὠφέλεια τῆς περιτομῆς are used almost synonymously.

15. τὰ λόγια τοῦ θεοῦ understood with Käsemann, *Röm*, 73 (E.T. 78f.) as the 'promise of the Gospel'.

16. E.g., Kuss, *Röm*, 100: 'the entire Old Testament revelation...the Law and above all...the promises'; Cranfield, *Romans*, I. 179; Stuhlmacher's view in *Gerechtigkeit*, 85, is too narrow: 'τὰ δικαιώματα τοῦ νόμου in 2.26 seems to be picked up again' but he too speaks of the 'character of promise in this divine law'. Herold, *Zorn*, 295: Rom 3.2 picks up Bar 2.20: 'God's wrath corresponds to his λόγια (cf. Rom 3.2).' Behind this arbitrary interpretation lies the integration of God's wrath in his δικαιοσύνη; e.g., 301: the tribunal of wrath as the revelation of δικαιοσύνη.

17. Käsemann, *Röm*, 67 (E.T. 73), on the basis of Flückiger, *Die Werke des Gesetzes bei den Heiden*, *ThZ*, 8, 29, understands τὰ δικαιώματα τοῦ νόμου in Rom 2.26 as the entirety of the Torah, which is defined by legal statements; but even apart from the fact that this expression refers to the Gentiles, of whom Paul cannot really say that they 'keep' the entirety

of the Law (and Käsemann, ibid., 68, E.T. 73, rightly sees that he cannot say so), it should be kept in mind that the context in which we find it does not substantiate the stated purpose of the argument in Gal.

18. See R. Meyer, art. περιτέμνω, *TWNT* VI.76.38ff. (E.T. VI.77.17ff.).

19. Michel, *Röm*, 105.

20. Klein, 'Individualgeschichte und Weltgeschichte' = *Rekonstruktion und Interpretation*, 205.

21. See especially Käsemann, *Röm*, 241ff. (E.T. 253ff.); Müller, *Gottes Gerechtigkeit*, *passim*.

22. Cf. also Dietzfelbinger, *Heilsgeschichte bei Paulus?*, 17.

23. Correctly ibid., 20: Paul bases the saving character of Israel's history 'in the divine offer and not in what Israel does'.

24. Cf. Luz, *Geschichtsverständnis*, 270: in Rom 9.6b 'the notion that "Israel" is a sociologically identifiable entity has already been abandoned in principle.' For Luz the hint has thus been given that 'Israel' does not derive its unity from the national entity so called. Rather we should say that 'God himself bestows on Israel its character *as* Israel' (ibid., 270). This is correct. We may even say that it has been splendidly formulated. Except that I am not sure whether Luz is not perhaps undervaluing the 'national entity' here. For after all it is to Israel and specifically to Israel that God gives this character *as* Israel. Dietzfelbinger, *Heilsgeschichte bei Paulus?*, 17, n. 40 is right, against Müller, *Gottes Gerechtigkeit*, 50, who considers the Jewish idea of God's people as destroyed in Rom 2.29 and 9.6ff.

25. Luz is correct, ibid., 270, n. 12 when he says that Paul's concern is not 'the substitution of the Church as the Israel of God for the Israel of the *sarx*'.

26. Cf. ibid., 274: 'Paul can speak positively of Israel in such a fashion as was never done to my knowledge in the Judaism of the period...'

27. Käsemann, *Röm*, 246 (E.T. 258).

28. It is only later that Paul comes to speak of the Gentile Christians, especially at 9.25ff. and 11.11ff., but linked to the subject of Israel.

29. Käsemann puts this splendidly in *Röm*, 251 (E.T. 263) with reference to the Israel according to the flesh as the bearer of the promise: 'For this (i.e., Rom 9.4f.) asserts continuity in the earthly sphere (Asmussen), which is partially contested in vv. 6b-7 and radically so in v. 8. Any attempt at harmonising blocks an adequate solution of the basic problem, which in view of the contradiction can only be dialectical and paradoxical.'

30. Käsemann, *Röm*, 254 (E.T. 267).

31. Luz, *Geschichtsverständnis*, 270.

32. Ibid., 273.

33. Ibid., 273.

34. See Section 1.2 of this investigation.

35. At most we could say that we have in Gal 2.9 part of an official agreement in that here we possibly have the arrangement made about the divided missionary activities. But as is well known not even this formula is clear: are we dealing with the separation of missionary areas? Mussner, *Gal*, 123, n. 120, finds in this text nothing but the Pauline interpretation of the agreement made at that time, but not the official text; the 'we' would by itself already tell against that. He thinks that it is erroneous to think of this agreement *merely* in geographical terms, as a division of missionary areas (ibid., 123, n. 120). For the view that Gal 2.7f. is a quotation from the official minutes of the Synod – a view somewhat differently supported in different writers – see Cullmann, *Petrus*, 19 (E.T., 2nd ed., 20); Dinkler, 'Der Brief an die Galater' = *Signum Crucis*, 279; and especially Klein, 'Gal 2.6-9' = *Rekonstruktion und Interpretation*, 106ff. Against this see Mussner, *Gal*, 117, n. 93. For Gal 2.7f. as the text of a minute we have the evidence of the repeated form of the name, 'Peter', which is unique in Paul. On the other hand, ἰδόντες is not quite appropriate to the introduction of a minute.

According to Klein the causal connection between vv. 7 and 8 can be explained incomparably better from the standpoint of the negotiations than from that of the *Auctor ad Galatas* (loc. cit., 119). But it could also be argued that vv. 7f., as a Pauline summary of a common opinion expressed at the Synod, have the function of providing a preparatory argument for the Galatians, to herald the summary of the resolution of the Synod contained in the conclusion of v. 9. Yet perhaps Mussner is not altogether wrong: 'Discussion on Gal 2.6-9 will probably never be brought to an end' (loc. cit., 117, n. 93).

36. Thus among others Kümmel, *Einleitung*, 261f. (E.T. 194f.); Wilckens, 'Über Abfassungszweck und Aufbau des Röm' = *Rechtfertigung als Freiheit*, 130; Eckert, *Verkündigung, passim*; Mussner, *Gal*, 25; Vielhauer, 'Gesetzesdienst und Stoicheiadienst im Gal' = *Rechtfertigung*, 541-555. On Jewett, see n. 1 of Section 1.1 of this investigation. For a survey of the various views on Paul's opponents in Galatia, see Mussner, *Gal*, 11-29 (= *Einleitung*, para. 4., Die Gegner). The considerations presented in this section (2.2) of our investigation also support the old thesis about Judaisers. Strobel also, in 'Das Aposteldekret in Galatien', *NTS* 20, 177-190, sees Jewish Christians at work in Galatia. In his view they would certainly be there with an official commission from Jerusalem, to introduce the 'apostolic decree' decided on after the Synod, and Paul would then as Romans shows have revised his original rejection of the decree. Thus Strobel's solution to the problem of the difference between Gal and Rom is different from mine. But his study too is an attempt to answer the question of the *theological difference* between the two letters.

37. Wilckens, 'Über Abfassungszweck und Aufbau des Röm' = *Rechtfertigung als Freiheit*, 136, n. 69.

38. Ibid., 136.

38a. See too W. D. Davies, 'Paul and the People of Israel', *NTS* 24, 12f.: 'He was probably aware that the opposition to him in Galatia was succeeding, and that his Jewish opponents in Jerusalem...would certainly be encouraged in their hostility by his failure in Galatia. It was, therefore, a matter of anxious urgency for him to gain the understanding support of the Roman Christian community – Jewish and Gentile – for his position as he went up to the Holy City.'

39. Baur, 'Über Zweck und Veranlassung des Römerbriefs', *Tübinger Zeitschrift für Theologie*, 1838, Heft 3, 59-178.

40. I mention here only the following: G. Harder, 'Der konkrete Anlass des Röm', *TheolViat* 6 (1959), 13-24; Marxsen, *Einleitung in das Neue Testament*, 85ff. (E.T. 92ff.); Klein, 'Der Abfassungszweck des Röm' = *Rekonstruktion und Interpretation*, 1969, 129-144; Jervell, 'Der Brief nach Jerusalem', *StTh* 25 (1971), 61-73; Bornkamm, 'Röm als Testament des Paulus' = *Geschichte und Glaube* II, 1971, 120-139; Wilckens, 'Über Abfassungszweck und Aufbau des Röm' = *Rechtfertigung als Freiheit*, 1974, 110-170; Schmithals, *Der Römerbrief als historisches Problem*, 1975; Suhl, *Paulus und seine Briefe*, 1975, 264ff.

41. Klein, 'Abfassungszweck des Röm' = *Rekonstruktion und Interpretation*, 139.

42. Schmithals, *Römerbrief*, 7.

43. Wilckens, 'Über Abfassungszweck und Aufbau des Röm' = *Rechtfertigung als Freiheit*, 141.

44. Ibid., 160.

45. Ibid., 130; the arguments for my view have been repeatedly expressed in this study. It is therefore superfluous to mention them here.

46. Naturally through messengers, as James and Paul might not have met again before the latter's renewed stay in Jerusalem.

47. When precisely this was so it is hard to say. Let us assume that Gal was written before 1 Cor (against Borse, *Der Standort des Galaterbriefes*; Borse's view is also affected by his approximating Rom and Gal too closely as to content). In favour of this view is first of all the completely different attitude in each letter. In Gal Paul is engaged in a fight on principle

against putting oneself under the Law. But in 1 Cor 9.20 he is able to say that to those who are under the Law he becomes as one who is under the Law. This passage sounds almost like a Magna Charta of pastoral tolerance. Deissmann, *Paulus*, 54f. (E.T. 80f.) already spoke in regard to 1 Cor and Rom of Paul as being sometimes very tolerant, but in regard to Gal he referred to the 'classic of intolerance'. Drane, 'Tradition, Law and Ethics in Pauline Theology', *NovTest* 16, 175, organises these circumstances into a temporal sequence which can be supported *theologically*: Paul condemns Peter in Antioch (Gal 2.11ff.), 'an action which runs quite counter to Paul's instructions on the very same thing in 1 Cor VIII and his statement of his own procedure in IX 19-23.' What Paul says in 1 Cor 7.19 is so modified in relation to Gal that 'he appears to be saying exactly the opposite of what is said in Gal' (ibid., 170). 'But in 1 Cor VII 19 Paul goes on to make a statement which would appear to be totally incompatible with his position on circumcision (i.e., in Gal)...' (ibid., 171). Drane also rightly sees that 'A new and distinctive element has appeared here (i.e., in 2 Cor) in contrast to both Gal and 1 Cor, namely the emphasis on the "new covenant", something mentioned for the first time briefly, and almost casually, in 1 Cor XI 25' (ibid., 171; see also n.3 of this section of our study). We cannot go further into Drane here. But it should be noted that he traces Paul's new attitude in 1 Cor to a theological modification in his thinking subsequent to Gal. Another circumstance favouring Gal's being written earlier than 1 Cor might be the fact that in Gal 3.27ff. the theologoumenon about the body of Christ does not appear – which would be very odd if Gal were to have been written after 1 Cor. The reappearance in Rom 14f. of the tolerance which finds expression in 1 Cor 8f. is the circumstance which to me is decisive for the chronological priority of Gal. If one sought to place Gal in between these two letters, the result would be a zig-zag line. For the chronological sequence Gal, 1 Cor, Rom, see also Strecker, 'Befreiung und Rechtfertigung' = *Rechtfertigung*, 480. The view that 1 Cor 16.1 rules out the temporal priority of Gal over against 1 Cor (thus again most recently in Suhl, *Briefe*, 222), loses its force when we consider that Paul revised his radically antinomian view and on that basis *too* a total break with the Galatian congregations is not at all so certain as has to a great extent been cheerfully assumed.

48. Bornkamm, 'Der Röm als Testament' = *Geschichte und Glaube* II, 137; on the theological significance of the Collection see especially Munck, *Heilsgeschichte*, 298f. (E.T. 303): the reason for Paul's bringing the Collection to Jerusalem in person despite imminent danger to his life lies in his view of the link between the Gentile Mission and the Jewish Mission. 'It is his intention to save the Jews by making them jealous of the Gentiles, who are accepting the Gospel in great numbers' (E.T. 303). Paul is thinking of Isaiah 2.2ff., Micah 4.1ff. and Isaiah 60.5f. Georgi, *Kollekte*, extends this thought: Paul inverts the idea in Deutero-Isaiah: 'It is not the Jews who preceded the Gentiles but the other way round' (p. 72). He speaks of the provocative character of the Collection (p. 84).

49. If this is right should one continue to speak as definitively of the provocative nature of the Collection as does Georgi? It is at least less provocative than the *nomos* conception in Gal. But certainly, however much Paul gives ground, an element of provocation does remain.

50. Fuchs, *Hermeneutik*, 191 (on which see Marxsen, *Einleitung*, 88, E.T. 94); Wilckens, 'Über Abfassungszweck und Aufbau des Röm' = *Rechtfertigung als Freiheit*, 167 (cf. Schmithals, *Römerbrief*, 34f.; Holtz's review and Wilckens, 'Rechtfertigung als Freiheit', *ThLZ* 101, 265).

51. Despite the diatribe style the questions raised by way of objection cannot then (only) be the work of fictitious opponents.

51a. In his study, *Paulus der Heidenapostel I*, Gerd Lüdemann objects to the ideas set forth here in Section 2.2. He says they are 'encumbered with the completely indemonstrable hypothesis' (we may ask what hypothesis is after all demonstrable!) that James received word about Gal or at least about its contents (p. 116, n. 139). But how can we reconcile this radical scepticism towards my conjecture with what Lüdemann himself writes about Paul's Galatian opponents? He says: 'Rather are Paul's opponents in Galatia to be regarded as Palestinian (!) Jewish Christians who were taking offence at Paul's preaching of the Gospel of freedom from the Law. For them the true Gospel could be taught only in Jerusalem or starting from Jerusalem and it included the observance of legal requirements' (p. 59). Thus at a decisive point Lüdemann even goes beyond what I have said; for I have not included the Palestinian origin of these people in my reflections, as it did not seem proven to me. However I do consider the Palestinian origin of Paul's opponents to be in every way possible. But if they were Palestinian Jewish Christians – i.e., people whose home was in Palestine – then contact with the Church leaders in Jerusalem is not merely to be supposed but must be accepted as a probability bordering on certainty! It is only with great difficulty that we can conceive of Palestinian Jewish Christians intervening in Galatia and getting to know about the letter to the Galatians there, and then returning to Palestine and failing to pass on even a single word to James and the other leaders in the Jerusalem community about the danger which in their eyes existed in Galatia! It was at all events a danger which in terms of their self-understanding concerned the very root of the Christian faith: the congregation was separated from the maternal soil of Israel and was thus robbed of its real vital power! It is *equally* a hypothesis not to assume contact between Paul's opponents from Galatia and the Jerusalem congregation! So reasons must be given by anyone wishing to banish from scholarly consideration this contact as a completely indemonstrable hypothesis. However, a methodical discussion of Lüdemann's position cannot be undertaken here in any thorough-going way. Let us confine ourselves to one question regarding his comments. Lüdemann wishes to establish a Pauline chronology which breaks through existing taboos, and in so doing he appeals in part to American or English work already published. His results constitute an interesting essay which does in fact enrich Pauline studies. Even if objections are raised to essential elements of his line of argument – and in my view they must be – he has nevertheless done us the service of tackling energetically a question which is far from having been exhaustively discussed. Lüdemann wishes to establish his chronology *solely* on the basis of external criteria, e.g., on the basis of Paul's pronouncements on the Collection. He explicitly refuses to use internal criteria, such as pronouncements by Paul which could be interpreted in terms of a theological development. Such an approach is highly debatable. Of course it means that Lüdemann is deliberately contenting himself with a partial view which is *conditioned and tailored by his method*. But if this is so, then he cannot raise the objection against another partial view that the latter, just because it is in fact only partial, is lacking in adequacy. Yet this is what he is doing when he reproaches me for having failed at any point to take the trouble of safeguarding my theses chronologically (p. 116, n. 139). Nor did this seem at all necessary to me, in that I am thinking in terms of that 'old' chronology which puts the Synod shortly before A.D. 50 and shortly thereafter 1 Thess. Also it seems to me – but this time using 'internal' criteria – impossible to read more from the data in Gal and 1 Cor than that Gal was written before 1 Cor, if the danger of over-interpretation is to be avoided. Even to take 1 Cor 16.1 as providing part of the proof for the priority in time of 1 Cor over Gal is purely hypothetical and needs to be argued out in relation to so-called internal criteria. See most recently my review of Lüdemann's book in *ThLZ* 107 (1982), 741-744.

52. Schmithals, *Römerbrief*, 106f.

53. Ibid., 93.

54. e.g., οὖν in 12.1 (ibid., 164); ἐπαναμιμνῄσκων in 15.15 (ibid., 166); the doublets 15.5 and 15.13 (ibid., 154ff.).

55. Ibid., 167ff.

56. Klein, 'Der Abfassungszweck des Röm' = *Rekonstruktion und Interpretation*, 129ff.

57. Schmithals, *Römerbrief*, 154, n. 9.

58. For 2 Cor see e.g., Marxsen, *Einleitung*, 72ff. (E.T. 77ff.).; for Phil see Gnilka, *Phil.*, 6ff.

59. Well worked out by Wilckens, 'Über Abfassungszweck und Aufbau des Röm' =

Rechtfertigung als Freiheit, 143ff.

60. For the difference in substance between the two statements see Section 2.4 of this study.

61. Schmithals, *Römerbrief*, 191ff.

62. Ibid., 178.

63. Betz, 'The Literary Composition and Function of Paul's Letter to the Galatians', *NTS* 21, 353-379.

64. Ibid., 354.

65. The weakest part of Betz's argument is the section on paraenesis, both as to basics and as to its delimitation. Thus, I cannot be persuaded that the *probatio* ends with Gal 4.31 and the paraenesis starts at 5.1. Because his own comments lack sharpness, his objection to Merk, 'Der Beginn der Paränese im Gal', *ZNW* 60, 83-104 (where Merk has the paraenesis beginning at 5.13) is unconvincing. He says Merk's deductions are not based on an analysis of the composition of Gal. Yet in the last resort he is unable to say anything about the place of the paraenesis in the 'defensive letter'. Significantly, Betz, loc. cit., 375 says, 'It is rather puzzling to see that *paraenesis* plays only a marginal role in the ancient rhetoric handbooks, *if not in rhetoric itself*' (my italics for end of sentence). And it is also significant that while all the other sections of Gal are given Latin designations, here the Greek word *paraenesis* has to serve! See on Betz too my forthcoming study 'Der Galaterbrief und das Verhältnis von antiker Rhetorik und Epistolographie', *ThLZ* 109 (1984).

66. Schmithals, *Römerbrief*, 163.

67. Ibid., 163.

68. See ibid., 152f.

69. Suhl, *Briefe*, 279.

70. Ibid., 280 and 280, n. 73; with Michel, Suhl takes Rom 1.16a οὐ γὰρ ἐπαισχύνομαι τὸ εὐαγγέλιον 'I am not ashamed of the Gospel', in the sense 'I acknowledge the Gospel' (ibid., 280f.). Thus Paul is prepared to come to Rome and preach the Gospel because he acknowledges it as the Gospel in which the righteousness that comes from faith is revealed, and in which therefore insistence on Jewish privileges reveals itself as an anachronism (ibid., 281f.). Herold, *Zorn*, 228ff. seeks to expound 1.16a otherwise: 'I am not brought to ruin by the Gospel'. As the roots bos/αἰσχ – are (says Herold) juridical categories for the Old Testament and Judaism, and imply active or passive condemnation in legal proceedings (ibid., 66 and frequently), and as this also holds good for Paul's usage, Herold also expounds ἐπαισχύνομαι in Rom 1.16 as follows: This form has the passive sense – 'I am not being ruined'. However he himself admits that the problem of this exposition lies in the relation of the verb to the direct object, but he thinks that there is a Hebraism here that can be demonstrated from Gal 2.7, 1 Thess 2.4 and 1 Cor 12.13 (ibid., 230f.). 'Thus he clearly relates a passive statement to an accusative of the object...' (ibid., 231). However these references can scarcely prove that Rom 1.16a is a Hebraism since in them transitive or quasi-transitive verbs are also construed *transitively* in the passive voice but ἐπαισχύνομαι never has the sense of 'to ruin' as a transitive deponent. Thus there is no real grammatical analogy between Rom 1.16 and the other Pauline passages. So we are left with οὐκ ἐπαισχύνομαι τὸ εὐαγγέλιον presenting a medial form with the accusative – a very peculiar construction in Greek (Kühner-Gerth, *Grammatik* II/1, 123f.) (probably not a passive with τί as Menge, *Wörterbuch*, 254, supposes). But above all else, the forms represented by Herold as Hebraisms are Greek in construction; see Kühner-Gerth, loc. cit., 125: '...it happens with some verbs which in the active voice have an accusative of the thing alongside the dative of the person, such as ...πιστεύω τί τινι (!), etc., that in the passive construction the dative of the person switches over to the *nominative*, while the *accusative* of the thing remains unchanged, as the Greek here too conceives the passive reflexively...Polybius 8.17.1 τοὺς Κρῆτας πεπιστεῦσθαί τι τῶν φυλακτερίων...' In addition to the references adduced in Kühner-Gerth, see also the

construction in Heraclitus B 32, which though not grammatically identical is related: "Εν τὸ σοφὸν μοῦνον λέγεσθαι οὐκ ἐθέλει καὶ ἐθέλει Ζηνὸς ὄνομα. Significantly, Rehkopf, in the fourteenth impression of Blass-Debrunner, has deleted from para. 312 the sentence Herold quotes: 'New Testament examples can admittedly rarely be directly supported from the classical language...'!

71. Thus, e.g., Marxsen, *Einleitung*, 91ff. (E.T. 98ff.).

72. Suhl, *Briefe*, 277.

73. Michel, *Röm.*, 330; Käsemann, *Röm.*, 377 (E.T. 395).

74. See Bornkamm, 'Röm als Testament des Paulus' = *Geschichte und Glaube* II, 138, n. 47: 'The verse stands clearly in the context of a restrospective reference to the missionary work by the apostle which has been concluded in the East (vv. 19 and 23) but as the scriptural passage quoted in v. 21 indicates (Isaiah 52.15), the verse is at the same time intended to provide a reason for the planned journey to Spain. (The Christians in Rome are not among those whom the Christian message has not yet reached!)' The sentence which comes immediately thereafter does however seem questionable in my view: 'It is no less important to note that the purpose of v. 20 is not to justify or excuse the apostle's visit to Rome, but to explain why it has been delayed (vv. 22f.).'

75. It is debatable whether Rom 2.1 is as yet concerned with the accusation against the Jews. διό is a difficulty: *Therefore* you, all of you, who judge, are without excuse. If the explanatory διό relates to what immediately precedes it, i.e., to 1.32, it cannot be the Jew who is being addressed but merely the Gentile (e.g., Zahn, *Röm.*, 104f. and 104, n. 2). But if we nevertheless try to relate it to the Jew, the διό must not be understood as if its purpose were to establish an explanatory connection with c. 1. Lietzmann therefore regarded this word as a 'colourless transitional particle' (*Röm.*, 39). Michel also has it that διό has lost its original meaning and has become a mere transitional particle (*Röm.*, 64). Fridrichsen's attempt to take διό as a misreading of δίς (*Symbolae Arct. Osloenses I*, 1922, 40; *RHPhR III*, 1923, 440) has – probably rightly – met with general rejection.

Bultmann proposed a very radical solution: he suggests that 2.1 should be regarded as a gloss. 'All the difficulties disappear if we remove the verse as a gloss the purpose of which is to summarise the purport of vv. 2f.; or to draw the appropriate conclusion from v. 3. We can then see that v. 1 should really come after v. 3...' ('Glossen im Römerbrief' = *Exegetica*, 281). This proposal is certainly very tempting (though the stylistic rigidity of the πᾶς ὁ κρίνων in the salutation has not been overcome but merely blamed on the glossator). Käsemann has also adopted it (*Röm.*, 49f. = E.T. 50). Michel in a note refers to Bultmann without contradicting him (*Röm.*, 64, n. 2). Nevertheless I do not find this radical solution compelling. First of all it should be clear – despite Zahn – that as of 2.1 a new group is addressed (Cranfield, *Romans*, I. 141f. is not convincing: '...in 1.18-32...it is not exclusively the sin of the Gentiles..., but the sin of all men. The διό then presents no difficulty.') The accused are those who judge those described up to 1.32. Such judgement is presumptuous; indeed they do the same thing themselves. Reference to identical guilt would be meaningless if one of the Gentiles previously accused were involved. Rather should the point expressed elsewhere in c. 2 – which tells against the Jews – indicate that already in v. 1 it is the accusation against the Jewish world that is involved. If we remember that Paul dictated the letter, some fuzziness of language or of precision in the trend of his thought is understandable. There is no difficulty in supposing that in dictating Paul finds his thoughts jumping ahead so that there is a prolepsis as to content: he already has the Jews in mind but he does not yet say so.

Then again, διό may be the short form of διὰ τοῦτο (Menge, *Wörterbuch*, 184). But Paul even so produces this διὰ τοῦτο elsewhere to refer to a reason *still to come*; e.g., 1 Thess 2.13: 'And we also thank God constantly for this (διὰ τοῦτο), that (ὅτι) you...' (See also 1 Thess 3.5: διὰ τοῦτο...μή...). But if we accept this function too for διό in 2.1 it would then be possible to paraphrase 1.32 and 2.1 thus: 'The Gentiles know God's legal demands in his Law and according to these demands those infringing them are worthy of death. They not only do the same, but make no concealment of their sympathy for those who do likewise. But for the reason that follows you too are without excuse – and here I am addressing *everyone* who fails to conform, *even* the Jews and pre-eminently the Jews: in judging the other person you condemn yourself; for you are judging even although you do the same yourself.' (No special explanation is needed for the fact that in Greek we can have τὰ γὰρ αὐτὰ πράσσεις ὁ κρίνων instead of τὰ γὰρ αὐτὰ πράσσων κρίνεις ; see especially Kühner-Gerth II/2.98!)

76. Wilckens, 'Aus Werken des Gesetzes...' = *Rechtfertigung als Freiheit*, 107.

77. Käsemann, *Röm.*, 83 (E.T. 89).

78. Schmithals, *Römerbrief*, 15.

79. Kümmel, *Römer* 7, p. 9 (following M. R. Engel) and elsewhere; but see Käsemann, *Röm.*, 182 (E.T. 192).

80. Zahn, *Röm.*, 337 disputes the idea that the focus of the question is on the identity of *nomos* and *hamartia*; Kümmel, *Römer* 7, p. 43, n. 1, accepts this. However, Zahn's argument – that the article is not present with ἁμαρτία – does not really have the force of evidence. Thus Kümmel himself points to Paul's varied use of νόμος and ὁ νόμος, ibid., 55. But the same would then hold good for ἁμαρτία: in Rom 7.7-13 Paul uses the form with the article six times and the form without the article three times without any discernible difference in content. Yet Zahn and Kümmel have noticed something which is absolutely right. For Paul does not wish to be confronted with the question whether *hamartia* can be used as a synonym for *nomos*. The point is rather whether the *nomos* is in essence determined by *hamartia*. Yet Gutjahr's expression, 'something partaking of the nature of sin' (*etwas Sündhaftes*), which gains Kümmel's approval, seems to me to be too indeterminate. Cranfield in *Romans*, I. 347 tends to avoid the issue: '...could indeed suggest that the law is actually an evil, *in some way* to be identified with sin' (my italics).

81. Lipsius, *Röm.*, 125; Bläser, *Gesetz*, 114.

82. Kuss, *Röm.*, 442.

83. Limitative ἀλλά 7.7 (Kümmel, *Römer* 7, p. 47; Michel, *Röm.*, 146; ibid. 147, n. 1; Kuss, *Röm.*, 442; not so Käsemann, *Röm.*, 184 (E.T. 193): 'adversative').

84. Kümmel, *Römer* 7, pp. 48f., has yet another view of the distinction: according to 3.20 the subject cannot recognise sin as such without the Law. But according to 7.7 no sin comes about without (the) Law. This means that in 3.20 we have a noetic but in 7.7 an ontic statement. But with H. J. Holtzmann, Kümmel sees the occurrence of sin in 7.7 as the emergence of *personal* sin, *conscious* sin. Then of course there is no longer such a sharp distinction between Paul's two statements; for if according to 7.7 only *conscious* sin arises, this too amounts to a noetic statement. It is of course true that Paul does not always use his terms consistently. Yet it we it does not appear that any different understanding of ἁμαρτία is being expressed here. That ἁμαρτία in 3.20 and 7.7 is synonymous is however indicated by the fact that ἐπίγνωσις in 3.20 and γνῶναι in 7.7 belong to the same stem. Also it is not said in 7.7 that sin and covetousness arise only because of the Law. It is of course correct that in 7.8 the cause – and so by implication the emergence – of *epithumia* is being discussed.

85. Lipsius, *Röm.*, 125: 'the experience in the Ego of the power of objective evil which is given through the commandment (i.e., the experience of ἁμαρτία which here too is personified)'; Michel, *Röm.*, 147.

86. Käsemann, *Röm.*, 184 (E.T. 194) and the literature there listed.

87. Niederwimmer, *Freiheit*, 129.

88. Käsemann, *Röm.*, 183 (E.T. 193).

89. Bornkamm, 'Sünde, Gesetz und Tod' = *Das Ende des Gesetzes*, 55: Paul 'leaves room for the possibility that ἐπιθυμία can express itself just as easily in antinomian as in legalistic fashion, i.e., in the zeal for one's own righteousness (Rom 10.3)'; Bultmann is more cautious in *Theologie*, 248 (E.T. I, 247): 'It may be that in these verses Paul does not reflect over the

question whether "desire" tempts man to transgress the Law or whether it misleads him to a false zeal for fulfilling it. Yet the latter must at least be included.' In the essay he wrote in 1927, 'Römer 7 und die Anthropologie des Paulus' (*Exegetica*, 198-209) (E.T. *Existence and Faith*, 173-185), he was not so cautious in his judgement.

90. e.g., Lipsius, *Röm*, I. 126; Käsemann, *Röm*., 185ff. (E.T. 196ff.); Cranfield, *Romans*, I 351.

91. Käsemann, *Röm*., 186 (E.T. 196).

92. Kümmel, *Röm* 7, p. 85.

93. Käsemann, *Röm*., 186 (E.T. 196).

94. Kümmel, *Röm* 7, p. 86.

95. Ibid., 86f.

96. Ibid., 87.

97. Bornkamm, 'Sünde, Gesetz und Tod' = *Das Ende des Gesetzes*, 58f.

98. We cannot here enter into a detailed discussion of the complex of questions raised by Rom 5.12 or 5.12ff. On the literature, other than commentaries, see especially: Bultmann, 'Adam und Christus nach Röm 5' = *Exegetica*, 424-444; Bornkamm, 'Paulinische Anakoluthe' = *Das Ende des Gesetzes*, 80-85, 89 and esp. 83f.; Brandenburger, *Adam und Christus*; Jüngel, 'Das Gesetz zwischen Adam und Christus', *ZThK* 60, 42-74 and esp. 51f.; Wedderburn, 'The Theological Structure of Romans V.12', *NTS* 19, 339-354.

99. Kierkegaard, *Der Begriff der Angst*, 1.2, 473f. (E.T. *The Concept of Dread*, 28); my italics.

100. With Käsemann, *Röm*., 187 (E.T. 197) though he wrongly (ibid., 137, E.T.) objects to Bultmann's use of Kierkegaard (*Theologie*, 251 = E.T. I. 251: 'sin came into the world by sinning'); on this see Hübner, 'Existentiale Interpretation der paulinischen "Gerechtigkeit Gottes"', *NTS* 21, 477, n. 9.

101. Kierkegaard, *Angst*, 1.2, 475 (E.T. 29): my italics.

102. Ibid., 1.1, 467 (E.T. 23).

103. Existential interpretation understood, of course, not as an 'individualistic *stretto*'! See Hübner, *Politische Theologie und existentiale Interpretation*, c. 1.

104. Westermann, *Genesis I*, 325: 'Evil or the power of temptation referred to in Gen 3 must be a human phenomenon just like sin and transgression...Adam represents humanity...This statement, which is extremely important for J, viz., that *there is no aetiology for the origin of evil*, was destroyed in the mythical interpretation where a precise origin is indicated.' But we shall not discuss here what Westermann means by 'mythical interpretation'.

105. Käsemann, *Röm*., 186 (E.T. 196).

106. Kümmel, *Römer 7*, p. 54: 'wholly unnecessary'.

107. Ibid., 50.

108. Ibid., 51.

109. Ibid., 52; cf. Käsemann, *Röm*., 182 (E.T. 191): 'revived'.

110. Kümmel, *Römer 7*, p. 53.

111. Ibid., 52.

112. What Heidegger says in 'Die Sprache im Gedicht' = *Unterwegs zur Sprache*, 74, regarding a poem of Trakl's, also holds good *mutatis mutandis* for Paul: 'The language of a poem is in its nature ambiguous in its own special way. We can hear nothing of what the poem is trying to say so long as our confrontation with it is merely with some unimaginative representation of a straightforward sense.' Here we may again draw attention to Lipsius's commentary on Romans which appeared as early as 1891 and contained much, clearly stated, which has only been able to establish itself in the present century as the common property of exegetes. We read there, p. 126, on Rom 7.9-11: 'The age in which man still "lived" without the law is simply that in which he was as yet unaware of the law – in terms of the Genesis story which is here in mind, it is therefore the period prior to God's injunction not to eat of the tree

of knowledge, Gen 2.17...*but this is at once related to man's individual experience under the Mosaic Law* and his coming to an awareness of sin only through knowledge of the Law; the age of childish innocence is not specially in mind.' (The italics are mine.)

113. Prümm, *Die Botschaft des Römerbriefs*, 14.

114. However, Rom 7 is still expounded by English-speaking scholars of repute as autobiography or as a description of the Christian life: Bruce, *Romans*, 147ff.; Barrett, *Romans*, 143: 'It is possible that Paul is...telling his own story in the light of Genesis.' Cranfield, *Romans*, I. 356, sees Rom 7.14ff. and Rom 8 as 'two different aspects, two contemporaneous realities, of the Christian life, both of which continue so long as the Christian is in flesh.'

115. Kümmel, *Römer 7*, p. 126.

116. Käsemann, *Röm.*, 190 (E.T. 200).

117. Ibid., 190 (E.T. 200).

118. I am in complete agreement with Käsemann, *Röm.*, 194 (E.T. 204) when he says with reference to Rom 7.14ff. that 'Paul...affirms, not just the contradictoriness of existence even in the pious, but the entanglement of a fallen creation in all its expressions in the power of sin. Hence he does not need to differentiate, as he would have to do from an ethical or psychological point of view. He does not leave open even the possibility of a battle which is not yet decided, so that it would be adequate to speak of torn or divided man as many do.' *Man does not recognise at all that at the deepest level he is 'divided' or 'torn asunder'*; this expression, which is mostly understood psychologically, is justifiable only when it is specifically *not* understood as a psychological conflict. See below for Bultmann's understanding of man's 'willing' under the Law as a 'trans-subjective tendency".

119. Ibid., 184 (E.T. 194).

120. Ibid., 184 (E.T. 194).

121. In parenthesis it may be mentioned that even in the Old Testament the idea too is not unknown of the recognition of sin as a revelation; see Knierim, *Die Hauptbegriffe für Sünde im AT*, 55. However for the theological idea of Romans this notion is unlikely to be of any significance, as Paul in Romans certainly still maintains the view he had in 2 Cor 3.15: a veil lies over the hearts of the Jews whenever Moses is read to them. But this means that as Jews and as men of the Old Testament they have not understood God's decisive revelation in the Law of the Old Testament. Consequently it will be possible for us to speak at most of a modification by Paul of this Old Testament idea.

122. Bultmann, *Exegetica*, 49.

123. Ibid., 49. (Klein, 'Individualgeschichte und Weltgeschichte' = *Rekonstruktion und Interpretation*, 193, n. 51: Paul, in Rom 2.17ff., wishes to 'establish empirically the presence of sin in Judaism'. Klein certainly therefore considers Rom 2.17ff. 'not to have the force of a principle' – 'the theological inadequacy of such a procedure' is here revealed (ibid., 193).) This criticism in no way implies denial that Bultmann's programmatic essay furthered New Testament research in a crucial particular. In the essay Bultmann went beyond the liberal view of Paul which evaluated the parenetic imperative as illogical in relation to the soteriological indicative. Paul bases the imperative precisely on the fact of justification; he derives the imperative from the indicative, ibid., 39.

124. Bultmann, 'Römer 7 und die Anthropologie des Paulus' = *Exegetica*, 198-209 (E.T. *Existence and Faith*, 173-185); quotation 207 (E.T. 183); similarly in *Theologie*, 246 (E.T. I. 246): 'This is the domination of sin: All man's doing is directed against his true intention...' Whether it is right to regard the θέλειν as 'the trans-subjective propensity of human existence as such', 'Röm 7', 202 (E.T. 177), may here be left unanswered. But see Käsemann, *Röm.*, 193 (E.T. 203): 'The description of the conflict as "trans-subjective"...has met with furious criticism, for it ostensibly does not do adequate justice to the subjective element...or to the specific application in the ethical sphere...It is undoubtedly misleading but yet it paves the

way to overcoming a *purely* psychological and ethical interpretation and was not at all as abstract as it sounded.' (My italics.) On Rom 7 see further Kertelge, 'Exegetische Überlegungen zum Verständnis der paulinischen Anthropologie nach Röm 7', *ZNW* 62, 105-114.

125. H. Jonas, 'Philosophische Meditation über Paulus, Römerbrief, Kapitel 7' = *Zeit und Geschichte*, 565; but the contrast Jonas draws is false: 'Thus Jesus takes the lowest and Paul the highest possibility as a critical object...' (ibid., 569); see on this Haenchen, *Matthäus 23 = Gott und Mensch*, 51!

126. Lipsius, *Röm.*, 115; Käsemann, *Römer*, 148 (E.T. 121) is right: the Law 'radicalises sin by allowing it to increase through transgressions'.

127. Michel, *Röm.*, 106, n. 3.

128. In Rom 'wrath' serves as a term for the judgement of God – which previously in Gal was expressed by 'curse'.

129. Is Käsemann, *Röm.*, 113 (E.T. 121) right in saying that *nomos* is figurative and (cf. Zahn) that Paul is offering a 'general truth' here? This is possible, but as Käsemann also admits, the focus in 4.15a – which is the logical consequence of 4.15b – is on the Mosaic Law.

130. Michel, *Röm.*, 126f.

131. Luz, *Geschichtsverständnis*, 202, n. 254, raises the objection against Brandenburger, *Adam und Christus*, 250f., that *paraptoma* cannot be shown to be *parabasis*. In that Paul looks at Adam and everyone who sins together (see above), we can agree with Luz when he writes, '"*Paraptoma*" is Adam's missing the mark; it determines history and reveals its power in the sins and transgressions of those who came later' (loc. cit. 202). However there is most likely a shift of nuance as to this term from vv. 15-17 to v. 20 and this is not made explicit by Luz. Käsemann, *Röm.*, 148 (E.T. 158) is right: the Law 'radicalises sin by allowing it to increase through transgressions'. But it is axiomatic that for Paul this 'activity' of the Law is subject to the reservation in Rom 7.7ff.

132. To different effect e.g., Jüngel, 'Das Gesetz zwischen Adam und Christus', *ZThK* 60, 68; Klein, 'Individualgeschichte und Weltgeschichte' = *Rekonstruktion und Interpretation*, 199, n. 70a.

133. Hübner, 'Existentiale Interpretation der paulinischen "Gerechtigkeit Gottes" ', *NTS* 21, 462-488.

134. Here we shall not deal with Luz's thesis in *Geschichtsverständnis*, 204ff., that Rom 5.12ff., the only general outline of history in Paul, is not a sketch of salvation-history but of its opposite.

135. Käsemann, *Röm.*, 304 (E.T. 316).

136. Bultmann, art., πείθω *TWNT* VI.11ff. (E.T. VI.10f.).

137. Käsemann, *Röm.*, 302 (E.T. 315); see also Ch. Müller, *Gottes Gerechtigkeit*, 78ff.; it is of course once again too vague when Müller thus expounds Rom 11.32 in the light of Gal 3.22f.: 'The law is there to bring men to sin or rather to the act of sinning. The characteristic expression συνέκλεισεν which in Paul occurs only in Rom 11.32 and Gal 3.22, distinguishes the factical effect of the law, viz., death, as an act of God's irresistible will' (ibid., 82).

138. Michel, art., συγκλείω, *TWNT* VII.744.45 (E.T. VII.746.18ff.).

139. However Michel's interpretation of 'Gal 3.22...in the sense of Rom 11.32' is hardly appropriate, where he says that scripture shows man's abandonment to the power of sin, and that God has placed men in custody by means of the Law, the effect of this custody being to protect them from self-destruction and from the influence of the powers of evil until faith is revealed (cf. ibid., 746.44ff., E.T. 746.35ff.)! Here neither the context of Gal 3 nor the predestinarian context of Rom 9-11 is taken in earnest.

140. K. Barth, *KD* IV/1 558 (E.T. CD IV/1 501).

141. Hübner, 'Das Gesetz als elementares Thema einer Biblischen Theologie?' *KuD* 22, 261.

142. Not so Gutbrod, art., νόμος, *TWNT* IV.1069.13ff. (E.T. IV.1076.32ff.): the dual command is the νόμος 'so that the command to love one's neighbour is ὁ ἕτερος νόμος Rom 13.8.' Again to different effect we have Marxsen, 'Der ἕτερος νόμος Rm 13,8', *ThZ* 11, 230-237: in antithesis to the law of the Roman state ὁ ἕτερος νόμος means the law of Moses; this view is supported by Merk, *Handeln aus Glauben*, 165 and Ulonska, *Funktion*, 199, n. 146.

143. Käsemann, *Röm.*, 345 (E.T. 360f.). Ulonska, *Funktion*, 200, rightly sees that in Rom 13.8-10 Paul is proclaiming 'the law as an ethical requirement in the implementation of love of one's neighbour'. But in part at least he misunderstands and in part he is off the point when he writes that 'the authority of the command to love is not derived by Paul from scripture...The command to love being qualified as "full measure" has displaced the partial standard of the Mosaic law. But full measure means that he who loves his neighbour no longer wrongs him!' (ibid., 200f.) But how far did Paul remove this notion of 'full measure' from the Torah? Ulonska's thesis cannot be said to be substantiated in terms of Nygren's fine sentence, *Röm.*, 307: 'Love can never "be fulfilled", but love itself is the "fulfilment of the Law" ' – which Ulonska quotes, loc. cit., 201.

144. Käsemann, *Röm.*, 345 (E.T. 361).

145. The expression καὶ εἴ τις ἑτέρα ἐντολή does indeed allow of the possibility, speaking purely formally, of thinking by implication of cultic legislation as well. But this is foreign to the line of argument in Rom. The subsequent reflections in this section also make this clear.

146. Hübner, *Das Gesetz in der synoptischen Tradition*, c. 4 and 'Mk 7.15 und das "jüdisch-hellenistische" Gesetzesverständnis', *NTS*, 22, 319-345; see also Paschen, *Rein und Unrein*, 155ff., and especially 185: 'Jesus' saying focuses the effect of impurity on internals – on the heart, the seat of decisions. An important and never forgotten part of the Old Testament ideas on purity is thus given absolute force.' Jesus appears as the one who 'declares food impurity to be...inoperative in contrast to pollution from within' (ibid., 186).

147. cf. Käsemann, *Röm.*, 359 (E.T. 375): 'Absolute certainty and apostolic authority form a principle (Michel). From this standpoint it is idle to debate whether the apostle is appealing here to a saying of Jesus (Zahn; Jülicher; perhaps also Michel) or not...'

148. Käsemann, 'Das Problem des historischen Jesus', *EVB* I, 207 (E.T. 39).

149. Käsemann, *Röm.*, 359 (E.T. 375).

150. Käsemann, *Röm.*, 344 (E.T. 359), rightly takes Rom 13.8-14 as a 'summary of the Great Exhortation'.

150a. Love = the subject of the sentence.

151. Neusner, *The Rabbinic Traditions* I, 338f.; against Neusner's argument see Hübner, 'Das ganze und das eine Gesetz', *KuD* 21, 249 and 249, n. 40.

152. Becker, *Untersuchungen zur Entstehungsgeschichte der Testamente der Zwölf Patriarchen*.

153. In his monograph, *Die Gesetzesauslegung Jesu*, Berger arrives at this result only on the basis of an extremely arbitrary assessment in the field of *Religionsgeschichte* – due to a material defect in methodology; on his methodological approach see Hübner, 'Mk 7.15 und das "jüdisch-hellenistische" Gesetzesverständnis', *NTS* 22, 319-345.

154. Marböck, 'Gesetz und Weisheit', *BZ* 20, 10.

155. Ibid., 13.

156. Hengel, *Der Sohn Gottes*, 106, n. 123 (E.T. 67).

157. See Hengel, *Judentum und Hellenismus*, 551f. (E.T. I, 267ff., esp. 268).

158. Hebrew text best accessible (partially) in Schlatter, *Der Evangelist Matthäus*, 483.

159. Michel, *Röm.*, 306f.; see also Paschen, *Rein und Unrein*, 71: 'Paul does not of course fully carry through the radical revaluation of the κοινός idea which we find in the apophthegm...'

3 ELABORATION

Up to now the individual sub-sections of Sections 1 and 2 corresponded. The study was deliberately structured in this way so as to give the clearest possible survey of the various stages in Paul's theological development from Galatians to Romans. In the course of the presentation, decisive and substantial points have already been made. However, if in the course of the presentation we have reached that stage in which things of substance have already been stated, this does not mean to say that these matters of substance could not be drawn out more with a consequent deepening and concentration of our understanding. Thus in a third section, the results so far obtained will be supported by even more exact attention to what the text says and by even more penetrating reading in and between the lines. I hope in this to have succeeded in avoiding the dangers of over-interpreting.

3.1 Boasting and Refraining from Boasting

That Paul did undergo a theological development can also be inferred from the way in which he handles variously in his letters the subject of boasting or 'glory(ing)'. This is especially important for our enquiry in so far as this subject is closely connected with the Law. Käsemann has rightly stressed that the verb 'to boast' is a key-word of Pauline theology.[1] This naturally also holds good for the corresponding substantives.

3.1.1 Boasting in Galatians

For Paul refraining from boasting is a decisive mark of Christian existence – or more precisely, it is refraining from boasting about one's own works before God. This statement, which goes right to the heart of Pauline theology, is incontestably true of Romans, but is it also appropriate for Galatians?

We note first of all that in Galatians the verb καυχάομαι occurs only twice

101

(6.13,14) and the substantive καύχημα (= glory, the subject matter of boasting or the justified presupposition for boasting) occurs only once (6.4). In the whole first, polemical part of the letter, in which the Mosaic Law is declared to be the sphere of servitude where freedom is lacking, we do not find the motif of glory. Paul allows it an appearance only in the last chapter; but then it does not look as if the news which had reached Paul from the Galatian congregations had spoken of boasting by those opponents of the apostle who demanded circumcision or even by the congregations themselves, as to the works of the Law which they had achieved or even merely as to their possession of the Law.[2] So how does Paul introduce the subject of boasting or 'glorying' in Galatians?

Let us first of all endeavour to understand the decisive verse in Gal 6.4 in terms of its immediate context. We are in the hortatory or paraenetic part of the letter. Paul is here addressing the Galatians as people who live in the Spirit and should therefore walk in the Spirit (5.25). In these Galatian congregations of Christians who are 'led by the Spirit' (5.18) there are however also some who have been 'overtaken' in a sinful deed (ἔν τινι παραπτώματι, 6.1). The spiritual Galatians (ὑμεῖς οἱ πνευματικοί[3]) are meant to help such people back on to the right road, and in so doing the individual should be particularly on his guard lest he also fall into temptation (6.1).[4] Critical self-examination therefore has the purpose of ensuring that one does not become similarly guilty. We would particularly stress that recognising one's own sin is not the point of this self-critical examination. Much though Paul intends to warn Christians by depicting their susceptibility to temptation,[5] he has no intention of charging the 'pneumatics' or 'spiritual' Galatians with actually having committed sins. The admonition continues with the well-known words that they are to bear one another's burdens 'and so fulfil the law of Christ' (6.2). The presupposition is that *each person* has for his part to bear burdens. These burdens are interpreted almost unanimously by the commentators as sin.[6] Mussner even says specifically 'not just any sins but those into which one has fallen.'[7] In this connection he refers to Andrea van Dülmen according to whom the 'burden' is to be interpreted above all in the light of the previous verse where there is a reference to the sin of a[8] member of the congregation. 'Thus the burden lies in the weakness, the susceptibility to temptation, the constant danger and man's repeated sin.'[9] However, this is not quite the same as what Mussner is saying, for he interprets 'burdens' only as a specific kind of sins. On the other hand, van Dülmen mentions in the one breath both susceptibility to temptation and sin, i.e., a disposition towards sin and sin itself. (When she also speaks at the same time of weakness, she probably means here too the disposition towards sin.)

We cannot dispute – nor is it generally disputed – that Paul sees the Christian as disposed to sin, in so far as he is precisely the scene of the struggle of 'spirit' and 'flesh'[10] against each other (5.17). Moreover this circumstance is sufficient in itself to justify talk of 'burdens'. Now if in 6.1 the 'pneumatic' or 'spiritual' Christian is warned against giving in to his susceptibility to temptation, he is being in fact addressed specifically as someone who *as yet* has *not* sinned. But in that case it is hardly probable that in the very next verse Paul should be imputing sinful deeds to *every* Christian.[11] It seems reasonable rather to suppose that what he wanted to say here was this: support each other as people who may fall into sin all too easily because of your susceptibility to temptation; but support each other *even if* you have yielded to temptation. Van Dülmen seems to me to come nearer to Paul's intention in so far as she mentions weakness, liability to temptation and the constant danger *alongside* repeated sins, but she still goes too far when she assumes in principle that, for Paul, every Christian not only has the disposition to sin, but also actually repeatedly sins.

6.3 continues by way of justification: 'for if anyone thinks he is something, when he is nothing, he deceives himself.' Schlier takes this sentence to mean that everyone is nothing. 'No one is in truth anything...And if he supposes that he is something, although he is nothing, then he deceives himself.'[12] Lipsius puts it otherwise: the admonition in verse 2 is justified 'by the point that those who without reason think themselves better than others and therefore qualified to judge, deceive themselves in the judgement they make...i.e., again those who in leaving the Law of Christ unfulfilled, boast in their Jewish legal righteousness. These consider themselves to be something (i.e., from an ethical standpoint) although they are in fact nothing...'[13] Now the motif of boasting in the righteousness of the Mosaic Law is not mentioned specifically here,[14] but in any event it is right to say that in verse 3 *not all the Galatian Christians are addressed* for Paul is simply drawing attention to the possible danger of self-deception. If however the verse were to be taken in an inclusive sense such that *every* believer had to consider himself as *completely nothing*, the central point of verse 4 would be meaningless – viz., the contrast of boasting in regard to oneself and boasting in regard to others. The trend of the argument however is to the effect that unchallengeable boasting can exist only in regard to oneself and that therefore in such boasting there is no room for comparisons.[15] However to say that looking at others leads to the loss of 'glory' makes sense only if it is possible to have genuine 'glory' or 'boasting' if one stops looking at others! Such authentic 'glory' is however allowed by Paul. In the literature on the subject this fact is largely acknowledged; however the explanation given for it varies extremely. As here we have now reached a decisive point in our reflections, we must draw more widely than usual on the literature, the more so as a comparison of various opinions will be extremely instructive just at this point.

According to Holsten, Paul starts from the position that each person has the 'glory' due to him on the basis of the examination of his actual existence, 'something of which he is able to boast and may legitimately boast as an expression of his real value'. However, he has this 'glory' only when he considers himself in isolation, for he will discover on examination that he has a weakness which is peculiar to him and which is lacking in his neighbour.

Consequently there will be an end of glorying in relation to the other.[16] Thus: just because one has other specific weaknesses than one's fellow Christian has, one is not to boast of one's, albeit undeniable, strong-points – which the other lacks, strengths and weaknesses being variously distributed in each case. Correspondingly, Sieffert – who insists strongly that the expression in verse 4 'to have a boast' should in no sense be understood ironically or as a parody[17] – thinks that what is meant is not an absolute 'glory', which according to Rom 3.23(!)[18] nobody possesses, but rather a *materies gloriandi* – a ground for boasting for the *individual cases* which is the product of examination.[19] There is it is true a certain inconsistency in Sieffert's argument in that he considers the phrase 'his own work' in verse 4a to refer to the totality of a person's actions.[20] For how can he then see the reason for a justified 'glorying' as lying simply in the individual case in each circumstance? Thus we now see that a great deal depends on how the phrase 'his own work' is to be understood: does it refer to a particular action which is under consideration in a particular case or to man as a whole, that is to the basic 'set' of his existence in so far as this finds expression in activity? It is just at this point that the commentaries prefer to make assertions rather than to justify them.

Oepke, too, in considering the claim to 'glorying', speaks of a 'striking positive turn of phrase' in verse 4. 'It is not meant in a directly ironical way, but we may properly read between the lines the sobering phrase "where appropriate".'[21] Thus Paul twists and turns as he develops his argument: 'glorying' is to be allowed but not all that whole-heartedly – the more so as Paul here, according to Oepke, also takes into account the need for recognition which is common to men in general. Finally, in Oepke's view we are concerned with the 'principle of individual responsibility'. 'Each person is to apply the *highest* standards *directly* to his life's work...'[22] Importantly 'his own work' is understood here as his life's work. However, there is, as it appears, a peculiar obscurity attaching to this. Oepke does not say that it is nothing, rather that the person concerned somehow or other has a claim to 'glorying' – but simply 'somehow or other'!

This solution is not satisfactory as it stands. Nevertheless the decisive questions which open the way to an understanding of these verses have meanwhile clearly revealed themselves:

1. Is there, according to Gal 6, a genuine claim to 'glorying'? (This question has meanwhile been answered positively.)

2. What is the nature of this 'glorying'?

3. Does the basis for this 'glorying' lie in individual deeds or in one's whole life's work?

Schlier too allows that there is a place for genuine 'glorying', in fact for the 'entire activity of a man in a particular case'.[23] There is a 'hidden justification' of the fact that critical examination of one's conscience embraces 'glorying' only in regard to oneself but not in regard to others. This lies in the fact that consideration of the other party includes comparison, and the comparison includes one's own measurable achievement.[24] Perhaps we may restate this as follows. The quantitative standard is inappropriate for the quality of action required of the Christian. This idea would of course have something to correspond to it in content in Galatians,[25] but is it really what is meant at this point? Perhaps more important for Schlier is the view of Paul which in his opinion lies behind these verses, according to which the 'glorying', which the believer actually has because of his works, depends in the last resort on *God's work* and on the grace of Christ. The self-examination which Paul demands allows one to recognise this grace which is made available for one's activity and one's life.[26] But this idea is the very one which cannot be traced in 6.1ff. It has been imported into the text by Schlier. He does indeed do justice to the point that, according to 6.4, there does exist a genuine claim to boasting or 'glorying'. However, as this seems to him to be somehow or other theologically disturbing, he has recourse to grace as a way out, and thus he reads the text under the influence of a dogmatic pre-judgement which is extraneous to it. In this way, he also fails to grasp the relation of verse 3 to verse 4. He does in fact refer to man outwith the grace of Christ when he similarly extends to *everyone*[27] the statement in verse 3 in which he who is 'nothing' is called upon not to deceive himself. This becomes clear also from the fact that he quotes the Council of Orange: '*Nemo de suo*(!) *habet nisi mendacium et peccatum*'.[28] However, in verse 4, according to Schlier, what is involved is the boasting or glorying which appertains to the *Christian* because of the grace of Christ. However, such a transition from existence outwith grace in verse 3 to existence in grace in verse 4 involves putting a construction on the passage which is not justified by the text. Verse 3 too is addressed to Christians who conceive of themselves as '*pneumatikoi*' ('spiritual') and are meant to do so. Thus Schlier's exegesis is far from convincing. It has an element of truth, of course, in so far as the 'work' of the Christian is the 'fruit of the Spirit' (5.22), that is, as it cannot be regarded as '*de suo*'; but according to Paul, this does not at all exclude the Christian's responsibility. According to 5.25 he demands of those who live in the power of the *pneuma* that they should also walk in the *pneuma* on their own responsibility.

Let us now take a look at one of the most recent commentaries on Galatians – by Mussner. Examination of 'one's own work' brings two things to light: either this 'work' – by which Mussner understands the entirety of man's activities[29] – is evil and sin, or because of the Lord's grace, it is good.[30] Dependence on Schlier is plain here. Mussner however differs noticeably from all the exegetes previously referred to. He sees the section in Gal 5.26-6.5 as a coherent whole which could rightly have the superscription: 'warning against striving for vain glory, κενοδοξία'.[31] It is this very context in which the warning of verse 4 is to be found: let each man examine his own work! Strict examination of this can lead to the conclusion 'that it is good and can maintain itself in God's sight'. 'This may...then be grounds for the one who does the examining to "glory" with reference to himself alone.'[32] This is plainly and indeed unambiguously formulated. The only thing is that we must then ask whether the further development of Mussner's argument is logically consistent. Initially, he leaves two interpretative possibilities open for the future tense, 'he will have glory':

(1) It is a logical future. In that case, what we have here is not, as many exegetes think, an expression of the apostle's bitter irony, but much rather a deep resignation: 'unhappily an honest self-examination shows that "one's own work" is *mostly* tainted with sin, so that any kind of self-glorying is only κενοδοξία.'[33] However, it may be asked how far the argument which says that in fact *not every* work of one's own is *in principle* tainted with sin (cf. 'mostly'!) leads us to see the expression 'boasting in oneself alone' as an expression of deep resignation. At all events, this exposition – even if Mussner does not say so explicitly – does imply that Paul believes there to be Christians – however few of them there may be – whose work does in fact stand up to a strict examination, as is in fact actually said at the beginning of the exposition of verse 4!

(2) Mussner, however, thinks it more probable that the future here is an eschatological one: if one's own work stands up to the critical appraisal of conscience, then the person concerned will have 'a subject for glorying at the coming judgement-seat of God'.[34] But then the statement must be understood ironically. The reason Mussner gives is this: 'an honest self-examination shows that no subject for self-glorying remains for the coming judgement!'[35] In this he appeals to Bultmann: 'faith implies the surrender of *all* self-glorying. But for those who stand in faith there may open up a new possibility of boasting...'[36] But what is the point of appealing *here* to Bultmann? In the extract from the TDNT quoted here, Bultmann was significantly not referring to Gal 6.4,[37] nor was he concerned there at all with the specific drift of the statement in Gal 6.1ff., but with an overall presentation of the basic Christian attitude to boasting or glory from Paul's perspective. But the question to be dealt with *here* is precisely whether Gal 6.4 was already considered from the same perspective as the statements made in Romans about self-glorying! However – even apart from the fact that Gal 6.4 is expounded by Mussner in terms of Romans – when he states that there is *no* remaining basis for self-glorying in the coming judgement (reading 'he will have' as an eschatological future) it is hard to avoid the question how previously he was able to allow[38] that 'a strict examination' can prove one's own work to be good to one's conscience, but[39] then can subsequently suggest that 'an honest self-examination' yields the opposite. What is the difference between a strict and an honest self-examination?

It is also questionable whether 6.5 means that self-glorying is excluded before God because each has to bear the burden of his own sin (φορτίον).[40] However, if Mussner were right here and if the future in this verse were further to refer to the eschatological judgement, our understanding of 6.3f. would in fact be put in question. Would the 'boasting' of verse 4 not then be relativised in such a way that Mussner's categorical statement that 'self-glorying is excluded before God' would now gain in probability as a résumé of the Pauline argument in 5.26-6.5? At all events, verse 5 is the justification for what has previously been said (γάρ!) and it is in verse 5 that we find: 'for *each* man will have to bear his own burden'.

Now it is certainly not settled that φορτίον means burden in the sense of the burden of sin. It has already been established in the exegesis of verse 2 that the burdens (βάρη) which each is to carry for the other do not, in principle, have to mean sinful deeds. But then neither is it obligatory here to conclude that φορτίον means the burden of sin. Thus Schlier interprets this term as the 'work' (ἔργον) for which the individual is responsible.[41] Konrad Weiss's view is similar, bringing in 2 Cor 10.12ff. and 1 Cor 3.10-15, 4.5 to expound Gal 6.5: 'If so, φορτίον is the "achievement" or "work" that each will bring with him for evaluation in the judgement.'[42] The 'work' *can* then be distorted by sin but it does not necessarily have to be.

This exegesis is reinforced if we ask *what it is* that verse 5 is after all justifying. In other terms, what is the *tertium comparationis* between verses 4 and 5? In verse 4 the reader is asked about his own work: this is the sole criterion for whether 'boasting' is appropriate for him. This is not to be established as a result of comparison with others but only – this seems the most likely interpretation – by comparison of the 'work' which is in each case one's own with the demand made on the Christian (5.14). We then have in verse 5 the justification for the critical look at oneself: examine yourself with a critical standard; for it is by *your* work *alone* that you will – or will not! – win through in the judgement. Be critical with regard to your work lest you fall short in the *krisis* of God! Probably Paul chose the term 'burden' instead of 'work' in verse 5 because it enabled him – in his typically shorthand fashion – to express this idea: 'for you will perhaps have to bring your work as a burden before God.' All the same, the person whose Christian life has not run its course without deeds of sin is not unconditionally lost; Paul after all asks the Galatians to 'set' such a one 'to rights' (6.1: καταρτίζετε) But then – to follow Oepke – the *tertium comparationis* in the two verses Gal 6.4 and 6.5 could be individual responsibility,[43] of which no one is relieved. To this extent, there would also be no contradiction between verses 2 and 5: verse 2 relates to being together day by day, while verse 5 refers to the eschatological judgement.[44]

However, if what is meant is 'one's own work' in the sense just outlined, it might well be that this should be understood – with Oepke, Schlier (?), van Dülmen and Mussner – as referring to one's entire life's work, and not – as Holsten, Lipsius and Sieffert suggest – as the result of one's behaviour in particular circumstances. If we further reflect that Paul considers the moral obligations of the Christian to be expressed in the *single* saying about loving one's neighbour, which thus constitutes 'the whole Law' for the Christian (5.14), that is, if one considers that this understanding of the Law implies looking at man as a whole, then one is led the more to suspect that the term

'work' in fact refers to the basic attitude and basic orientation of the
Christian's existence, expressed in his activity as a whole. The contrasting of
the many works of the Mosaic Law and the single work of the Christian would
fit in excellently to the trend of thought in Galatians as we have understood it.
   In the presentation of the detailed exegesis of Gal 6.1-5 or rather 5.26-6.5
and in discussion thereof, something essential in the understanding of this
section has become clear. It is clear that Paul does recognise a genuine claim on
the part of the Christian to 'glory' on the basis of his life's work and sees this
work as something which is relevant to judgement. Of course he does not
introduce this idea as a deliberate climactic statement, but simply in the course
of his reflections on how Christians ought to behave towards each other. In the
course of developing this argument, he does certainly make it quite clear that
he assumes there is a claim to 'glory' before the final judgement of God, not
indeed for works of the Law which have been duly performed, but indeed
rather for a Christian life understood as a 'work'. Accordingly, Gal 6.5 is of
first-rate importance, not for Paul who is in fact only introducing a marginal
comment here, but rather for us who ask whether a comment made in passing
may not disclose something important to us. Once again we find in the
linguistic overloading which is characteristically Paul's that a double climactic
statement is articulated in a *single* sentence:
   (1) It is *only when* someone examines accurately his own life's work and
arrives at a positive result because of this truly critical assessment[45] that he has
a claim to 'boasting' or 'glorying' for the eschatological judgement (emphasis
on τότε).
   (2) Even where there is a positive outcome resulting from as strict an
examination as possible of one's own life's work, the claim to 'boasting' holds
good *only* in regard to oneself (emphasis on μόνον).
   Now in Galatians, however, the subject of 'boasting' is once again taken up,
antithetically, in the letter's conclusion written 'in Paul's own hand'. Jewish
Christian agitators are demanding circumcision of the Gentile Christian
Galatians[46] in order to 'glory' in their 'flesh' (ἐν τῇ ὑμετέρᾳ σαρκί) (6.13). It is
not greatly relevant to the problem of 'boasting' or 'glory' in Galatians
whether this is historically so or not. We can therefore exclude this question.
We may also pass over the question whether the agitators, as 6.12 says, were
for their part under pressure[47] or whether Paul merely 'implied'[48] that this was
so – because this was his way of looking at things, from within his perspective
and in accordance with his experiences and his associative mechanism. It is,
however, of importance for us that Paul, as a former Pharisee, probably very
familiar with the questions of the Jewish mission and perhaps even himself a
Jewish missionary prior to his call (5.11), is able to see the successful
endeavour to have others circumcised as a legitimate justification for self-
glorying from a Jewish angle. He must see such an endeavour specifically as
the acquisition of a title to 'glory' which made one safe from Jewish
persecution. For it would allow one to argue skilfully against the Jews to this

effect: you cannot persecute us for we have made Israel greater, we have in fact
won proselytes for Israel – the fact that these proselytes also now consider
Jesus of Nazareth still as Messiah need not in *these* circumstances disturb you
any longer. Thus Paul's purpose is to display the *actual* intention of the
trouble-makers to the Galatians concerned: 'those who wish to compel you to
be circumcised are not preachers but evil agitators; for their stated intention of
ensuring your salvation is only a *pretext*. In reality they want to acquire 'glory'
for themselves in Jewish eyes by making proselytes, that is, by demanding
circumcision in order thus to escape being persecuted themselves (6.12). Their
demand for others' circumcision is simply intended to procure themselves an
alibi. They are not really concerned about you, the Galatian Christians, at all.
You are only a means to an end. The agitators say: 'we desire your salvation
before God', but they mean: 'we desire our salvation before men'. (One might
ask in passing: does the expression 'they do not keep the Law' (verse 13a),
alongside its precise meaning of actual non-fulfilment of what is commanded
in the Law (3.10!), also perhaps mean to say that they are in reality not in the
least concerned about the Law? This would be possible if Paul sees them as
Jewish Christians of the type whom he believes had at one time at the Synod in
Jerusalem agreed to his theology that the Law was incapable of providing
salvation.[49] But this cannot be said with any certainty. In any case, however,
Paul wants to expose the true interests of these people.)

However are we not going too far in this interpretation? Does Paul really
want to castigate the preaching of his opponents as the height of hypocrisy? At
all events 6.12 initially suggests as much: 'they would compel you to be
circumcised *only* (μόνον) in order that they may not be persecuted for their
preaching of the Cross of Christ.[50,51] Thus Paul asserts that it is only this base
motive which concerns these people, and nothing else. Naturally we may ask
first whether the exclusiveness of the language ('only') is not rhetorical
exaggeration. But what above all gives cause for thought is that if Paul really
sought to claim as the decisive purpose of those agitators who were demanding
circumcision that they themselves should remain unmolested, he was aiming in
his polemics in 6.11 in a *completely* different direction from that of the overall
tenor of Galatians! There the point is in fact that the Galatians must be clearly
shown that the followers of the religion of Law are deceiving themselves *about
themselves*. In this, as we have seen, Paul is engaging in 'ideological criticism' in
which he is laying bare *unconscious* interests which are concealed from them.
He 'unmasks' the intentions which determine the actions and judgements of
the pious champion of the Law without such a person being able to see through
them and thus through himself. On the other hand, in the addendum to the
letter in 6.11ff., 'ideological criticism' is not involved, for here those who are
attacked know indeed only too well what they are doing. It is *not* necessary to
open *their* eyes about themselves; no, it is the others, in our case the Galatians,
who have to recognise by what dishonest egoists they are being taken in. Thus
in the last section of Galatians we are concerned *no longer with a demonstration*

of the true character of the religion of the Law but with the unmasking of those who are misusing the religion of the Law for their own personal advantage.

But that is to say that it is in fact questionable whether Paul's intention in 6.11ff. really was to unmask those who preached circumcision as merely opportunistic representatives of the religion of Law who were basically unconcerned about the Law itself. Indeed the disclosure of such a *misuse* of the Law almost becomes an apology for the Law in the bygoing! But we would then have to ask whether Paul has not gone too far in the heat of the conflict by the exaggerated portrayal of his opponents[52] – so far in fact that it escaped him how he was damaging his real theological polemics by over-aggressiveness, and how by personal vituperation he was blunting his theological purpose itself: in brief, how clarity of argument gives him the slip in his emotion. However, we would also have to ask whether there does not lie concealed behind the inconsistencies of Paul's argument the conviction that the religion of Law itself is responsible for its representatives sliding imperceptibly into an attitude in which they egoistically misuse the Law even in relation to others, this time consciously or deliberately. This might be all the more readily supposed if the preachers of circumcision were not, as Lietzmann supposed, Gentile Christians, but were Jewish Christians whose ultimate motives – even according to Paul! – were to be looked for in their rootedness in the Torah. The way these people acted would then be determined by a peculiar mixture of conscious and unconscious intentions.

If we are right in what we have just said, then Paul did not see the self-glorying of his opponents simply as a tactical move in relation to the Jews. Rather for him tactical behaviour and self-confident boasting are then intimately bound up with each other. In verse 14, then, too, Paul is *not merely* opposing a tactical self-glorying which is Jewish in conception to a self-glorying appropriate to the Christian 'in the Cross of our Lord Jesus Christ'. This means, for otherwise the relationship of verse 14 to verse 13 would be incomprehensible, that Paul is trying to say that one should not glory in what one has done for the Law for, as something attained merely externally, it is only 'carnal'; but one should boast in the Cross – and there lies the paradox, for one is to be 'self'-glorying in respect of something which is in fact *not* the product of one's own efforts. Mussner makes this point very finely: 'the opponents glory in something which is their success, whilst the apostle glories paradoxically in something which has come into being completely independently of him...'[53] The Jews glory in salvation through their own activity, the Christians glory in the salvation wrought by God's activity. Through the Cross, that is, through God's redeeming activity[54] the world is crucified for Paul and he is crucified to the world. But the world is precisely symbolised by the Law. Thus for Paul the Law is crucified and he is crucified to the Law. He is dead to the Law. He is now 'a new creation' (6.15) as which, therefore, being dead to the Law, he lives to God (2.19).[55]

Can 6.12-14 throw light on 6.1-5 (or 5.26-6.5)? There we did indeed see the possibility of a genuine claim to 'glory' on the basis of one's own particular 'work'. This 'glory' – according to our exegesis – is *not fundamentally* relativised by one's own failure, but in individual cases it may be so. The relativisation of glory which is the aim of this section consists only in forbidding a comparison with other people: the glory of one's own work is invalid as soon as it is played off against others. By contrast, in 6.12-14 we hear of 'glory' only in the paradoxical sense of boasting on the basis of something which is in fact not one's own work. However, is the admission, previously made, of a glory on the basis of one's own particular work not in the last resort thereby paralysed, more or less, in that so long as one still makes one's judgements on the basis of the narrow perspective of one's own particular work, it is indeed possible to concede a 'genuine' claim to glory? On the other hand, as soon as one judges from the perspective of the redeeming act of God in Christ – which for Christians should be a matter of course – the assertion of one's own particular glory becomes farcical, comic play-acting.

But it is wrong to compare the two passages in Gal 6 with each other precisely in this way, for in so doing we attribute by implication a common standpoint to both pronouncements, whereas this does not exist. 6.1-6 unmasks a false glorying in respect of what others do, based, that is, on a sense of one's own superiority, but in 6.12-14 there is contrasted with the false glorifying of 'success' in the old, illusory order of 'salvation' the authentic glorying on the basis of the real act of salvation which is God's doing alone. The *tertium comparationis* in the two discussions is therefore *solely* 'glorying' as such, and we must above all note that in 6.4 we are concerned with glorying which is acceptable to God[56] and which cannot be played off against others, while in 6.13f. we have to do with the *act* of glorying or boasting in front of others *inasmuch* as the reason for such boasting is one's state of redemption whether this springs from one's own activity or from the activity of God.

Thus considering again everything that is said in Galatians on the subject of glorying or boasting, we can see that the apostle's later view, that *renunciation of glory before God is of the substance of the self-understanding of the person who believes in Christ*, has not yet been enunciated in this letter.

3.1.2 Boasting in 1 and 2 Corinthians

In 1 Cor 1.29 we have an absolute veto on boasting: *no human being* (μὴ...πᾶσα σάρξ) is to boast *in the presence of God*. Does this mean that here at last the idea expressed positively in Gal 6.14, that one is to boast only in the Cross, is now further explicated by its negative formulation in such a way that any boasting in human qualities, whatever they may be, is in principle forbidden in the presence of God? *The idea* of a further theological development of Gal 6.14

in 1 Cor 1.29-31 would be readily acceptable if we put Galatians chronologically before 1 Cor.[57] But does this further development actually occur in such a way that what in the terminology of Gal 6.4 is called 'work' is now in substance also included in the veto on boasting? The context of Paul's demand for such a fundamental renunciation of boasting is his polemic against the demand of the Corinthian 'Greeks' for wisdom (1.22). Human wisdom however is for Paul a symptomatic expression of all sorts of earthly qualities which one might use as the basis for a claim to glory in the presence of God. Now it is true that there is no direct statement in 1.18-31 to the effect that moral conduct also appertains to these earthly qualities, but in view of the insistence on preaching Christ crucified (1.23; cf.2.2) who has become righteousness, sanctification and redemption for us (1.30),[58] it is reasonable to assume this. We do in fact have, as Conzelmann shows, God's wisdom 'in Christ' as something 'alien';[59] thus we possess *only* an 'alien' righteousness and sanctification (sanctification being a synonym here for moral behaviour since in 1.30 righteousness and sanctification explicate the 'alien' wisdom).[60] Thus the 'quotation' from Jer 9.22[61] might then be paraphrased thus: let him who boasts do so in Christ as his 'alien' righteousness and 'alien' sanctification. Thus the tenor of the entire argument in this section is that the Christian, as he is regarded in the presence of God, owes himself *entirely* to God's saving activity.

Does Paul thus also wish to exclude as illegitimate boasting about the 'work' which is achieved on the basis of this *'alien'* righteousness and sanctification? We cannot cite verse 29 in support of this view; for here the point is the devaluation of those human qualities which are demonstrable outside the sphere of being 'in Christ'. To this extent we may perhaps take the phrase 'no flesh' in the strict sense of the term; no one is to boast in the presence of God in so far as he is only flesh.[62] In other words, no one who still remains in the sphere of 'the flesh' can boast, but only those who are already living in the contrasting realm of being 'in Christ'. We would then have to interpret the quotation from Jeremiah thus: let those who boast do so as people who are '*in* Christ'.

Accordingly, the drift of the argument of 1.26-31 certainly points to the belief that those who boast '*in* Christ' boast only in what constitutes 'being in Christ', viz., the saving activity of God *by itself*. In this way the question of the 'work' which the believer who is 'in Christ' does, being set as he is in the sphere of an 'alien' righteousness and sanctification, would be frankly inappropriate. Nevertheless the question of boasting in one's 'work' is still not disqualified in principle (see 1 Cor 3.13ff.; cf. also 2 Cor 5.10!). This only happens in Romans as is still to be shown.

Paul's dialectical statements in the 'four chapter letter' (2 Cor 10ff.), and above all in the 'fool's speech' we find there, caricature and treat ironically the thirst for glory of Paul's opponents in Corinth. But the subject of his deliberations here is certainly in no way – to use Bultmann's words – 'the basic

Christian attitude to boasting' but 'apostolic self-boasting'.[63] To be sure, the two questions merge into each other (something moreover that becomes very clear from Bultmann's article in the TDNT): but without overlooking essentials, we may dispense here with further treatment of 2 Cor 10ff.[64] The other passages where apostolic self-boasting is involved will also be left out of account here.[65]

3.1.3 'Boasting' in Romans

The theme of 'boasting, boasting of self' is a dominant one in chapters 2-4. As must on no account be overlooked, it makes its various appearances there only in a *polemical* context. It is first emphasised that the Jew boasts of his *possession* of the Mosaic Law (2.23), but his boasting in God, which is based on this, is perverted by the fact that he 'takes his rest' on his supposed possession of the Law (2.17).[66] (That there is also a genuine boasting in God is shown by 5.11!) In fact the possession of the Law which is assumed is really illusory. It is lack of possession, since the Jew too, and the Jew in particular, offends against the Law (2.21ff.) and thus he too 'falls short of the glory of God' (3.23) – like the disparaged Gentile of chapter 1! His possession of the Law has vanished into thin air because the Law is something only when it is done (2.25). In that case, of course, it does even bestow life (7.10, 10.5).

Does the Jew boast only in his possession of the Law? Or does he also boast in having done the Law? Within the section 2.1-3.18, at all events, nothing is said about his being proud of having done the Law. The apostle's reproach is rather to the effect that – as Lipsius already said – the Jew is relying on the Mosaic Law just as if mere possession of it were itself a merit.[67] But then that is to say that Paul does *not* here *accuse* them of 'righteousness by works'!

This may perhaps receive further corroboration from 2.25-29. There the subject is in fact circumcision – linked with the question of the Law! As Michel rightly sees, 2.25 is in the form of a thesis: circumcision is of use when (but also only when) you do the Law.[68] Circumcision too can indeed – like the Law – be understood as a 'possession' and that means that it can be misunderstood. We might thus paraphrase: you who think yourself sure of your salvation on the basis of just this 'possession' of yours, as a Jew whose Jewishness is characterised by circumcision and Law, have forgotten that it is in fact circumcision which presses for the fulfilment of the entire Law (cf. Gal 5.3, where we saw Paul's understanding of circumcision which derived from his pre-Christian period: circumcision is by its very nature an obligation to obey the Torah entirely!)[69] Did Paul himself know the rabbinical principle expressed in ExR 19(81c), viz., 'the circumcised do not go down into Gehenna'?[70] The argument in 2.17-29 and above all in 2.25-29 would certainly come into greater relief and thus standing out in relief would be the more readily intelligible as a polemic against this principle. As against this, of course, there is the view that Paul is heir to another rabbinical view of circumcision, viz., that which is reflected in the passage mentioned, in Gal 5.3. Thus if Paul had already known, as a *rabbinical* principle, the principle in ExR 19 that is first attested for a later period, then his polemics against it would be again formulated on the basis of a rabbinical principle. Thus Paul would have been conducting in Rom 2 merely a polemic within the confines of rabbinic thinking. Thus although Paul wanted to attack Judaism *as a whole*, he would have attacked an attitude which was held only within one element in Judaism. It consequently seems to me not indeed impossible but hardly very likely that Paul did know that principle.[71] But then in that case, 2.25, although it is written in a didactic tone and in the form of a thesis, is not a thesis directed against a particular rabbinical view.[72] Paul's intention might therefore be best correctly understood thus: the fact that the Torah was given to Israel misled and misleads Israel into misusing it as a 'possession'. Accordingly Paul is not denouncing a self-glorying by *works* of the Law, but precisely the opposite, viz., a self-glorying because of one's possession of the Law but *without* works of the Law.[73] In the current commentaries this contrast is certainly not given adequately sharp expression.

Before Paul returns to the subject of boasting (3.27-4.2), the accusation against *the* Jew, which itself already contains a certain tendency to generalise, is given more precise form as an explicit statement of the sinfulness without exception of *all* Jews (and Gentiles). Here however what we find Paul saying is: we have already (i.e., in our demonstration in 1.18ff.)[74] accused everyone of being under the power of sin[75] – all Jews and all Gentiles (3.9). It is clear that, in this summary accusation, what Paul is talking about is being under the *power* of sin, not, that is, about an individual's own sinful deeds for which he is responsible. Paul's introduction of sin (here for the first time in Romans it is 'sin' in the singular understood theologically)[77] as a power, at the point where he looks back to his previous discussion of personal guilt,[76] raises the question of the *necessity* or inevitability of sinning: man lives in a world which is the world of sin. His 'being-in-the-world' (Heidegger) is in fact understood precisely as a 'being in sin'.[78] Is this here an anticipation then to some extent of the dialectic of guilt/fate which we find clearly expressed in 5.12?

Quotations from the Old Testament are used to justify the idea of 'being under *hamartia*' against which the accusations are directed. Only, in these quotations Paul is concerned again solely with the fact *that* all men are guilty, but not with a demonstration of existence *under* sin, nor with a demonstration that man cannot escape from the field of force of this sin by his own efforts. It is thus remarkable that Paul immediately after this can state that not a single person can become just in the sight of God through *works* of the Law (3.20). Is he in 3.20 intending *more* than merely to state the fact of failure through neglect of the works of the Law, as the earlier use (3.9) of the singular, 'sin', leads one to suppose? Do we find a first intimation here of the idea of the intrinsic impossibility of justification by *works* – the more so as Paul continues: *for* through the Law comes (only) knowledge of *hamartia* (again in the singular!)?[79]

There follows the section 3.21-26 which is so important for the structure of Romans, in which section the δικαιοσύνη of God is expounded in elaborate terms as the δικαιοσύνη by faith and grace of the *righteous* God. In this (if you like) dogmatic passage which is positively overloaded with theological specialist terms and which gains its special stamp from the fact that objectivising terms from the inherited tradition have been interpreted by Paul in a specific way (emphasising the factor of faith),[80] the polemic against glorying is significantly not to be found. However in verse 27 the solemn tone which can be discerned in 3.21-26 and is difficult to overlook suddenly breaks off. What has been called the 'diatribe' style now introduces movement, not to say a hectic pace, into what follows.

And immediately, too (in 3.27a), Paul asks the 'triumphant question':[81] 'what then is left for the Jew to boast about?', only to answer it with the succinct answer that 'such boasting is excluded!' It almost looks as if the apostle had specifically introduced the dogmatic section only because he could thereby ask all the more effectively the question regarding boasting – i.e., this is dogmatic exposition serving a polemical purpose! But *what is it* that is now excluded: is it the possibility of boasting about the possession of the Law or about the works of the Law which have been performed? This is the cardinal question which arises of necessity out of our discussions so far.

Paul himself interprets his terse answer by pursuing the trend of his thoughts with a renewed question in 3.27b: 'by what Law?' Translated more precisely, διὰ ποίου νόμου would have to read: 'by what kind of Law?' That is to say, how must the/a Law be contrived such *that* (in the consecutive, i.e., *not* in the final sense of 'in order that') the possibility of self-glorying or boasting is thereby excluded in principle? The reply to this question which is formulated in a typically terse Pauline manner, and is consequently much in need of interpretation, mentions the 'law of faith' which is opposed to the 'law of works'. Mostly the term 'law' in the expression 'law of faith' is understood only in the improper, non-literal sense, say as an ordinance or standard, or perhaps more specifically as the order of salvation.[82] Since G. Friedrich's essay, 'Das Gesetz des Glaubens Röm 3,27'[83] this interpretation has been in dispute. Friedrich, in fact, understands the law of faith as the Mosaic Law in so far as it proclaims faith: 'the law of faith in Rom 3.27 is the Law which testifies to righteousness by faith in Rom 3.21.'[84] Other exegetes have subsequently subscribed to this view, even if with minor modifications.[85]

How the 'law of faith' is to be understood in our view is something we shall reserve till Section 3.3 of this enquiry. Let us leave this question still open at this point and attempt to interpret 3.27 from within its context – an interpretation which is not as yet dependent on the exact sense of the phrase which is in dispute. Paul then states that boasting or self-glorying is excluded by that *nomos* which is appropriately designated the *nomos* of faith. More sharply formulated, boasting or self-glorying is excluded only by the law of faith and consequently in no case by the 'law of works'. Even if it is in dispute how we are to understand the 'law of faith', there is still agreement to a great extent that the 'law of works' means the Torah. However, as Paul here designates the Mosaic Law by the phrase 'law of works' which is for him an odd one, we may suppose that he sought to look at it from a very particular point of view. Usually he speaks of the 'works of the Law' (six times in Galatians – 2.16, 3.2,5,10; twice in Romans – 3.20,28). Now however – in linguistic terms – the inversion of the *functor* and the *argumentum* in Rom 3.27 must certainly have been occasioned among other things by the question 'by what kind of law?' Yet it might be assumed as of the highest probability that the change in the drift of the content due to the inversion of the semanteme was intended by the author: Paul expresses by means of the defining genitive 'of works' the standpoint from which he intended to regard the Mosaic Law at *this* point in the argument – in other words, if Paul *here* describes the Law as the 'law of works' what he wants to say is that boasting or self-glorying is not excluded in so far as the Law is regarded from the standpoint of 'works'. And we may certainly go a step further: for those who take it as a 'law of works', but also only for those, the Law aims of *necessity* at boasting or self-glorying.

The same point also emerges clearly from a consideration of the connection of verses 27 and 28. For verse 28 does in fact function as a justification for verse 27: 'our theological judgement (λογιζόμεθα, lending extreme emphasis to his pronouncement!) is as follows: man is justified by faith – that is to say without the works of the Law!' If then accordingly it is justification by faith, as the righteousness that counts in the presence of God, which is incompatible with self-glorying then this certainly cannot be true of the righteousness *aimed at by means of* works. This is also clear from the nature of the case. For if the Law is defined as the sum of commandments which when complied with make man righteous, and if furthermore being righteous means being righteous in the presence of God, then the whole point for the man who understands the Law in this way is that he claims recognition in the sight of God for the works he has achieved. Yet more: he is in fact dependent on so doing, he must claim recognition for them in the sight of God. But this means no more nor less than boasting in the presence of God. If *righteousness through works* is legitimate – and this in fact refers to the view which understands the Law as a 'law of works' – then *it implies the legitimacy of self-glorying or boasting* – in fact the duty to boast in this legitimate way. Behold, O God, here are my righteous works! Behold, here I am in my righteous works as you have commanded me to submit them to you! Behold, here I am as the realisation of my works! Here are works *as* my righteous self![86]

Paul's starting-point in his thought is the new order of salvation. In *it* the theological judgement of verse 28 has its validity. But is it then permissible to infer from this verse that the old order of salvation which rested on righteousness through works is intrinsically worse than the new one which rests on righteousness through faith? We need to put the question more sharply. For the way in which the question is presently articulated does not by any means point us in exactly the right direction. It must in fact be asked whether – even if a temporal moment is constitutive for the whole argument because of the νυνί in Rom 3.21 – it is really entirely correct to speak of a *new* order of salvation in the strict sense of the term. Is there not already in 3.28 an attack being made on a perverted understanding of the 'old' order of salvation, as in fact the linguistic alienation or transmutation of the Torah into the 'law of works' with its denigratory tone leads us to suppose? Must we not then distinguish between an authentic 'old', a perverted 'old', and a 'new' order of salvation – the last somehow in continuity with the authentic 'old' one? Is then the 'old' order of salvation really based on that foundation which is to be regarded, according to 3.27, as righteousness through works? Let us for the time being leave this question aside and simply note here that the genuine old order of salvation involving the Law *can* in the light of the argument of Rom 1.18-3.28 be interpreted in such a way that according to it boasting or self-glorying in works of the Law which have been achieved is certainly not excluded but is rather demanded. This would also be true if the phrase 'law of works' were to articulate an aspect of the Law which belongs to it essentially. The phrase 'law of works' would then not be a linguistic expression for the misuse of the Torah. Much of course tells in favour of the idea that the 'law of works' does mean the perverted Law – above all, this interpretation would eliminate the difficulty of the holy Law of God demanding self-glorying of necessity (7.12). However, for the time being, it is sufficient simply to note that from the course of the argument in Romans up to 3.28 inclusive, it cannot with certainty be established that the use of the phrase 'law of works' is laying an accusation against an *abusus legis*. So long as we still cannot clearly see here what the truth of the matter is, we shall have to consider (at least for Romans up to *3.28* inclusive) Ulrich Wilckens's view: 'At all events Bultmann's verdict does not meet the case for Rom 1-3: "it is their very intention to become righteous in the presence of God by fulfilment of the Law and not just their actual evil works, their transgressions of the Law, which make the Jews reprehensible in the sight of God..." '[87]

Rom 3.31 is a much disputed verse. The discussion is concerned above all with the meaning of 'we uphold the Law'. Important though this question is, it will concern us less in the present context (the verse will be the subject of a more detailed exegesis in connection with the still outstanding question of the exact meaning of 'the law of faith' in 3.27). Here let it be said merely that 'law' in 3.31 means the Mosaic Law. The verse indeed has an apologetic sense. What is being asked is in fact whether the 'new' order of salvation has done away with the Law, that is with the principle of the 'old' order of salvation. Paul answers this with a decisive 'No', the sense of which is drawn out in Rom 4.[88]

It is widely recognised that the Abraham Midrash in Rom 4 is intended as the justification of the theological judgement in 3.28 (which is then to say, the verse in 3.28 which provides the justification for what precedes it [γάρ!] is now in turn justified itself). Thus chapter 4 also sheds light on 3.27 with the phrase 'law of works'. Might it be that in the light of Rom 4 we have to revise some of the exegetical judgements which have already been made? At all events, as has been shown, there are indeed in Rom 1-3 statements which are still open to interpretation and in need of interpretation. Above all, there is the decisive theological question: if the new ('new'?) order of salvation with its righteousness from faith has invalidated the old ('old'?) one with its righteousness from works, did that happen – and we know this question already from the treatment of Gal 3 – only because all men have in fact fallen short, or because the new order of salvation is superior to the old and therefore has been intentionally introduced by God because of the Law's function of unmasking sin? Is Bultmann then perhaps not still right in his judgement – which Wilckens rejected – according to which a man is not to achieve salvation in principle through works of the Law[89] – if we look not only at Rom 1-3 but also take Rom 4(ff.) into account? In other words: is an isolated interpretation of Rom 1-3 a false track from the start because what Paul says in these chapters could be formulated in such a way only in the context of the *overall* plan of Romans, i.e., because Rom 1-3 may be expressed as it is only on the basis of Rom 4ff.?

Paul asks what 'Abraham, our ancestor according to the flesh' found (4.1). We do not need here to go into the complicated text-critical problem in the verse as it contributes little to our question. For the latter, it is sufficient that, despite the fact that the text cannot be reconstructed with certainty, we can see that Paul is asking about the significance of Abraham in so far as he is the physical ancestor of the empirical Israel.[90] More important is our understanding of verse 2. Are we concerned here with something which is a reality or something which is not such?[91] Is Paul reckoning with the possibility that Abraham did in fact become righteous in terms of a righteousness of works but that this kind of righteousness brought him no glory in God's sight? Or is he trying to suggest that Abraham, even if he had been righteous in the sense of righteousness from works – which however in reality he was not at all! – would not have been able to assert this 'glory' in the presence of God but only in the presence of men?[92] It is clear from 3.9ff. that only the second view fits in compatibly with the other reflections of the apostle: within the sphere of the validity of the Torah, Paul cannot accord any righteousness even to Abraham; for no one is righteous and therefore neither is Abraham. It is reasonable to assume that Paul knew about the opposing view of the synagogue.[93] Once again we can see clearly how strongly the subject of 'glory' or boasting in Romans is given a polemical slant. Even the one of whom you tell such great things – says Paul against the Jews – is the one who as scripture shows was not righteous because of his works.

However, the idea that Abraham is a sinner also emerges from 4.3ff. According to Gen 15.6 which is quoted in Rom 4.3 he was justified by faith; this faith was counted to him as righteousness. However, according to 4.5 this faith is defined as faith in the God who acquits none other than the godless; it is *this* faith, and this faith alone, which is reckoned by God as righteousness (the verb λογίζειν is taken up in verse 5 from verse 3 or Gen 15.6!); it is this faith and this faith alone on which Abraham's righteousness solely depends. And finally David or Ps 32.1f. is quoted, where the imputed righteousness based on justification without works is explained as sin which is not imputed. Thus, to follow Wilckens, Abraham is indirectly taken as being a justified *sinner*.[94] He is right to make the point so emphatically, thus: justification by faith means the justification of the *sinner* who cannot be made righteous on the basis of the works of the Law.[95] But the decisive *theological* question now takes this form: *is the fact of Abraham's being a sinner, which is indirectly stated in 4.3ff., identical with his deficiency in righteousness through works* which has been inferred from 3.9ff.?

Let us again look at 4.2 because it is here that we can already discern the real point of Paul's argument: even if there had been a justifiable claim on the part of Abraham to glorying in the presence of men, and even if he had 'done justice' to what a righteousness on the basis of works demands, this simply would have had no validity in God's sight! Now quite suddenly the new idea, revolutionary to Jewish thought, has been pronounced, and now at last the specific element in Pauline theology has been clearly stated: *even complete righteousness on the basis of works within the framework of the Torah does not mean righteousness in the sight of God*! Kuss puts it well: 'But for him the *realis* of Judaism is an *irrealis* from the start, and furthermore he immediately interrupts himself and deletes the whole thing in a *train of thought which is not strictly logical*: "but not in the sight of God!" – there is no human self-glorying or boasting in the sight of God at all.'[96] And, in fact *this* train of thought is not logically connected with what has previously been said! This 'not in the sight of God' is certainly not what we would have expected after all that has been said. Paul's argument in chapters 1-3 was concerned to establish the point that all, including the Jews, had failed to satisfy the claim of the Law *as* a Law which requires works, not to make the point that fulfilment of this claim was inadequate as such. Well, is the 'not strictly logical train of thought' in fact illogical? Not at all! We must rather ask on what new level Paul is carrying on the discussion. We recall that in 3.27ff. his starting-point is the new order of salvation, but at that point it was not clear whether the new order of salvation was qualitatively superior to the old one, or whether it was simply a matter of a 'vicarious emergency solution'.[97] Now the argument in 4.2 by contrast hardly admits of thinking of Christ as an emergency solution, for in this verse *righteousness from works is disqualified as such*, as has just been shown; that is to say, the very starting-point which made possible the argument in Rom 1-3 in the first place appears to be disqualified!

Now one might be able to draw the sting of the interpretation just attempted by taking 4.2 in this way: if Abraham had become righteous on the basis of works of the Law, it would not have been allowable for him to boast in the presence of God despite the righteousness he had acquired thereby which is a full and true righteousness; for as a matter of principle one does not boast in the presence of God! It is unbecoming for man, even for the just man. Then the question in 4.2 would not be that of the impossibility of boasting in the presence of God, but of the impropriety of such behaviour. However, against such a *toning down of a theological into a moral point*, there speaks in the first instance the fact that here we have to do not with the act of boasting (καύχησις) but with the fact of glory (καύχημα), that is to say, with something which is the possible basis for glorying.[98] However, an exposition of this sort still leaves us, above all, with the difficulty that verse 3 supports verse 2 with the scriptural quotation from Gen 15.6. Thus the idea that even Abraham as someone who was righteous because of his works – should such an Abraham have existed! – would have had no glory in God's sight, i.e., would not have been righteous in

God's sight, is supported on this view by the theologoumenon of justification through faith in the God who justifies the *sinner* (verse 2 taken together with verse 5). But then the consequence is that *even the perfect man* – once again were there such, but there is not such! – *is a sinner!* The moral exegesis of verse 2 is therefore impossible. Thus the only interpretation that remains is that being 'righteous' on the basis of works means nothing in God's sight. *Anyone who is 'righteous' on the basis of works is simply not righteous.* Nor may we take the term ἐδικαιώθη in the strictly forensic sense (as for example in 3.20). On no account may the word be translated straightforwardly by 'he has been pronounced righteous'. Nor indeed is this passive form at all well suited to the statement in verse 2, having as it does associations for the reader of a *passivum divinum*. If, nonetheless, Paul brings it in, he does so probably with the intention of literary ironical alienation. Thus Paul is once again 'playing' with his terms. Accordingly we should put ἐδικαιώθη in quotation marks. For what is the point of a passive linked to the expression 'on the basis of works' and what is its point in association with a statement which expresses the entire activity of man! If Abraham is 'pronounced righteous' in virtue of his own activity, then it simply is not God who pronounces him righteous. The presupposition made here is of course that Paul does not view the divine judgement as an analytical judgement.

Those who see their righteousness as a righteousness on the basis of works, *see themselves* as righteous on the basis of works. They see their existence as a righteous one because it is made up of their own activities. In their 'limited' horizon of ideas (they set limits against God!) they are able to comprehend only a righteousness thus construed as the highest possible quality of righteousness. As a human quality, however, this is not one for which thanks are due. In defining what is to count as such a quality, God is left entirely out of consideration. We may remember that we have come across similar presuppositions in Galatians even though the theological terminology was different. In Romans we similarly find Paul energetically denying that one's own self can be understood as a *homunculus*. Those who define themselves in terms of their righteousness on the basis of works have misunderstood themselves because they are trying to see themselves as their own creator. But this is the cardinal error: those who approach God's Law and thus God's holy will on the basis of works have perverted the *Law of God into the 'law of works'* and have laid upon themselves chains which bind them to present themselves before God with their 'works' and to 'pro-stitute' themselves before God (*prostituere* in Latin literally means to set oneself before something or someone, hence there is a latent pun in the German). Among other points in favour of this interpretation is that according to Rom 10.3 the Jews misunderstand the righteousness of God (at the same time misunderstanding themselves) as is shown by the fact that they strive to call into being their own righteousness and to establish it (τὴν ἰδίαν [δικαιοσύνην] ζητοῦντες στῆσαι).

Now if the points we have just made are correct, Rom 4.3 then means with reference to 4.2 that Abraham was justified by God because he recognised that he could not become, either by his own works or by his own activities, what he ought to be in God's sight: *man who owes his very being to God*. He recognised that sin consists above all in elevating oneself in God's sight. Paul thus considers *Abraham to be a sinner in two ways*: first, he has *not fulfilled the righteousness that comes from works*, and second, he has *sought to be righteous as a result of his works*. However, because he believed God both things were forgiven him. The question, whether what is said indirectly in 4.3ff. about Abraham's being a sinner is identical with his deficiency in righteousness on the basis of works which was deduced from 3.9ff., must thus be answered in the negative.

Rom 4.4f. provides confirmation of our findings so far.[99] Michel takes the man who receives his reward according to what is due to him, that is, the ἐργαζόμενος, to refer to a man who bases his relationship to God on works; whilst whoever rejects such an attitude, the μὴ ἐργαζόμενος, can be described as a believer and as someone who has been pardoned.[100] Käsemann takes ἐργάζεσθαι to mean 'to be concerned with works'.[101] Both want to show that Paul energetically rejects a relationship to God as a legal relationship arising out of man's interest – a relationship in fact in which man 'establishes' his rights in God's sight by what he does. Perhaps we may restate the argument even more sharply thus: it is in the nature of 'works' that the 'person doing the works' (ἐργαζόμενος!) understands himself *and thus* his relationship to God – according to Paul there is no self-understanding which does not imply the *coram Deo*! – as a sum of works with which he shows how good he is in the sight of God. The 'law of works' means, from an anthropological standpoint, a self-understanding as 'one who works' and thus the exclusion of a self-understanding as one who owes one's being to God. From the drift of the argument it can be seen that in this the term 'works' (deliberately plural in order to emphasise the quantitative factor) is used pejoratively. 'Works' thus does not mean simply doing what is commanded in the Law but doing what is commanded *with a very deliberate purpose in mind*: I want to meet the requirements of the Law so that *I* am the person who does this, so that *I* may attain the life which is the intrinsic intention of the Law. But this is radical evil, this egocentric use of the Law as a misuse of the Law in the form of works, and – picking up the formulation which has already been used before – its perversion into a 'law of works'. The person who does the Law for the sake of his own life does it in 'works' and thus precisely by so doing fails to achieve life. The Law is in fact a life-giving Law only where the aim of the person who follows it out is not his own life (cf. Mk 8.35!). The *'law of works'* is correspondingly the 'law' of *that person* who perverts the true Law, i.e., the Law of God. But in that case, the term 'righteousness by works', which up to this point we had still treated in a relatively positive way, is now revealed as a *contradictio in adjecto*: the person who seeks to become righteous through works becomes only 'righteous'. Righteousness *on the basis of works is therefore not righteousness on the basis of the Law*. It is thus probably significant that in 2.17-29 the term 'works' does not occur, for the person there addressed is in fact not aiming at righteousness on the basis of works at all. And it is similarly also probably significant that in 2.1ff. this term appears only in the quotation from Ps 62 where of course it does not have the precise sense it has in 3.27-4.2. We must therefore agree with Michel when, as already said, he sees in the term 'law of works' an articulation of an understanding of the Law as something which analyses obedience into individual acts and thus misunderstands God's will. He rightly sees that the works of the Law correspond to the law of works on man's side, and thus that the Jewish understanding of the Law (according to Paul!) necessarily evokes boasting on man's part.[102] Bultmann has also seen this clearly when he writes: 'But Paul goes much further still, he says not only that man *cannot* achieve salvation by works of the Law, but also that he is not even *intended* to do so... The way of works of the Law and the way of grace and faith are mutually exclusive opposites (Gal 2.15-21; Rom 4.4f...). But why is this the case? Because *man's effort to achieve his salvation* by keeping the *Law* only leads him into sin, indeed this effort itself in the end *is already sin*.'[103] 'It is not merely evil deeds already committed that make a man reprehensible in God's sight, but man's intention of becoming righteous before God by keeping the Law and thereby having his "boast" is already sin.'[104] So in the end Wilckens's objection to Bultmann is unjustified.[105]

It is not a large step now from rejection of righteousness by works as the fulfilment of the Law for the sake of one's own righteousness to Paul's paradoxical statement that we boast in the hope of God's glory, but that this coincides with our boasting also of suffering or distress (5.2f.).[106] This dialectical relationship of boasting in hope and boasting in the sufferings of the present does however determine the believer's boasting in God (5.11) which has nothing in common with the Jew's boasting in God (2.17), apart from the name.

Let us return once again to the question whether the old order of salvation by the righteousness of works has been cancelled by the new order of salvation by the righteousness of faith. The above reflections should have shown that the old/new pattern cannot be applied without qualification to Rom 3.21-4.25. There is of course no question but that, because of the Christ-event, signalised by the Greek word νυνί in 3.21, there is a new order of salvation, just as there is equally no question but that the old order of salvation has been cancelled out in this respect. But Paul cuts across this chronological pattern by regarding Abraham as already, in the full sense of the word, justified. Günter Klein can therefore rightly say: 'this much is at all events clear: the contingency of Abraham as a figure of the historical past plays no part in these verses (viz., 4.3-8), and Paul simply uses Abraham as a model for demonstrating the structural elements of the event of justification. *Everything which has been offered in verses 4-6 by way of an exegesis of the two quotations could, without more ado, be transferred to every believer today...*'[107] Only this must not be absolutised to the effect that 'the history of Israel' is judged as 'radically de-sacralised and paganised'.[108] Rom 9.4f. tells against this. One-dimensional thinking is not appropriate to the dialectical thought in Romans.

This interweaving of 'old' and 'new' orders of salvation because of the common faith in the God who justifies the godless has its counterpart in Paul's handling of the thesis in Rom 3.25 which he takes over from the tradition. For it is only with the addition of the interpretative phrase 'by faith' that one is able to utter it – an indication that the Cross and resurrection of Christ can be understood theologically only in the context of the faith which is also constitutive for Abraham.[109] To be sure Paul's thinking springs from his engagement with something radically new which has become a reality in the Cross and the resurrection (2 Cor 5.17!). Certainly the misuse of the Law as the 'law of works' is plainly unmasked from this angle, but it is just as clear that the 'new' order of salvation stands in continuity with the 'old' order of salvation in that the latter was not aiming at righteousness on the basis of works (something which Israel however – *despite* Abraham! – nevertheless attempted to gain).

Let us take another look at the formulation according to which Rom 4.2 disqualifies righteousness by works, i.e., seems specifically to rule out the very starting-point which made the argument in Rom 1.18-3.20 possible in the first place. We have deliberately said '*seems* to rule out' for, to take up a further formulation in this section, in Paul's argument up to 3.20 the concern was not with righteousness on the basis of works but with righteousness on the basis of the Law. Up to Rom 3.20 there was no suggestion that justifying works resulting from obedience to what the Law commanded were to be performed in order to procure justification. The argument up to that point was, in grammatical terms, consecutive rather than final: from the failure to do what is commanded, unrighteousness follows as a consequence. Taken in this way there is no inconsistency between the sense of Rom 3.21-4.25 and of the argument in 1.18-3.20 – however much there may be an ultimate terminological disharmony which springs from the *esprit* with which Paul expresses his thoughts.

To sum up: The peculiar development of ideas by Paul in Romans in regard to the subject of glorying or boasting can be set out as follows:

(1) The Jew's boasting in God coincides with his *boasting in the Law*, but since *he does not keep the Law*, this boasting is *sin* (2.17ff.).

(2) Furthermore the Jew is in error because he boasts of (an alleged) *fulfilment of the works of the Law*. For those who understand the *Law of God* as a *'law of works' pervert* it. The requirements of the Law cannot be fulfilled as 'works'. Those who fulfil the Law with the purpose of making themselves righteous are acting egocentrically, and in order to gain their life are in fact bargaining it away.

(3) The boasting in God of the person who believes in Christ reaches its climax in *boasting of sufferings*. It is a *total reversal of the egocentric orientation* of boasting in works of the Law.

As we look back we notice that it is not boasting as such, nor glory as such, that is excluded. Käsemann has probably rightly recognised that Paul, in true Semitic fashion, considered boasting or glory as an 'existential' element of human existence (so too Schlatter and Kuss), i.e., as an expression of human dignity and freedom. 'For this very reason it is easily perverted whether in terms of its object or the way it is demonstrated. If as Paul sees it existence is defined by its lord, the basic understanding of existence comes to expression in boasting. In this, a person tells to whom he belongs.'[110]

3.2 God's Righteousness and Righteousness

We turn now to the Pauline idea of 'the righteousness of God'. We shall not of course attempt to deal fully with the complex and often rather diffuse discussion of the term, just as we shall have here particularly to resist the temptation to become involved in interesting discussions of detail. For this reason we are offering at the start only a very rough outline of the problem.

Let us begin with Bultmann.[111] He regards δικαιοσύνη as a *forensic* term. 'It does not mean the ethical quality of a person. It does not mean any quality at all, but a relationship. That is, δικαιοσύνη is not something a person has as his own; rather it is something he has in the verdict of the "forum" (= law-court – the sense of "forum" from which "forensic" as here used is derived) to which he is accountable.'[112]

At the same time this righteousness is an *eschatological* term since it is related to the final judgement.[113] As distinct from its sense in Judaism, however, it has a present meaning as it has already been imputed to man in the present.[114] There is a further contrast to its sense in Judaism in respect of the condition attaching to God's judgement of acquittal: as *God's* righteousness it is bestowed without works of the Law, or rather on the basis of faith. That is to say, it is a sheer gift, since faith is to be thought of as a radical contrast to boasting or self-glorying.[115] Finally, this righteousness has its origin in God's grace, in χάρις.[116] On balance then: 'The reason why "righteousness" is called *"God's righteousness"* is just this: its one and only foundation is God's grace – it is God-given, God-adjudicated righteousness (Rom 1.17; 3.21f.,26; 10.3).'[117] The sense of the genitive θεοῦ is clearly indicated by Rom 10.3 as a *genitivus auctoris*.[118]

Ernst Käsemann has in particular energetically objected to this view.[119] To him it is quite impossible to accept that the theology and view of history which we find in Paul are conceived primarily with the individual in mind. The righteousness of God is indeed a gift, but at the same time it has the *character of power*. Thus existence for Paul is in every case determined by him to whom we belong. 'If a transformation of our existence is really effected in baptism and if God's Word does effect a new creation, this cannot help but mean a change of lordship.'[120]

Now it would be possible to characterise the rest of the literature and indeed to classify it, simply in terms of how far it follows either Bultmann or Käsemann, at least in its general drift.[121] In the continuing discussion attempts have been made at closer definition, as when Stuhlmacher sought to strengthen Käsemann's thesis by trying to demonstrate that the phrase δικαιοσύνη θεοῦ has the character of a formula: in his view Paul took over the expression 'the righteousness of God' as an already existing formula.[122]

Of particular importance is J. A. Ziesler's monograph which appeared in 1972, *The Meaning of Righteousness in Paul: A linguistic and theological enquiry*. He distinguishes between the meaning of δικαιοῦν on the one hand, and the noun δικαιοσύνη and the adjective δίκαιος on the other.[123] 'If we take the verb as essentially relational or forensic and the noun and the adjective as describing behaviour within relationship...we arrive at an exegesis which satisfies the concern of both traditional Catholicism and traditional Protestantism.'[124] Ziesler may be allowed to have taken the discussion a good deal further.[125]

We notice one thing immediately: in Galatians, there is no mention of the δικαιοσύνη θεοῦ. The same is true of 1 Corinthians. Philippians, which is difficult to date, has only the phrase τὴν ἐκ θεοῦ δικαιοσύνην (3.9). Thus the late 2 Corinthians is the earliest evidence we have for the Pauline use of this term (2 Cor 5.21). We leave aside the question whether Paul has taken over the whole complex 5.19-21 from the tradition.[126] For what we have in mind, it is however important that in 2 Cor 5.21 the term 'righteousness of God' is not used in precisely the same sense as in Romans; for – to adopt Ernst

Käsemann's apt assessment – the term describes 'the reality of the redeemed community' in 2 Cor 5.21, whereas it 'appears in Rom 1.17, 10.3ff. in personified form as power.'[127] Thus if we wish to define the subject of Romans as the statement that 'it is the gospel in which the righteousness of God has been revealed' we could expect that would not yet have pin-pointed the subject of Galatians. To get a clearer picture here it may be advisable for us to start off in the opposite way from what we have been doing so far: this time let us first look at the theological structures in which δικαιοσύνη θεοῦ and δικαιοσύνη appear in Romans, and then look back from there to Galatians.

It would be possible to paraphrase Rom 1.16f. as follows: 'I confess the gospel. It is in fact the presence *of God* in his saving power for those who believe, first for the Jews then for the Greeks. *In the Gospel*, in fact, God reveals himself as the *righteous one*, that is, as the one who makes those men righteous whose existence is founded entirely in faith. It is written, in fact, that it is the person who is righteous on the basis of faith who will live.' Corresponding to this, we have what Käsemann says: 'The Gospel is...the epiphany of God's eschatological power pure and simple.'[128] We can further agree with Käsemann when he understands the righteousness of God as a power *and* a gift.[129] It must of course be asked what in fact is meant here by 'power'. *What* is God able to do? What is the *proprium* of his *dunamis*? Käsemann rejects the interpretation put forward first and foremost by Lyonnet,[130] according to which the righteousness of God is to be regarded as the *activitas Dei salvificans*.[131] Rather, he thinks, the phrase 'righteousness of God' in Paul speaks 'of the God who brings back the fallen world into the sphere of his legitimate claim...whether in promise or demand...'[132] Thus it is not just (in the sense of an understanding of what is meant by forensic which is too narrow in its scope) the power 'merely' to pronounce man righteous.[133] Justification and sanctification do indeed coincide in Paul![134]

If our paraphrase of Rom 1.16f. matches what Paul was actually after, 'faith' implies the right behaviour in relation to this God of power who brings the world back into the sphere of his right. This divine rectitude with its plenitude of demanding claims is then determinative for the faith of the Christians. At all events in the preface to his letter Paul already emphasises the *obedience*[134a] of faith (1.5) in connection with the great emphasis placed on his apostolate, that is on his mission for the gospel of *God*. God as the One who pronounces us righteous, i.e., as the One who makes us righteous, God as the One who reveals his righteousness, i.e., who reveals himself as the righteous One (apocalyptic context!), faith as obedience – all these things belong to the same terminological field. This whole context already leads one to suppose that the obedience of faith is something more than merely 'giving credence to' a message. It leads one to suppose that the obedience of faith implies an activity corresponding to the 'righteousness of God', that is, an activity for which somehow or other the predicate 'righteous' or 'just' holds good – naturally not in the Aristotelian sense according to which he who does what is just is just![135]

Consistently with these considerations, Paul opposes the righteousness of God, that is God as *the Righteous One*, to the unrighteousness (ἀδικία) of man (3.5f.). God as this Righteous One has remained faithful to his covenant with Israel (3.3: τὴν πίστιν τοῦ θεοῦ).¹³⁶ But the unrighteous man is the faithless man (3.4: ἀπιστία).¹³⁷ He is a liar (3.7). The *unrighteousness* which is here mentioned in the *context of the righteousness of God* is therefore that unrighteousness which is taken as a consequence of failing in God's Law – whether it be the Jews' failure with the Mosaic Law or the failure of the Gentiles who are a law unto themselves (2.14f.).¹³⁸ But the opposition of God's righteousness and man's unrighteousness is then an indication that in Paul's sense *God's righteousness cannot be thought of as fully detached from the righteous activity of man which is prescribed in the Law*. If God is the One who makes men righteous, as the reader of 3.5 already knows from 1.17, then the meaning of 'the righteousness of God' could (also) be supposed – simply from the obvious connection of these two passages for this reader – to be the conquest of human unrighteousness, which however, in accordance with the argument in 1.18ff. and above all 2.17ff., consists in unrighteous activity. But, we must hasten to emphasise, to say this is in no sense to open up the way for an interpretation of Romans in the sense of the doctrine of the *tertius usus legis*!¹³⁹

Directly after the theological judgement in principle in 3.20 which is enunciated in forensic terms (δικαιοῦσθαι = to be pronounced righteous),¹⁴⁰ we have in 3.21 a reference to the righteousness of God with the striking new start, νυνί. What was formulated programmatically in 1.17 in positive terms (the righteousness of God on the basis of faith) is now explained in a negative direction: the righteousness of God is manifested 'without Law', which in the context means, 'without works of the Law'. The fact that Paul here does not speak of *works* of the Law as in 3.20 may well be occasioned solely by his wish to make the paradoxical contrast: χωρὶς νόμου – ὑπὸ τοῦ νόμου. The master of linguistic nuance is again at work. 3.21a may then be paraphrased: without man's deploying works of the Law, God has now revealed himself as the One who makes men righteous. The νυνί...πεφανέρωται indicates the irruption of the Eschaton into the present and thus the *modification* of apocalyptic thinking with the aid of apocalyptic terminology (πεφανέρωται as an equivalent for ἀποκαλύπτεται; see 1.17f.).¹⁴¹ The positively formulated statement of 1.17 however is taken up again immediately in 3.22: διὰ πίστεως (instead of ἐκ πίστεως). In 3.24ff. God's righteousness is again shown to be God's activity with man. Although up to verse 26 inclusive an interpretation which remains within the confines of the individual verses does not exclude an understanding of these verses in the sense of a 'purely' forensic imputative justification, this is ruled out because of the wider context. The dogmatic section 3.21-26 does indeed prepare for the theological climaxes which now follow in 3.27ff., including the proof from scripture in chapter 4 relating to Abraham. Abraham, as we earlier established in Section 3.1 of this enquiry, did what the Lord commanded because of his justification in such a way that he was not obeying a 'law of works'. He is therefore the one who is paradigmatically justified, for whom being pronounced righteous and being made righteous coincide. If our reflections on Rom 3.27ff. and 4.1ff. are correct, then the direct connection between 3.21-4.25 and the 'forensic statement' (Ziesler) of 3.20 again shows very clearly how little the category of the forensic can be reduced to a 'merely' declaratory factor – even perhaps in the sense simply of 'as if'! Paul's highly individual style of theological argument prompts the question whether relocating God's final decisive judgement in the Christian's present experience – i.e., what later is expressed by Luther in the term 'certainty of salvation' – viz., whether the historicising of God's judgement does not make it possible to understand this judgement *also* as a realisation of righteous action: if God justifies the sinner, then 'putting things right' becomes manifest as a righteous activity of man. 'The righteousness of God' thereby obtains a dimension of depth in regard to its content. From the angle of the person justified this could be put thus: it belongs to the existence of the person who is *pronounced* righteous that he *is* someone who acts in righteousness. If we isolate the forensic happening, we make it lose its meaning. We then theologise from a detached standpoint *about* the God who pronounces men righteous and *about* the man who is pronounced righteous, and thus we objectify the judgement of God – the divine 'forum'. But if we take responsible theological talk of the judgement of God to be talk arising out of an existence affected by that judgement, then it is only talk originating in such an existence that is unable to exonerate itself on the basis of its own conviction of acting righteously.

The only other place where we find a reference to the 'righteousness of God' in Romans is at *Rom 10.3*. To see what it means in this passage we must take into account its *dual reference*. First of all, it is contrasted with one's 'own righteousness', i.e., human righteousness, or more precisely, with being righteous on the basis of one's own activity in terms of works of the Law, and asserting this over against God. Thus in this narrower context it means the righteousness which man *owes* to God as his gift. From the viewpoint of the believer's self-understanding, we can say that it describes the person who is righteous because of his faith, and who owes to God the fact of his being righteous, or, to put it more concretely, who owes his own self as a righteous self to God. 'The righteousness of God' however in this verse is also related to the behaviour of the Jews. They have not subordinated (ὑπετάγησαν) themselves to it. Such a definition of the term 'righteousness of God' is however almost incompatible with the idea of 'being righteous because of ...'. Subordinating oneself is something one does to the person who has the appropriate authority. When however authority is spoken of here, the terminological field of 'power' is introduced. Consequently the righteousness of God in 10.3 is *also* understood as power. Here we can again paraphrase: the Jews have not submitted themselves to the righteous God, that is to say, the God who makes righteous. It thus appears that the 'righteousness of God' even in 10.3 is not a term that can be given a unilinear definition.[142] Rather it embraces both the being of the justified man as someone who exists *iustitia aliena* and also – which becomes clear against the negative reflection of the Jews – the relation of the man who is justified to the God who justifies. For the self-understanding of the justified man is that of someone who knows that he is righteous because of God, *and* who therefore knows that he is 'subject' to the righteous God. However, let it be expressly stated that this division into two elements represents a division which is only terminological and that therefore the self-understanding referred to is of course only a *single* self-understanding. This means however that those who know they have been given the *gift* of God's righteousness know that they are in this way *at the same time* determined by the *power* of the righteousness of God.

In his interpretation of Rom 10.3, Stuhlmacher starts from the entire complex of Rom 9-11. In his view these chapters centre on the subject of the righteousness of God understood as a 'manifestation of the eschatological creative power of God'.[143] As the emphasis in this phrase most probably lies on the word 'eschatological', it exactly describes *one* aspect of the term. We can also agree with Stuhlmacher in understanding 9.32b-10.2 as 'to some extent the salvation-history variant of Rom 7.7ff.'.[144] Thus: '10.3 sums up the idea that Israel has failed to achieve God's will as a righteous will and as a creative will...because Israel endeavoured to oppose to God's creative power its own δικαιοσύνη.'[145] Here of course where Stuhlmacher speaks simply of the creative will instead of the eschatological creative will, there is at least the possibility that a faulty interpretation may be suggested. When Stuhlmacher then goes on to state that some of the ground is taken from under the current interpretation, viz., that the righteousness of God in Rom 10.3 means God's gift, because what is involved is the destiny of peoples so that our passage is in no way to be expounded as relating to the individual,[146] he fails to realise two things:

(1) In Paul's theology of justification, it is not possible to separate sharply the individual and the collective elements. The two overlap. Certainly in the context of chapters 9-11 Paul's reflections on the righteousness of God relate to the collective entity of Israel. And yet precisely in 10.3 the singular 'Israel' is in fact not used but rather the third person plural, so that we *also* find a linguistic expression of the individual responsibility of each person in Israel – just as the overall argument of Romans would be meaningless without this individual aspect. It is precisely here that we can see the fruitfulness of the existential interpretation rightly understood, with its dual starting-point in man's inwardness and his 'being-in-the-world' which is therefore fundamentally opposed to any kind of individualistic mode of interpretation.[147]

(2) The dual aspect of God's righteousness which was set out above is not properly developed in Stuhlmacher. And yet it is just this dual aspect which is essential for Ernst Käsemann, in whose interpretation of Paul the character of

power in the righteousness of God is such a fundamental feature. In regard to
Rom 10.3 Käsemann says: 'in the eschatological *gift* of justification the *Giver*
comes on the scene as *Lord* and Creator'.[148] It is after all Käsemann who never
tires of emphasising that power and gift are not in essential contrast![149] But we
cannot then say with Stuhlmacher that in the total context of chapters 9-11
God's righteousness can be only (!) the power of God activating itself as an
eschatological creative power, directing history and human destiny.[150]

To sum up: In Romans 'the righteousness of God' means that gift of God
which manifests itself in essence in its character as power. For Romans what
Käsemann puts so well is true at least in relation to the 'righteousness of God':
'In Paul's theology change of existence always takes place as a change of
lordship, thus with the relation to another lord, and is nothing other than entry
into a new relation. A person's reality is decided by what lord he has.'[151] Either
hamartia is man's master or the righteousness of God; either the power of sin,
almost personified by Paul (5.21), or the just God who makes men just!
Hamartia, however, is no longer to dominate us because as Paul says in a
sharply contrasted formulation, we are no longer under the Law but under
grace (6.14).

Can something similar also now be said of 'righteousness' in Romans? Let us
first underline the fact that δικαιοσύνη without the determinative genitive
θεοῦ occurs precisely in the context of the statements about δικαιοσύνη θεοῦ.
Significantly, the term 'righteousness' in Rom 4 thus means the righteousness
imputed to Abraham and consequently to all believers (the verb λογίζεσθαι
occurs nine times in chapter 4 with the meaning 'impute'!). If in 3.21 it is said
that the righteousness *of God* is testified to by the Law and the prophets, the
proof from scripture is now given with regard to the righteousness imputed to
the believer, but this means that in Romans Paul means by 'righteousness', at
least in chapter 4, *the individual realisation and concretisation of the
righteousness of God*. Can we conclude from this that the righteousness of God
and righteousness are in Romans generally to be distinguished in the sense that
the term 'righteousness of God' implies the idea of power, while the term
'righteousness' expresses more the being of man which is bestowed upon him,
i.e., the gift? As an argument for this view 5.17 could be quoted (οἱ τὴν
περισσείαν τῆς χάριτος καὶ τῆς δωρεᾶς τῆς δικαιοσύνης λαμβάνοντες!). But
Paul then produces, in chapter 6, statements about righteousness which make
it possible also to understand it clearly as 'power'.

Now it would initially be possible to expound 6.13 by pointing to the manner
in which it is not righteousness but God that is contrasted with the power of
sin: in the service of *hamartia* there stand the weapons of unrighteousness
(ἀδικία can certainly be understood here as a human 'quality'!), but in God's
service stand the weapons of righteousness. However, if unrighteousness
means the unrighteous behaviour of man, why should not righteousness then
mean his righteous behaviour, or, to put it more precisely, the behaviour of the
person who has received his quality of being righteous as a gift from God? We

can find a similar exegesis of Rom 6.13 in Martin Luther: '*Iustitia tota generalis conversatio ex fide seu fides cum operibus suis* ...'[152] Even 6.16 could be interpreted as belonging to this line of argument. After the initial statement that man always has a master or lord and that having a master is a fundamental feature of being a man, here too the lordship of sin is not actually contrasted with the lordship of righteousness. Rather, it is said that just as being a slave to *hamartia* leads to death, so too obedience (i.e., towards God) leads to righteousness. One might actually have expected that the sentence would end with the words: '...or to righteousness which leads to life'.[153] Only then would we have an antithetical formula which was self-consistent, and in which the individual elements do also really correspond to each other. Theologically the relationship of obedience and righteousness is the prime difficulty here: ὑπακοῆς εἰς δικαιοσύνην. For up to now Paul has set the greatest store by the idea that the true righteousness of man is a gifted righteousness! And now suddenly we have: εἰς δικαιοσύνην! According to Kertelge this is, and remains, a formulation which is unclear.[154] So much is certainly true. But at the same time it must be emphasised that in no circumstances does Paul wish by this phrase to assert the righteousness of man to be even only in part a deed or achievement of man! Unless we wish to reverse the whole drift of Pauline theology, the interpretation which suggests itself is that obedience towards God is geared to man's being constantly maintained in the righteousness which he has received.[155] To put it otherwise, the gift is such when and only when it is understood as a task. If this interpretation matches the sense intended by Paul, then 6.16 confirms our interpretation of the relationship of chapters 3 and 4, according to which it belongs to the existence of the person who has been pronounced righteous actually to be someone who acts in righteousness – this simply because Pauline theology can be understood only as a theology worked out in relation to man's existence. Thus in 6.16 the phrase εἰς δικαιοσύνην indicates the effect of God's action in pronouncing one righteous, as seen from the standpoint of the righteous activity of the person who has been justified.[156] This of course does not mean, as Käsemann rightly emphasises, that one should therefore think of the moral standard of honesty or uprightness as a new ideal.[157]

If in the light of these reflections it appears that the only possible interpretation of the term 'righteousness' in 6.16 is as a gift, i.e., as the gift of being righteous in the sense of righteous activity which is itself a gift, nevertheless this verse does also show – though of course only allusively – the character of power which attaches to the righteousness of God. That is to say that if Paul contrasts 'for death' with 'for righteousness', it must not be overlooked that already in 5.12, along with the quasi-personified *hamartia* as a power, he also introduced the quasi-personified *thanatos* as a power.[158] 6.17f. are the verses which finally show clearly the character of power which righteousness has, although there is no explicit mention here of the righteousness *of God*. Man is always subject to a Lord or master – this idea is repeated here. Now it is formulated from the standpoint of temporal succession: you were the slaves of *hamartia*; but now you are in your freedom from this dominion 'enslaved' to righteousness, ἐδουλώθητε. Now at last *sin* and *righteousness* are specifically named as the *two powers which determine existence*, than which there is no other.[159] Since in 6.13 God is contrasted with *hamartia*, so that righteousness and God appear in the same semantic field, the contrast of sin and righteousness can also be articulated as a contrast of (quasi-personified) *sin* and the *righteous God* (see also 6.22!), and since the Christian is addressed as one who is justified, as the one who has died to sin because of baptism (6.2ff.), the term 'righteous God' can here be explained as: God who *has* made one righteous. In brief: he who is free from *hamartia* serves righteousness, i.e., the God who has justified him or made him righteous; he is specifically 'defined' by his being enslaved to this righteous God.

In 6.19c this imperative is derived from the indicatives which have already been stated: 'so now yield your members to righteousness for sanctification (εἰς ἁγιασμόν)' (τὰ μέλη ὑμῶν = a circumlocution for the entire person of the one addressed with regard to responsible action). Thus here the εἰς ἁγιασμόν corresponds to the εἰς δικαιοσύνην of 6.16,[160] and the phrase δουλᾶ...τῇ ἀνομίᾳ εἰς τὴν ἀνομίαν in 6.19b serves as an interpretative aid for the change from the accusative of purpose, εἰς δικαιοσύνην, 6.16 to the dative τῇ δικαιοσύνῃ in 6.19c. Here expression is now given with complete clarity to the character of power which resides in lawlessness *together with* its being actually implemented. But in that case the interpretation of Rom 6 which sees it as setting out the dual character of δικαιοσύνη will not be wrong: that character of power which distinguishes the righteousness of God according to 1.16f. does in fact belong properly to δικαιοσύνη. But in Rom 6 δικαιοσύνη also means 'righteousness of life' (Lipsius: *Lebensgerechtigkeit*) in which the man who is justified by God gives evidence of his having been pronounced righteous. Naturally the term δικαιοσύνη does not mean both these things in the deepest sense at each point in this chapter. For example one must certainly ask whether δικαιοσύνη can be expounded in the sense of 'righteousness of life' in the so palpably pointed antithesis of 6.18.[161] But it is very much Paul's way of handling his theological terms to give them life by illuminating their spectrum of meaning differently every time he uses them. Pauline theology if presented as a system of closely defined terms, with the emphasis on the limitation definition implies, would no longer be Pauline theology; but if we keep in mind this continual movement in Pauline thinking then – but admittedly only then! – what Ziesler says about the understanding of δικαιοσύνη in Rom 6 is true: '...a power...at the same time what one does', 'a certain kind of behaviour, plus the role of a power'.[162] Here Ziesler rightly points to the analogy of sin. For sin too conceived as a power is not simply something set over against man. It operates in fact in the deeds which man has to answer for; as Rom 5.12 shows it is fate *and* guilt. Or – to remain within the horizon of ideas in Rom 6 – we may say that in the person who is liberated from the power of sin by baptism this power of sin must not rule again – through the person's thus liberated as it may be obeying again *his* own desires.

We may add merely in parenthesis a thought which follows on from what has just been said about the concept of δικαιοσύνη. In his programmatic essay which has meanwhile become a document in theological history, 'Das Problem der Ethik bei Paulus' (1924) Bultmann contested the idea that either sin or δικαιοσύνη in the Christian was something perceptible in the empirical man. Δικαιοσύνη, he says, is not in fact an alteration in the moral quality of man, nor is sin to be considered as identical with moral failings.[163] 'That is to say, the identity of the justified man with the empirical man is something which is *believed*.'[164] Bultmann has in substance sustained this thought right through to his *Theology of the New Testament.* We have already mentioned in this section that in the latter work δικαιοσύνη, which he takes as a forensic term, is not understood by him as an 'ethical quality of a person. It does not mean any quality at all, but a relationship'.[165] In Käsemann the gap between sin and moral failings or between δικαιοσύνη and the moral qualities of man has been attenuated. 'What is usually called ethics…goes beyond the moral sphere as certainly as it expresses itself in that sphere, because sin has moral implications for Paul even though it is not a moral phenomenon.'[166]

Bultmann's endeavour to overcome a moral interpretation of sin and δικαιοσύνη has its proper place. It is understandable as a reaction against a moralistic distortion of Pauline theology; it was moreover, in the theological situation of that time, an urgent necessity. But today a kind of reversal is necessary and we have to understand afresh the category of the moral, starting from Paul's basic theological approach. *It is not 'morals' which have to determine what is theological* – a view moreover which again, even today, is having a new lease of life (frequently with astonishing superficiality) – but *'morals' which must be understood in terms of the fundamental theological structure of Pauline thought in such a way that we can recognise how it is entirely integrated in this.* 'Ethical' δικαιοσύνη[167] must not be downgraded to the status of a mere appendix, of an application of the Pauline doctrine of justification which is at most to be tolerated. Rather, 'ethical' δικαιοσύνη, which finds concrete expression in obedience to the God who pronounces man δίκαιος and equally, therefore, in love to one's neighbour, has its foundation in Christ's act of obedience (Rom 5.19: διὰ τῆς ὑπακοῆς τοῦ ἑνός; cf. 1.5: εἰς ὑπακοὴν πίστεως). We however have been linked with the obedient Christ in baptism into his death, that is, we have been baptised into his decisive act of obedience.[168] But this means that God's δικαιοσύνη and God's love (5.8) are realised in us, for the moral demand of love which does indeed mean the fulfilment of the Law as the holy and just will of God (13.8-10) has its ultimate basis in God's act of love (5.8!). The reflections in Section 2.3 showed clearly how the term 'sin' in Romans embraces moral failings but cannot be understood in its real nature on this basis. The dimension of depth in the term δικαιοσύνη also corresponds to the dimension of depth in this term (thus when we are talking of 'morality' in connection with Pauline theology, the association must not be made between morality and 'bourgeois morality', for the 'moral element' in Paul has nothing to do with 'bourgeois morality' or what is taken to be that). One thing of course must be conceded: what we look for in vain in Romans is a *terminologically exact correlation* of 'being acquitted' or 'counted righteous' and the new being effected through the Spirit which finds its expression in love. In Rom 8 the new being (κατὰ πνεῦμα) with its intentionality (φρονεῖν: *Aus-Sein-auf*) is simply contrasted with the old being (κατὰ σάρκα).

Looking back on the reflections offered in this section, the dialectic of the dominance of *hamartia* and the dominance of δικαιοσύνη or of the δικαιοσύνη θεοῦ or of the justifying God should appear clearly as an outstanding fundamental statement of Romans. In fact, Käsemann's very fundamental statement is true of Romans, viz., that 'a person's reality is decided by what lord he has'.[169] 'For Paul no man is ever without a master or on his own.'[170] Here we could in fact speak of a *theological 'existential'*: from the standpoint of Paul in Romans being a man always implies having a master. Being a man *is* in principle and in every case *either* being under the dominion of sin *or* being under the dominion of the righteousness of God.[171] However, this *dialectical-existential* statement is also made in the context of the theology of Law. It sounds like a theological axiom when Paul justifies the immediately preceding statement in 6.13 by saying in 6.14: 'you are not under the Law but under grace'. If anyone should happen not to read this passage in the light of Galatians, but rather should read Romans in isolation and should persist in reading it continuously as far as 6.14, he will perhaps become a little suspicious. For so far nothing has been said of a being *under* the Law. Up to this point the only power we have seen determining man in a negative way was sin and death. Otherwise up to 6.14 nothing at all has been said about the Law which might suggest that it is a power deleterious to man.[172]

No independent proof is necessary of the fact that Paul with his ὑπὸ χάριν in 6.14 is still in the terminological field of the lordship of δικαιοσύνη. But then the antithetical formula 'under the Law/under Grace' in fact makes the reader suspect initially that Paul is now suddenly regarding the Law not only as incapable of providing δικαιοσύνη but also as a power for ill. It is very hard to escape the impression that being under sin and being under the Law are here seen as one and the same thing. And it is indeed likely that Paul really intended to say that anyone who is under the power of the Law is at the same time under the power of sin. It is the selfsame person who exists with dire consequences under both régimes. *However, the coincidence of these two régimes does not mean that the two 'rulers' are identical.* Paul himself fears that an identity of this kind will suggest itself to the reader, for in Rom 7.7 he in fact asks whether the *nomos* is *hamartia*. It may well be that this question was actually asked of him often enough. The fact that 7.7 is in the *style* of a diatribe[173] cannot in any way demonstrate that Paul is not quoting an objection that had been raised against him.[174] The apostle refutes the view which had been, or could have been, attributed to him, viz., that the two 'rulers' were identical, with the thesis that the sinfulness of sin reveals itself precisely in the fact that sin brought death through what was good, i.e., the Law (7.13).

However, being 'under the Law' does not mean doing what is commanded by the Law. Without going any further 13.8-10 tells against this. What it means is rather that only when the Law has been perverted into a 'law of works' (3.27) does it take on an enslaving function. But then the phrase 'under the Law' means the same as 'under the dominion of the perverted Law' (one might wish perhaps to cite Rom 7.1-6 against this interpretation, but on this passage see Section 3.3 of the present investigation). However much Paul may stress the idea that the Christian is free from the dominion of the perverted Law, that indeed being a Christian *is being free* from the perverted Law, nevertheless for him the force of the statement does *not* in Romans lie on freedom *as such*. Once again: this judgement is true only of Romans. In Romans *freedom* is – like dominion – a *dialectical idea*. Freedom is an existential concept. Thus Paul can say in an almost disconcerting way: 'you were free from the dominion of righteousness' (6.20). There is a freedom which is evil, but 8.21 shows that Paul can nevertheless speak emphatically of freedom.[175] However here too freedom appears linguistically as something which is determined (ἀπὸ..., τῆς...). Romans is not written as a *magna charta libertatis* – despite the considerable stress which is laid on freedom in Christ. Theological reflection forbids a use of the word and of its derivatives in any too absolute way. Paul always says *what* kind of freedom is meant and what kind is not.

In sum: In his theological reflections in Romans Paul is striving to reach a balanced presentation of the peculiar dialectic of dominion and freedom. In this he is concerned to show how a distinction must be made between freedom from the Law and freedom from sin. Both kinds of freedom, or of the corresponding lack of freedom, are, to be sure, given as an interdependent 'package', but freedom from the Law in no way means freedom from the Law understood as in principle a power deleterious to salvation. The Law remains even for Christians a determinative factor. It would be possible to extend Paul's line of thought and say: *freedom from the perverted Law is the dominion of the Law of God* – properly understood, of course.[176] Paul does not indeed say this in so many words, but it is implied in the theology of Romans. In so far as in fact the command of the Law is just, δικαία (7.12), and the fulfilment of the Law is, we may probably assume, the doing of the 'just' command of loving one's neighbour in which the Law is summed up (13.8-10), freedom from the perverted Law implies the service of a slave in relation to the righteousness of God, i.e., to the righteous God; and this is a service which is necessarily evinced in 'just' deeds. The idea of obedience in this sense has its linguistic source in the expression δικαιοσύνη θεοῦ which does not occur in Paul, as we saw, until 2 Corinthians. Whether he took it over as an established usage (Stuhlmacher, etc.) can in this context be left unresolved.[177] At all events it is certain that in its final stage Paul's theological development has been given its character substantially as a result of this concept – so substantially indeed that the essence of the theology of Romans can be 'conceived' on the basis of this concept.[178]

Looking back now at *Galatians*, we have here another picture. The entire letter is a passionate appeal to the Galatians not to betray their freedom whatever they do. Those who are *free* are the Christians (where it is the notion of freedom which provides the key for interpreting what it is to be Christian)! 'For freedom Christ has set us free!' (Gal 5.1a). This sentence can be written only with an exclamation mark although it is formulated as an indicative. And so there follows also at the same time the imperative 'stand fast therefore and do not submit again to a yoke of slavery'(Gal 5.1b). Whoever is a slave, Paul contends, cannot be a Christian! What we have just denied of Romans is the more true for Galatians. It is the *magna charta libertatis*. In it the question posed with genuine intensity of feeling is that of 'freedom *from*', i.e., freedom from the Law, a freedom which is put on the same footing as freedom from the elements of the world and the demonic powers. It is at the same time freedom from the supra-individual power of *hamartia*. In Galatians there is no trace of what Paul is so much concerned about in Romans, i.e., to distinguish between sin as the actual power which works against salvation and the Law as the power which is merely misused by sin.[179] In this letter Paul does not find it necessary at any point to say that slavery under the Law's sphere of dominion contradicts the specific nature of this Law. The positive statement about 'the whole Law' in 5.14 does not in fact refer to the Torah at all. The tenor of the letter is therefore 'you Galatians are freed by Christ; so do not gamble away your freedom'. This freedom is not understood dialectically as a basic existential element. Freedom here is in no sense something to be spoken of in connection with pre-Christian existence. Freedom from the powers of evil is understood simply as freedom – no more, no less.

Similarly in *Galatians justice or righteousness* (δικαιοσύνη) is spoken of *only as a gift*. For none of the occurrences of this term (2.21; 3.6; 3.21; 5.5) are there any compelling grounds for inferring the sense 'power' from the context. Furthermore at no point does this meaning make any sense. (This holds good all the more for the derivatives.) As we have already pointed out on several occasions the expression δικαιοσύνη θεοῦ itself does not occur at all in Galatians. The entire argument in this letter in fact even makes it possible to suppose that at the time of writing Galatians Paul was not even familiar with the term δικαιοσύνη θεοῦ. If he had known of it at the time – or rather let us say more carefully, if he had at the time already been aware of the theological scope of this term – he would in all probability have formulated many statements differently. This much is at any rate clear: *Paul in Galatians does not think of the* δικαιοσύνη θεοῦ *as the powerful epiphany of the just and justifying God.* Nor in Galatians does he know that obedience to the δικαιοσύνη θεοῦ which would at the same time be obedience to the Mosaic Law freed from its perversions.

Taken together, depreciation of the Torah and the absence of the term δικαιοσύνη θεοῦ account for a determinative characteristic of the Pauline letter. We shall not attempt here to resolve the question whether Paul himself developed the term δικαιοσύνη θεοῦ from 1 Cor 1.30 where, in my view, there is an advance in christological reflection over against Galatians, or whether he gratefully picked it up from some other source as a welcome linguistic tool for the development of his theology. Let us therefore hold on to the point that the dialectic of the *existentialia* freedom and slavery, which is so typical for Romans, does not occur in Galatians.

Yet there are in Galatians the *first signs* of a dialectical view of freedom, viz., in 5.13, i.e., that sentence which finds its justification in the well-known theologoumenon in 5.14. Once again Paul establishes the programmatic point, 'you are called to freedom, brothers'. Thus once again there is an absolute statement about freedom without any qualification to suggest that it is a merely delimited freedom. All at once there is a warning against a possible (?) misunderstanding of freedom, viz., as licence: 'only do not let your freedom become an opportunity for the flesh!'[180] For this would be to squander one's true freedom.[181] But 'the flesh' is the individual location of the transubjective *hamartia*. And where the flesh, as a kind of Trojan horse for *hamartia*, makes it possible for sin to take control, freedom is at an end. The misuse of freedom cancels out freedom as such. After this warning we have the admonition 'rather serve each other in love'. Love, which is the sole law for the Christian (5.14), is accordingly understood as slavery. Liberating faith finds expression, according to 5.6, in love; it is this very liberating faith which is in fact the energy of love. It is however precisely the love made possible by the faith which liberates which is interpreted as δουλεύειν. Here we find the germ already in principle of that existential dialectic which is to be seen in Romans. To be sure, certain terminological elements are still missing which will be decisive for its development. Only with the term δικαιοσύνη θεοῦ and with a new valuation of the Torah will Paul be given the necessary presuppositions. One thing of course Paul has already recognised and clearly formulated in Galatians: freedom cannot be defined in terms of the individual for such a narrowly defined freedom is no freedom at all.

3.3 Legem statuimus! (Rom 3.31)

Let us make a final effort with Rom 3.27-31! Let us try to grasp even more precisely the real drift of this argument; let us try to listen even more closely to what is being said here – literally what is being *said*, for Paul dictated the letter to be read aloud – and to catch what his own specific intention was.

Having established that God is righteous and consequently makes the man who exists on the basis of faith righteous, Paul exclaims – and we can hear the sense of satisfaction in the tone of his voice – 'where now is the boasting (of the Jew)? It is out of the question!' Adopting the argumentative style of a diatribe he goes on to press his question: 'by what kind of law is the boasting excluded? Is it perhaps by the Law which has been perverted into a "law of works"?' The phrase 'law of works' in fact means, as was shown in Section 3.2 of this investigation, quite concretely the Mosaic Law of God *in so far as* it has been degraded and depraved into a means of having to assert oneself before God. However, if the reference in the 'law of works' to a specific view of the Torah is unmistakable, then this expression means the Torah in so far as it is a misused Torah – see Rom 10.4: Christ is the end of the misuse of the Law – and then it is only logical to assume that Paul's answer 'no, but by the law of faith' also has some reference to the Torah. The supposition cannot of course simply be dismissed that, arguing – as is not untypical for him anyway – elliptically, the apostle no longer understands by 'law' in the answer 'no, but by the law of faith' what he had understood immediately before in the question by this term. But we should first try for an explanation which presupposes a steady development in the author's train of thought. It is only when such an explanation cannot construct such a *continuum* otherwise than by a *tour de force* that we should argue in favour of a leap in the thought (as, e.g., in Gal 3.10). Here, however, it is perfectly possible to interpret the passage without the supposition of a leap in Paul's thinking: Paul is asking – I paraphrase – 'is it possible that the compulsion to boast is excluded by the Torah seen as a "law of works"?' The answer runs: 'on no account!' (for anyone who understands the Torah in this way has no alternative whatever to taking up a sinful stance before God). Rather boasting is excluded only by the 'law of faith', that is by the Torah as soon as this is seen with the 'eyes of faith'. Such an exposition comes close to that offered by Gerhard Friedrich: 'the law of faith in Rom 3.27 is the Law which testifies to justification by faith in Rom 3.21'.[182] The closeness of the interpretations arises because like Friedrich we take 'the law of faith' to be the Torah. It is of course true that the interpretation submitted here differs from that of Friedrich in so far as the standpoint from which the Torah is viewed in each instance is different: the Law as a witness to justification by faith, or the Law from the perspective of the man of faith. If Paul had intended in 3.27 to refer back to 3.21, then we would expect him to have said 'by the law of the δικαιοσύνη θεοῦ'. But in 3.27 we are confronted in each case with *a different attitude to the Torah* based on a *view* of the Torah which is in each case totally different: misuse of the Law resulting from the misunderstanding that it has to be used to establish a righteousness produced by oneself, or a right use of the Law which is possible only on the basis of faith.[183] No special demonstration is needed for the suggestion that here understanding the Law as 'the Law of faith' is of course possible only for those who also understand the Law as a witness to the righteousness of God in the sense of 3.21. To that extent Friedrich's exposition also coincides with ours in this point. But it must be noted that despite the common terminological field in which the Law stands as a witness of faith and faith is the true horizon of the Law, the perspective is in each case a different one; in the one instance God's activity is the point, but in the other, man's activity, or more precisely the activity of the believer.

Is Paul then not playing, as Bultmann supposes, with the term *nomos* in Rom 3.27?[184] And does not this term consequently mean in this verse, as Käsemann for example says, rule, order, or norm? And does not the 'law of faith' then mean the new order which is paradoxically so called?[185] Before we can answer this, we shall have to clarify what is to be understood by rule, order, or norm. The suggested understanding of νόμος πίστεως as the 'new' order of salvation in which the Law is not misused in order to establish one's own righteousness points to something entirely correct, in that Paul's thinking incontestably rests on the new situation of salvation which has become a reality through Christ. However, this new order of salvation is something which has been willed and established by God. Now our exegesis has shown that the expression 'law of works', which is so striking, does not mean an order of salvation established by God, does not mean the 'old' order of salvation laid down by him, but is the expression of a fundamentally misplaced human attitude towards the Torah which comes from God. But it is then *not possible to see in the two 'laws' of 3.27 two different orders of salvation both intended by God and chronologically replacing each other*, – i.e., two orders of salvation, one of which no longer holds good. However, if we start by assuming that the 'law of faith' means the right attitude to the will of God as this finds its expression in the Torah, while the 'law of works' denotes the false attitude to this same will of God, then of course we must ask whether when exegetes speak here of 'a new order' they are in fact right, at least *in so far* as there is an order of salvation established by God which does in fact correspond to the attitude or behaviour of the man who has faith. The 'order' which brings destruction would then match the Law of works, and the order of salvation would match the Law of faith. Given the broad spectrum of meaning which Pauline terms have, we can certainly also assume in our case overtones of such complementary correspondences of meaning. For when Paul speaks of man, he is in fact either thinking of him as already within the sphere of influence of sin or already within the sphere of influence of the righteousness of God. Paul simply cannot speak of man as if he could be thought of in isolation from this basic structure. If then in our verse the subject is right and wrong attitudes in man, then this statement implies the basic structure that has been mentioned. In every human decision either the reality of *hamartia* as a power or God's activity is *always* presupposed. The man of the Law of works *is* the man of the 'order' of this 'Law', and the man of the Law of faith *is* the man of the order of salvation in which the demands of the divine Law hold good.

These remarks are not intended as an attempt at a facile harmonisation of the view represented here with that of Käsemann. The difference in the two interpretations of the verse is still clear to see, yet perhaps the intention *underlying* Käsemann's exposition of 3.27 and that *underlying* ours are not all that far apart. And in particular it may, as I hope, have become clear that what Bultmann says about Paul's playing with his terms does apply to 3.27 even if the phrases 'Law of works' and 'Law of faith' refer on both occasions to the Torah; for it is precisely by the linguistically skilful manipulation of the genitives that Paul is able so to liberate the term 'law', which is so definite as it is generally preconceived, that he can re-articulate what is specific to the Jew in thus freeing the term from too close a definition.

The theological judgement formulated in Rom 3.28 follows as a justification of what has been said in 3.27 in the style of a diatribe. If every compulsion to boasting, and thus logically boasting itself too, is excluded by the Law in so far as this Law is seen in the horizon of faith, then it is this very faith by which man is justified – without the works of the Law. The instrumental use of πίστει can be best understood here as a subsumption and continuation of the διά of verse 27: if boasting is annihilated by the Law as seen from the perspective of faith, then it is this faith which defines the perspective of the Law 'by' which man is justified.[186] This 'by' however does not indicate the logical subject of justification, which naturally is and, of course, remains God. However, it is not without reason that Paul in verse 28 no longer speaks of the 'law of works' but as earlier in 3.20 of the 'works of the law'. For here the question is again about what the Law can achieve and no longer about one's attitude towards the Law. Consequently the defamatory formulation in verse 27 is also absent. The universalism implied in 'man' in verse 28 which determines the subsequent discussion in chapter 4 is explained here in a preliminary way in verses 29f. (It is of course a universalism which does not theologically cancel out the history of Israel; to this extent Käsemann's objection[187] to Klein[188] is justified: a 'desacralisation and profanation of Judaism'[189] is unknown to the Paul who wrote Romans.) It is of course possible to agree with Klein in speaking of a 'jump or kink in the sequence of thought'[190] as regards the transition from verse 28 to verse 29. On the other hand, however, the doctrine of justification and the universal horizon are so interwoven in the basic theological conception of Romans that the transition to verse 29 should not seem all that abrupt. *Rom 3.31* then asks, as the argument unfolds, whether the Torah has been made void 'by faith', a question which may be made more explicit by the suggestion that this would take place if we were to deny to the Torah the function of justifying, and do so on a universal level. The answer is given with apodeictic brevity: 'by no means, rather we establish the Law!'

In the two terms καταργεῖν and ἱστάνειν used here by Paul, Michel sees an equivalent to the rabbinical contrast between *battel* and *qayyem*.[191] To be sure Cambier contests this with the argument that for 'Law' in 3.31 it would then be necessary to presuppose the sense 'the totality of the stipulations of the Law' (*'loi—ensemble de préceptes'*);[192] but that here what is involved is the legislative word of God (*'loi—parole de Dieu'*).[193] Cambier's critical question needs however to be stated in a more fundamental form: where in fact does this pair of Hebraic/Aramaic terms stand in relation to the Torah? Does it in that context refer at all either to invalidating scripture (or a passage of scripture) or to leaving it in force? Was this pair of terms in any case part of the current exegetical and theological terminology of the Rabbis?

It is at least worth noting that Bacher lists the key-word *battel* neither under the heading of the Biblical exegetical terminology of the Tannaites, nor of that of the Amoreans. And even under the heading *qum* or *qayyem* he nowhere mentions *battel* as a negative counterpart to *qayyem*.[194] As a rabbinical *terminus technicus* the latter means maintaining a word of scripture or confirming a Bible passage by means of another.[195] In his *Wörterbuch über die Talmudim und Midraschim* Levy refers under the key-word *bittel*[196], as found in connection with the Torah, to *Aboth* 4.9, that is, to the very passage which Michel refers to in substantiation of the equivalence that he has asserted. There in fact we do find the contrast between *qayyem* and *battel*, or more precisely the Hebrew contrast *hameqayyem 'eth hattorah* and *hamebattel 'eth hattorah* in an antithetical parallelism, only here it is precisely not a question of upholding the meaning of a passage of the Law or of invalidating it, nor indeed even of either upholding or invalidating the Torah itself. Rather the contrast intended is clearly one between neglecting or not neglecting the study of the Law. Levy nowhere cites a passage from which emerges the idea that *battel* (or its derivatives) had the sense of invalidating the Law or a stipulation of the Law; which is to say that Michel's reference to *Aboth* 4.9 tells us nothing which would help us in understanding Rom 3.31.[197]

However, if in all probability there is no conventionally accepted rabbinical pair of terms lying behind the two verbs in 3.31, then it is more reasonable to suppose that Paul was taking up a reproach made against him by his opponents (and one which at least for Galatians would have been apt earlier on!) with his question 'are we then annulling the Law by faith?' Now it is a striking fact that the commentaries and monographs, when they turn to the interpretation of ἱστάνομεν, attach very little importance indeed to the relationship of ἱστάνομεν to καταργοῦμεν. However in view of what we have just discussed this is not serious.

Paul's assertion that he 'establishes' the Law is interpreted in the literature in three ways, if we may make use of a rough-and-ready grid:
(1) In the light of *Rom 3.21* 'the "establishment" of the Law clearly takes place in the testimony of the "Law and the Prophets" to the *righteousness of God* which has become manifest in the Christ-event.'[198]
(2) In the light of *Rom 3.20* '"we establish the Law" (verse 31) is intended here to refer only to its effect of bringing sin in practice *into the realm of experience* and so setting a seal on the guiltiness of all (3.20) but thereby (!) at the same

time to testify, as it points beyond itself, to the righteousness of God on the basis of grace (verse 21).'[199]
(3) In the light of *Rom 3.31a* the Law is conceived in 3.31 as a *moral demand*. It is this which Paul does not wish to set aside.[200] Accordingly when he establishes the Law he wishes to maintain the moral demands of the Law.

Let us take each of the three proposed solutions in turn. Against Wilckens, and thus against the first interpretation, Günther Klein has advanced 'difficulties which are quite insurmountable'. Klein points out that 3.31b is speaking only of the Law, but that in 3.21 Paul is appealing to the Law *and* the Prophets. He furthermore says that the 'Law' in verse 31 is clearly a reference back to the same term in 3.27f. Nor is there any mention of the term γραφή as one might have expected in 3.31.[201] Now Klein's concern is to attack the continuity on the basis of the Torah[202] which Wilckens asserts in terms of the history of election, i.e., to attack a salvation-history understanding of Romans. We shall set on one side here the question of salvation history, but Klein's other objections remain and are damaging. The connection of 3.27 and 3.31 is clear and in 3.27 the 'Law of faith' does not in fact, at least not directly, mean the Law which testifies to faith[203] but, as we suppose, the Law seen from the perspective of faith. It is then at least difficult to see in verse 31 a direct reference to verse 21.

However the solution proposed by Bornkamm of interpreting 3.31 on the basis of 3.20 is also not without its difficulties, for from 3.21 onwards and even more from 3.27 on the concern in the context of 3.31 is primarily with God's justifying righteousness or with faith. But then it is hardly probable that the destructive element of the function of the Law is to be so strongly emphasised in verse 31. Finally it seems improbable that 'moral demands' are the theme of 3.31. The drift of the argument tells against this – quite apart from the fact that in the context of this verse no distinction between the moral and cultic prescriptions of the Torah is made.

Käsemann sees 3.31 as making the transition to chapter 4. In this verse, he says, there is a reference back to the statement in verse 21b according to which the Law is also(!) a witness to justification by faith. *Nomos* in verse 31 is the will of God laid down in the Old Testament.[204] At all events Käsemann is right when he regards this verse as making the transition to chapter 4. Friedrich's arguments for this view are convincing.[205] If however verse 31 in fact has this transitional function, is chapter 4 then not an explanation and concretisation of 3.21b? And do we not have in that chapter the μαρτυρεῖν of the γραφή which is mentioned in verse 21 – the more so since, according to rabbinical usage, a Pentateuchal passage is quoted together with another passage from scripture? 'In accordance with rabbinical methodology the saying from the Torah is reinforced by the saying from the Psalms.'[206] However doubts now arise about whether the arguments brought by Klein against Wilckens 'are really decisive once we look at the inter-connectedness of 3.31 and the proof from scripture in chapter 4 on the one hand, and at the drift of the argument from 3.27ff. to 3.31 on the other hand, and, further, at the very reasonable supposition that chapter 4 is in fact an explanation of 3.21b. Thus the question arises whether the manifestly double reference of the proof from scripture in chapter 4, alluding as it does both to 3.21 (Law [and Prophets] in the sense of 'scripture' = witness to justification by faith) and also to 3.27ff. (the right perspective of the Law as the sacred demand of God) also demands the assumption of a directly intended double reference of 3.31 to 3.21 and 3.27ff.? This is true in a certain respect but we shall have to make some modifications: it is of course incontestable that in the argument regarding Abraham in chapter 4 the Law has the function of a witness to justification by God or through faith. Rom 4.3 with its scriptural proof from the 'Law' (Gen 15.6) in fact lies on the line of argument running from 3.21. But the argument regarding Abraham is certainly not merely concerned with the 'Law' as scripture which bears witness, but also and pre-eminently with what it bears witness to: the Law testifies of itself that it does not seek to be the 'Law of works'. More precisely: *the Law in so far as it is 'scripture' testifies of itself that in so far as it is a divine demand its intention is not to be a 'Law of works'*. Within the framework of this line of thought, however, 3.31 can be best understood as follows: 'we establish the Law' by contesting that it has the purpose of being the 'Law of works'. We establish the Law by categorically rejecting its false Jewish interpretation. We establish the specific original intention of the Law by energetically championing God's intention with the Law. There is then indeed continuity from 3.21 to the scriptural proof in chapter 4, but *what* is proved and *what* is, according to the drift of 3.27ff. to 3.31, 'established', is the complete inappropriateness of seeing the Law as the 'Law of works'.

The 'we' in the expression 'we establish the Law' should perhaps be given still closer consideration. This verbal form, in the first instance, speaks of an activity of man in regard to the Law. That in this context *Paul* is not concerned with such an activity is incontestable. If therefore we wish to remain in line with the Pauline statement and not allow ourselves to be misled by the active form of the first person into an activistic interpretation, it will be advisable to restate this form so that its real point, which is concealed by the *grammatical* form, becomes clear. Let us keep in mind the point that the verb ἱστάνειν or ἵστημι is extremely well suited to making *God's* activity explicit (e.g., the idiom στήσω τὴν διαθήκην μου in Gen 6.18 LXX and frequently elsewhere).[207] Now Romans is the very place where Paul uses the same verb for the presumptuous attitude of the Jews which usurps God's activity: to *establish* their own righteousness, 10.3! Thus we should come closer to what Paul had in mind in 3.31 if we paraphrase by saying: 'we maintain the validity of the Law by recognising God as subject. God is the subject of the righteousness which goes along with the Law and is the subject of the life which goes along with the Law. We acknowledge the validity of God's position as the subject of righteousness, as Abraham did. We establish the Law by allowing God to establish his righteousness.' Ἱστάνομεν then, in our context, no longer means so much 'we

bring into force'[208] as rather 'we acknowledge', or in yet another turn of
phrase, 'we give free scope to the activity of God in us and we put nothing in the
way of this activity'.

*But anyone who can speak in this way is already someone who 'walks according
to the spirit'* (8.4). The link between 3.31 and chapter 8 is clear from the
retrospective element in this chapter.[209] Christian existence – or, to stay closer
to Paul's language, the existence of the believer – can only be described as
existence in the spirit of God. The object of the thought and efforts (φρονεῖν)
of this spirit, or in modern terms, what this spirit is 'out for', and, together with
that, what the man who lives in the spirit is 'out for', is life and peace (8.6).[210]
He who establishes his own righteousness – and thus not the Law – is the one
who perverts the Law into the 'Law of works' because, according to 8.4, he
'walks after the flesh'. His intentionality (*Aus-Sein-auf*) is identical with what
the 'flesh' is out for, and, since the flesh is the individual locus of trans-
subjective *hamartia* in each case, is identical with the intentionality of this
fearful and cruel *hamartia*. Even without taking 8.2 into account, we already
have as Paul's view the idea that so long as man walks according to the flesh, he
establishes the Law for himself as a law of death, while the real intention of the
Law is life (7.10).

Paul however speaks of the Law in a special way (8.2-4) in the very context of
his discussion of the existence which is determined by σάρξ and πνεῦμα. 8.2
first of all contrasts the law of the spirit of life with the law of sin and death.
(We need not here take any special interest in the point that the two
formulations of contrast do not entirely correspond to each other. What is
perhaps important for our purposes is to see from them how much Paul makes
his formulations on the basis of the situation, and how little Pauline theology
may be understood as a firm or even rigid system of fixed and closely defined
terms.) According to our reflections on 3.27, the genitives occurring there, 'of
works' and 'of faith', define the Law in regard to the perspective of the moment
from which it is regarded. From this alone one might suppose that the same is
also true of 8.2. It is this very exegesis of 3.27 which supports Lohse's
hypothesis that Paul, at the beginning of chapter 8, understands by *nomos*
'unambiguously the Old Testament Law'.[211] Let us try to provide a further
basis for this to some small extent.

First of all, the expression 'law of the spirit' most likely refers back to 7.14:
'the law is spiritual, πνευματικός'. In 7.14, however, it is clearly the Torah
which is meant. Thus it has to do with the *pneuma* by its very *nature*. Thus by its
very nature it has to do with that power which is the power of the justified man.
The point that the Torah is by nature pneumatic is however made within the
context of a discussion of its death-'effect' (7.13). Thus Paul can even say
shortly before: ἡ ἐντολή...εἰς θάνατον (7.10).[212] Thus the expression 'the Law
of *hamartia* and of death' in the sense of 'the abused Torah' can also be seen to
have its beginnings in chapter 7; if the *nomos* is transferred from the sphere of
the *pneuma* into the sphere of *hamartia* which brings death, then it is deprived

of its real intentionality – what it is really 'out for' (*Aus-Sein-auf*), viz., of its
being 'out for life'.[213] If we further consider that Paul repeatedly introduces
even non-existential ideas for existential matters (5.12ff.!) 8.2 can then be
understood as follows: those *for whom* the *nomos* is the Law of the spirit, i.e.,
those who exist in the spirit which is the giver of life (cf. 8.10f.) are, when they
look at the Law, freed from the perverted Law, that is from the compulsion to
misuse the Law as the 'Law of works' under the dominion of *hamartia* and thus
from the fate of being abandoned to death. Thus 8.2 confirms that *for those*
who 'walk according to the flesh' the Law appears to be, and is, a death-
bringing power of destruction[214] which is all the more frightful and terrifying in
that the person concerned – above all, the more zealously he pays homage to
the Law of works as an idol – is not aware of his tragic fate at all (7.15).
However, *for those* who 'walk according to the spirit', i.e., according to what is
the true character and substance of the Law, it does appear to be, and is,
spiritual and therefore life-giving. Because God's spirit is the spirit of the
believer, because therefore the intentionality (*Aus-Sein-auf*) of the spirit of
God coincides with that of the justified man, the latter does 'of himself' what
the spiritual Law, the Law of the spirit and of life, 'demands', and not on the
basis of a merely external stimulus, but as being 'driven by the spirit' (8.14).
This spirit-theology of Paul is hardly a theology of the *tertius usus legis*.

Before we pass on to 8.3 let us take a further look at 7.21ff., for there the term
nomos is handled in a distinctly peculiar way. There the subject is the 'Law of
God' and further the 'other law in my members', 'the law of my reason, τοῦ
νοός μου', and finally 'the law of sin in my members' or simply 'the law of sin'.
It was these verses which made Bultmann speak of Paul's playing with the term
nomos: here, as he put it, *nomos* had 'the general meaning of a norm or of
compulsion, constraint'.[215] Above all, the phrase 'law of *hamartia* in my
members' in 7.23 must stand out when considered in the light of 8.2. Are we to
suppose that Paul here too meant the Law of God seen from a false
perspective? Is *this* not the place, if anywhere, that it is appropriate to take
nomos as not in any way referring to Torah? Bruce, who in verse 23 explains the
'other law in my members' and the 'law of my reason' in Bultmann's sense as
two opposed principles can however say in regard to the 'law of sin': 'And yet it
may be asked if there is not a sense in which "the law of sin" could be an aspect
of the Law of God.' And, appealing to 8.2, he continues: 'Can the Law of God,
which is by definition holy, be described as "the law of sin and death"'? Yes, *in
so far* as it stimulates sin and passes sentence of death on the sinner.'[216] Thus
Bruce does not go so far as Lohse who also in 7.21ff. interprets every
occurrence of *nomos* there as Torah.[217] Bruce considers also the 'law of the
spirit of life' in 8.2 not to be the Torah. If Paul there speaks thus he is doing so
only for the sake of the verbal antithesis: '...the *law* of the spirit is the spirit's
vitalising principle or power'.[218] But even if in 7.23, 25 the 'law of sin' is not the
perverted Torah but is intended to mean the sinful principle in man, this does
not prove that in 8.2 the 'law of sin and of death' must be understood in the

same sense. Rather we should then assume that Paul in 8.2 wants to show by this expression how devastatingly the Torah can be perverted if it can be covered by the same predicate as the 'law in my members'.

Returning to the course of the argument in 8.2ff.: in 8.3 the expression ἐν ᾧ is not unambiguous. It can be understood modally ('in which')[219] or causally ('by which').[220] Our interpretation of verse 2 might indeed best favour a causal interpretation of the elliptical sentence: 'as to the incapacity of the Law (to give life to the sinner) it may be caused by the fact that the Law is weakened by the flesh. Therefore God has now sent his Son...' This understanding of the verse is wholly continuous with Paul's consideration of the relationship of Law, sin and flesh: the Law has *become* incapable of providing life because man has perverted the Law because of his σάρξ into the 'Law of works' (chapter 7).

There are few who would dispute that δικαίωμα τοῦ νόμου in 8.4 means a legal demand (thus most exegetes) or legal claim of the Law.[221] However, there is a difficult question as to what Paul then seeks to say when he speaks here of the fulfilment of the legal demand. Käsemann, who assumes that Paul is here using an expression taken from the tradition, thinks that the various explanations offered of the statement show how dangerous and open to misunderstanding it is. A literal reading, so Käsemann, would suggest an interpretation according to which 'it is natural as in Matt 5.17ff. to see in love a radicalising of all the commandments and a new law'.[222] As an example from a more recent period, we may quote Henning Paulsen: 'according to 13.8 the δικαίωμα τοῦ νόμου consists in the fulfilment of the command to love, in mutual love'.[223] Against this view, Käsemann says: 'In contrast to his expositors Paul unmistakably sets forth the alien work (*opus alienum*) and in so doing pays the price for the fact that his argument is affected by motifs from another source. His intention is clear. Only the spirit gives freedom from the powers of sin and death.'[224] The last sentence is entirely correct, and is indeed scarcely contested, but the decisive question is, as Käsemann shrewdly sees, whether in fact the Gospel becomes a means for the fulfilment of the Law if, say, loving activity is identified with the guidance of the spirit.[225]

These considerations bring us right into the central questions of Paul's theology of the spirit. At this point it once again becomes clear that we cannot tackle a central theological problem without other central questions coming into the foreground. Theological monographs therefore always remain somewhat torso-like. Because they seek to limit themselves to a single theme, they necessarily broach more questions than they are able to answer. The question which Käsemann puts can therefore not really be answered here if the monograph is not to broaden out into a 'duograph' on the Law and on the spirit (nor would it remain at a 'duograph'). Nevertheless we ought at least to attempt a tentative reply.

First of all attention must be drawn to Käsemann's basic thesis that justification means the putting into effect of God's justice or Law. The thesis has, as is well known, been much criticised but should nevertheless be accepted in principle provided it is not contrasted too sharply with a theology of existential interpretation.[226] The more it is intended to hold fast to the idea that what is involved in justification is the justice of God, the more must it also be seen that in the Cross and Resurrection it is not only God's justice but also his love which is manifested (Rom 5.8ff.!). The justice and love of God cannot be separated. Human love and man's doing of what is right are, however, to be seen in the context of the justice and love of God. Human righteousness and righteous activity belong to the realisation of the universal divine justice. If it is only the spirit of God that frees man for love, then it is not to a 'love' which is commanded by the letter of the Law if love is still to be love. Therefore Bruce, for example, rightly points to 2 Cor 3.6[227] and (if a relatively longer quotation than usual be permitted here) we must agree with him when he writes: 'For in Rom viii. 1-4 Paul echoes the sense, if not the very language, of the new covenant oracle of Jeremiah xxxi. 31-34. In that oracle there is no substantial difference in content between the Law which Israel fails to keep under the old covenant and the Law which God undertakes hereafter to place within his people, writing it "upon their hearts". The difference lies between their once knowing the Law as an external code and their knowing it henceforth as an inward principle. So for Paul there was no substantial difference in content between the "just requirement of the Law" which cannot be kept by those who live "according to the flesh" and the just requirement fulfilled in those who live "according to the spirit". The difference lay in the fact that a new inward power was now imparted, enabling the believer to fulfil what he could not fulfil before. The will of God had not changed...'[228] 'The reference to the spirit should remind us that Paul's teaching here points to the fulfilment not only of Jeremiah's "new covenant" oracle, but also of the companion oracles in Ezekiel xi. 19f. and xxxvi. 25-27 where God promises to implant within his people a new heart and a new spirit – his own spirit – enabling them to do his will effectively.'[229]

There is an echo of 2 Cor 3.6 in Rom 7.6: We are separated from the Law in so far as it is *gramma*. We are dead to the Law *as gramma* (7.4). The Law's demand for justice is therefore not a demand as *gramma*. Käsemann's question whether the gospel will become the means for the fulfilment of the Law sounds horrendous so long as the Law is understood as *gramma*, for who would want to make the gospel into a dogsbody for the *gramma*! However, if in the gospel the powerful righteousness of God becomes manifest (1.17!) and if man's righteousness, given by God, is one with his existence in the spirit of God, then what Paul calls the fulfilment of the Law's demand for justice may no longer be interpreted in legalistic fashion. For this demand of the Law may not be defined in fact on the basis of a preconceived general idea of law, but *it is the spirit of God* which *shows what the Law of the spirit is*. Because of the spirit, the Law has been rescued from the perversion and legalisation to which up till now it has been subject, and rescued in such a way that everything which up till now set it in a bad light has disappeared. *Existence in the spirit of God now says what*

Law is, but Law does not say what existence in the spirit is.[230]
Thus it is just here that open questions remain. It remains uncertain how
existence in the spirit with its implicit spontaneity of action is to be expressed,
so that Schrage's concern (with individual commandments!) here becomes
clear. For the spontaneity does not mean an abandonment of concrete
paraenesis. The still more difficult problem remains, how we are nowadays
linguistically to put across the point that God's spirit is the spirit of the
believers. How do we here transcend objectifying language so that Paul's real
concern in Rom 8 can today be comprehensibly stated? Questions on
questions! In our present context they must simply be allowed to remain such.
But even in this context they should at least be stated in the brevity which the
circumstances dictate.

To conclude, let us hear what Eberhard Jüngel has to say. He too sees Rom
3.31 as related to the subject matter of Rom 8.2: justification by faith
establishes the Law by doing away with it as a way of salvation. Consequently
in Rom 8.2 Paul can speak of the law of the spirit of life and of the law of sin
and death. The genitives in this verse are taken by Jüngel in the possessive
sense: 'the νόμος does not bestow the spirit any more than it has produced sin.
But it does give validity to the spirit just as it showed up sin as sin in a decisive
way.'[231] In our exegesis we have always been talking of the varied relationship
of man to the Law. Jüngel fills out this idea when he speaks of the relationship
of the Law to man. This relationship, he suggests, has now fundamentally
changed (in Christ). 'Even the νόμος has its *new locus* in Christ (Rom 8.2).
There it becomes (!) the νόμος Χριστοῦ (Gal 6.2).'[232] Now of course this kind
of juxtaposition of Romans and Galatians does not agree with what we have
said. But in regard to Romans alone the idea of the change of locus for the Law
may be allowed to describe the basic theological point. We should admittedly
ask whether in fact the Law, having previously stood *over* man, now stands
alongside him. Should one not rather, following the argument of chapter 8,
speak of the spiritual Law *in* the spiritual man? However, Jüngel is certainly
right when he considers the Law of Christ – letting this term from Galatians
also hold good on this occasion for Romans – to be the 'end of the period
under the Law'.[233] And we would further agree with him that 'the fact that the
νόμος is qualified by the genitive τοῦ πνεύματος brings out the idea that the
Eschaton which *was* there in Christ as the end of the Law, *remains* there as
spirit'.[234]

This idea can be carried further if we take Rom 10.4 as the 'end of the Law of
the carnal man' which corresponds to the 'end of the Law perverted by
hamartia and *sarx*'. But then Rom 3.31 says 'we establish the Law of the life-
giving *pneuma*', '*we accept the Law of the pneuma with its pneumatic claim to
justice*'.[235] But this is now not what is being said in Galatians. In fact, we could
place over that letter too the superscription: 'Christ is the end of the Law'. But
this sentence would then be saying that 'Christ is the end of the Mosaic Law'. It
would not have the kind of differentiated sense we find in Romans, viz., 'Christ

is the end of the carnal misuse of the Law'.

3.3.1 Notes on an Essay by Ferdinand Hahn

One of the most important of contributions to our subject is Ferdinand Hahn's essay in *ZNW* 67. While our way has frequently led us from Galatians to Romans, Hahn looks back on Galatians from Romans, which he treats first of all, in order then to work towards some overall conclusions. In somewhat rough outline, Hahn's view of Romans agrees at decisive points with the interpretation of Romans offered here. In the explanation of Galatians we differ rather strongly. While I trace the difference between the two letters to an understanding of the Law which is essentially different in substance – though the theological concern, justification by faith alone, remains the same – and therefore assume a real theological development on the part of Paul, for Hahn the difference lies essentially in the different perspective from which in each case Paul tackles the Old Testament texts: 'Paul in Galatians has looked at the question of the Law one-sidedly from Jewish premisses...In Romans, on the contrary, from 1.18 onwards, all the emphasis is laid on the idea that not merely sin and death but also Law and the works of the Law concern all men (2.14ff.; 4.3ff.; 5.12ff.; 7.7ff.), regardless of whether they be Gentiles or Jews.'[236]

I am delighted that Hahn and I agree in decisive questions related to the interpretation of Romans. The view put forward here, in Section 2.3, that sin is recognisable only to the believer as *hamartia* in the full Pauline sense of that term, and that therefore the 'knowledge of sin' in Rom 3.20 is simply not possible in the proper sense of the term for those who have not yet attained to faith, is given very pronounced expression in Hahn: 'In this respect, however, even with the aid of the Law there can be no real "knowledge of sin"...1.18-3.20 does not offer insights which can be acquired independently of the message of the Gospel, however universally these statements may apply... Men...are led to a knowledge of their sin simultaneously by the Gospel which grants them redemption...'[237]

We further agree that phrases like νόμος πίστεως in Rom 3.27 or ὁ νόμος τοῦ πνεύματος τῆς ζωῆς in Rom 8.2 refer to the Old Testament Torah. And we both build on findings of Gerhard Friedrich and Eduard Lohse. Here Hahn repeatedly hits on formulae which are excellent and meet the case precisely. I quote merely (as to Rom 8.2-4) the following: 'But this then means that the Law, liberated from its involvement with sin and death, points beyond itself to the salvation and life granted in Christ, and can be recognised and followed specifically in its δικαίωμα too as the expression of the divine will. This is already hinted at in 7.4 with the expression καρποφορεῖν τῷ θεῷ.'[238] Above all,

'the decisive point is that for Paul the Law never stands on its own and on no
account can it be made the basis of an effort aimed at a salvation which men
themselves choose – i.e., as a νόμος τῶν ἔργων. Fundamentally it is to be found
in a context and linked to a subject-matter, whether that of sin and death or
that of promise and of fulfilment effected in Christ.'[239] I shall not go into minor
differences where my judgement would be other than that of Hahn.

However, as regards Hahn's comments on Galatians, the reservations I
have are not insignificant. Is it really true that in this letter the subject of Law is
handled more or less exclusively with an eye to those who formerly were
Jews?[240] As to the Gentiles in Galatians, is there only, other than in Romans, a
discussion of the promised participation in salvation, but not of the problem of
the Law?[241] Symptomatic of our difference in approach is Hahn's exegesis of
Gal 3.13 where Paul quotes Deut 21.23. The verse begins with the words
Χριστὸς ἡμᾶς ἐξηγόρασεν. While Mussner makes nothing at all of the ἡμᾶς in
his commentary on Galatians, Schlier writes, 'The ἡμᾶς includes
everybody...even the Gentiles'.[242] Contrariwise, Hahn says, 'Thus he has
"purchased our" freedom, who were formerly Jews, just as at the same time he
has effected for the Gentiles participation in the blessing of Abraham and in
the promised gift of the spirit (verse 14).'[243] But where does Paul, in Gal 3,
speak in the first person plural in order to bracket himself with the Jewish
Christians, *as opposed to the Gentile Christians*? It may be solely a question of
judgement, but the fact that Paul at the beginning of chapter 3 specifically
addresses the Gentile Christian Galatians does initially make it possible to
suppose that the vicarious assumption of the curse by Christ is not simply an
event affecting the Jewish Christians. And if we are entitled to consider Gal
3.22 in close connection with our passage, this lends support to our
reservations. For in verse 22 we read that τὰ πάντα,, though in the sense of 'all
men', are concluded by scripture under the power of sin. And it is in fact the
exclusive mode of argument in 3.10ff. which is taken up again in 3.22.

If however the intention was to contrast 'us' in verse 13 with 'the Gentiles' in
verse 14, then we would have: 'Christ has bought us Jews free from the curse of
the Law so that the Gentiles may receive the blessing of Abraham'. But in what
way is this purchase a presupposition for a blessing for the Gentiles? Is it
perhaps so in the sense of a straightforward *conditio sine qua non* which cannot
be given a specific justification? But in what sense is the death of Christ then a
universal salvation-event (*Heilsgeschehen*)? And what then is the meaning of
Gal 1.4, that the Lord Jesus Christ gave himself for our sins (here really for the
sins of all men including those of the Gentiles)? Thus in Hahn's interpretation
of 3.13f. the death of Christ in relation to its saving function is to say the least
unclear. Let us however once again stress that up to the present our objection
might well be understood to be more in the nature of a matter of judgement.

However the following argument is more decisive exegetically in my view. If
we look at the drift of the argument in the section 3.19-4.7 we notice that Paul
introduces an interweaving of first person plural usages, both for statements

formulated with the Jews in mind *and* for those with a Gentile orientation. 'We' have been kept under the Law, 3.23, 'we' are no longer under a tutor, 3.25; thus too 'we' when immature (besides 4.2 see also 3.25!) were under the (Gentile!) elements of the world, 4.3. How were 'we' – including Paul as a Jewish Christian! – under powers which were demonic in a Gentile context? Does not the whole thrust of the argument lie in the idea that in the persistent 'we' Jewish Christians and Gentile Christians are bracketed? Why does Hahn pass over 4.3 with the expression 'we under the elements of the world'? At the end of the first paragraph of p. 56 one might at least have expected a brief comment from Hahn on this verse. Discussion with Hahn could certainly be very fruitful if this verse were brought in. Finally, in 4.4f., God sent his son... born under the Law, so that he might redeem those born under the Law, so that we (!) might receive sonship.

On Gal 5.14, it is still unclear how far the *whole* Law, which is now suddenly viewed positively, is fulfilled in the single command to love – where important stipulations of the Law such as circumcision or food laws have nevertheless been abrogated. Reference to the reality of the spirit is not an answer to this question. In my view we escape from this dilemma only by means of the philological solution proposed in Section 1.4. The relation of Gal 5.14 to 5.3 is of course also in mind here.

A further marginal note may be made. Hahn states explicitly that Gal 3.21 is as a culmination of the train of thought contradictory to the promise from Lev 18.5 which is quoted in 3.12.[244] On this old *crux interpretum* it remains to be said that either it must remain as a contradiction or that the contradiction is resolved by the fact that the apparently contradictory statements can be traced back to different intentions (see Section 1.3).

However I am again at one with Hahn in saying that the *interpretatio Christiana* of the Old Testament has been up till now a task still awaiting mastery.[245] One of the most important theological tasks confronting exegetes today in particular could be the question of the theological relationship of the two Testaments. The study here submitted may be taken as a preliminary effort to this effect – viz., as a preliminary study for a draft theology of the New Testament, its subject being the use of the Old Testament by the New Testament authors.[246]

3.3.2 Notes on books by E. P. Sanders and H. Räisänen

In 1983 E. P. Sanders's *Paul, the Law, and the Jewish People* was published in Philadelphia. The author has presented his book to a very large degree as a discussion of my thesis, seeing me very much as a theological follower of Rudolf Bultmann. (This is only partly true.) I cannot of course deal with

Sanders's argument in detail. To do that, in view of the detailed manner in which he has examined or, more precisely, has attempted to refute my thesis, would require a book of its own. Thus I will restrict myself to drawing attention to one or two passages where symptomatically his arguments seem less than convincing.

Towards the beginning of his discussion Sanders states the following as fundamental to his understanding of Paul: 'The subject of Galatians is not whether or not humans, abstractly conceived, can by good deeds earn enough merit to be declared righteous at the judgement; it is the condition on which Gentiles enter the people of God.'[247] Sanders's insistence on this thesis would carry more conviction if Paul in his argumentation in Galatians did not immediately link the question of circumcision with the question of Law pure and simple. It is of course beyond dispute that the question of circumcision is one about 'the condition on which Gentiles enter the people of God'.[248] But for Paul the question of circumcision is necessarily identified with the question of an existence *in accordance with* the Law (5.3!). Thus in starting with the question of the condition of entry into the people of God Paul's argument is concerned principally with the existence of the Christian which is given *after* such entry. This of course means that Sanders's suggestions about the actual theme of Galatians cannot be sustained. Now it is true that he himself says that the Galatian controversy is principally concerned with the rite of admission - 'centers on the admission rite'[249] - while admitting that it does also embrace other aspects of the Torah, such as dietary laws and festivals. Yet this in itself seems to me to show up a clear weakness in his argument. It is however necessary to go a step further. For it is simply not true that 'the controversy centers on the admission rite, circumcision';[250] rather Paul expends all his energy on decrying theologically the *condition* of those who exist under the Law. Thus there is no alternative but to reject Sanders's initial thesis. He has misconstrued 'the subject of Galatians'.[251]

According to Sanders the argument in Gal 3 is directed against Christian missionaries, not against Judaism. Among scholars who hold such a view (that Paul is arguing against Judaism) he mentions, along with Hans Dieter Betz, Ferdinand Hahn and Ulrich Luz, me. But apparently he has not understood what it is that he is arguing against. For if Paul does indeed argue against a Jewish view of things in Galatians then he does so only *because his opponents see their Jewish Christianity as Judaism*! Yet Sanders, who describes Paul's opponents in Galatia as 'right-wing Jewish Christians', himself says that 'Paul's opponents take the standard Jewish (!) view that to enter into the Biblical promises one has to accept the Biblical condition: the Law of Moses'.[253]

Sanders takes vigorous exception to my view (and consequently to the view of the overwhelming majority of exegetes) that in the quotation of Deut 27.26 LXX in Gal 3.10 it is the words πᾶς and πᾶσιν which are of greatest significance for Paul's argument. Sanders counters this with a 'terminological argument'. According to him Deut 27.26 is the only expression in the LXX in which *nomos* is linked with 'curse'. Paul was looking for an expression which said that *nomos* brings a curse. And he therefore quoted the only reference which he could find in Scripture: 'Thus I propose that the thrust of Gal 3:10 is borne by the words *nomos* and 'cursed', not by the word 'all' which happens to appear.'[254]

Thus Sanders's argument runs as follows: *Because* Deut 27.26 is the only place in the LXX where law and curse occur together he quoted it. And it is therefore clear that πᾶς and πᾶσιν occur in this sentence only accidentally and are without importance for Paul. An argument of this kind is known as a *petitio principii*: the two words are not to be seen as constitutive of Paul's argument, therefore Paul has only included them because they actually occur at this point. The idea that Paul might be interested in the occurence together both of the idea of curse on the one hand and of *nomos* in its quantitative totality on the other, even though this is what is actually suggested in 5.3, is therefore deliberately not even considered.

Sanders seeks to support his arguments for his understanding of Gal 3.10 with a second proof. He rejects 'a fairly common view that one should interpret what the proof-texts say in order to discover what Paul means'[255] for the following reason: 'I think that what Paul says in his own words is the clue to what he took the proof-texts to mean'.[256] This assertion – and the 'I think' admittedly hides the assertive character of his thesis – provides him in his view with a further argument for his contention 'that the emphasis is not on the word "all" '.[257]

In the third argument for his interpretation of Gal 3.10 - 'the place of Gal 3:10-13 in the argument of 3:8-14'[258] - he surprisingly mitigates the force of his second argument by referring to none other than verse 8 as the 'main proposition', in other words to the very verse which makes explicit reference to scripture. For in that verse Paul proves *his own* expression ἐκ πίστεως δικαιοῖ τὰ ἔθνη ὁ θεός by means of a scriptural quotation. Nor does Sanders pay any attention to the decisive γάρ in verse 20.

Thus Sanders' whole argument against the usual interpretation of Gal 3.10, which as he rightly sees is a linchpin of my understanding of Galatians, has feet of clay. I am truly grateful for any criticism, not least when it is directed against the foundations of my overall argument, because others may well be able to see from their own different perspectives weaknesses in my argument more clearly than I. Because I know that scientific theses, particulary in the historical field, are always hypothetical in character I welcome every *advocatus diaboli* of my hypothesis. The obvious weaknesses of the criticisms of one of the foundations of my understanding of Paul however leave me with a greater feeling of confidence in this conception.

New Testament studies owe a particular debt of gratitude to the Finnish New Testament scholar Heikki Räisänen for his study *Paul and the Law* which was published in 1983 in the series *Wissenschaftliche Untersuchungen zum Neuen Testament* (vol. 29). It is written with great attention to methodological rigour and presents an interesting contrary thesis to mine. Räisänen also constantly engages in debate with me. At this juncture however I cannot enter into discussion with him as I am to publish a detailed review of the book in the *Theologische Literaturzeitung* (Leipzig). I must therefore ask the reader to refer to the review at the appropriate time. Here I can make only a few remarks about the content of the book. In the introductory chapter Räisänen gives a review of the history of research particularly with reference to attempts to explain the tensions within the Pauline epistles. He distinguishes three methodological approaches:

1. 'The first alternative to be mentioned might be regarded as a sophisticated version of the dialectical approach.'[259] Räisänen singles out Hans Conzelmann for particular mention in this respect.

2. 'A few interpreters solve the tensions in Paul's letters violently by attributing large parts of Galatians and especially of Romans to later interpolators.'[260] The prime example of this is O'Neill.

3. 'By far the most attractive device to do away with the difficulties caused by the tensions in Paul's thought are theories of development.'[261] Representatives of this hypothesis mentioned are 'Dodd, Buck and Taylor, and, most recently,...Drane, Hübner and Lüdemann.'[262]

His own thesis is based on the following conception: '...there are already obvious tensions in Paul's thought on the law in Galatians, and even more in Romans. Neither letter is internally consistent.... To suggest that both Galatians and Romans are beset with internal tensions and contradictions is to anticipate my own conclusions.'[263] In the end however I do not find Räisänen's thesis convincing because he underestimates the difference between the quality of the contrasts between Galatians and Romans as against the quality of the contrasts within the two Pauline epistles themselves.

Notes

1. Käsemann, *Röm.*, 64 (E.T. 69).
2. This hypothesis would be the more compelling were it true that the coupling of circumcision and obedience to the Law was first introduced into the discussion by Paul.
3. According to Mussner, *Gal.*, 398, there is no trace of an ironical tone to be found in this salutation.
4. Consider the unexpected transition from the second person plural to the second person singular. As a result of this stylistic device the salutation becomes a plea; cf. Burton, *Gal.*, 328.
5. Cf. Schlier, *Gal.*, 271.
6. E.g., Lipsius, *Gal.*, 59; Schlier, *Gal.*, 271.

7. Mussner, *Gal.*, 399.
8. Mussner, ibid., 399, n. 20, wrongly quotes 'of the' instead of 'of a'.
9. Van Dülmen, *Theologie*, 66.
10. *Sarx* not as an anthropological category but as a theological one because it is a complementary term to *pneuma*. It is the individual locus in each case of trans-subjective *hamartia*. So its power is that of *hamartia*. Man's openness to temptation is because it is precisely his *sarx* that is involved. So for the *sarx* the dual character of sin also holds good: the latter is a given quantum and an act which involves responsibility in a historical context. But the Christian, having crucified his *sarx* with its *epithumiai* (5.24), is in fact not someone who is sinning, in that it is only the act which involves responsibility that *makes* the *sarx* manifest and turns it into an agent of *hamartia*. The undoubted theological correctness of Luther's '*peccator simul ac iustus*' formula cannot therefore be given its justification simply by reference to the *existence* of the *sarx*.
11. Thus we have Burton, *Gal.*, 329, exhibiting a correct caution when he says, 'The reference of τὰ βάρη is clearly to...the burden of temptation and possible (!) ensuing sin.'
12. Schlier, *Gal.*, 273; similarly we have Mussner, depending on Bisping, in *Gal.*, 400; likewise Oepke, *Gal.*, 148: 'So who is "something"? Nobody!'
13. Lipsius, *Gal.*, 59.
14. Lipsius in fact deduces it too only from the expression 'law of Christ' in v. 2.
15. This is clearly recognised by Sieffert, *Gal.*, 347f.
16. Holsten, *Ev. des Paulus* I/1, 130.
17. Sieffert, *Gal.*, 348: this is 'already ruled out by οὐκ εἰς τὸν ἕτερον.'
18. But are we dealing here with a statement about Christians?!
19. Sieffert, *Gal.*, 347f.
20. Ibid., 347.
21. Oepke, *Gal.*, 149.
22. Ibid., 149; Oepke's italics.
23. Schlier, *Gal.*, 273; what is meant by 'in each particular instance'? If Schlier is referring to the parallels in 1 Peter 1.17 and Rev 2.2 (plural!), we might assume that he takes ἔργον to be the work of a life which is the subject of examination in any particular instance. Of course the expression is also open to interpretation as 'the entire work of the man in the concrete situation concerned'.
24. Schlier, *Gal.*, 274.
25. See the rejection of quantitative thinking in regard to anthropology, Gal 3.10; 5.3!
26. Schlier, *Gal.*, 274.
27. Ibid., 273: 'No one is truly something.'
28. The text continues significantly thus: '*Si quid autem habet homo veritatis atque iustitiae, ab illo fonte est, quem debemus sitire in hac eremo...*(S. Prosper)' (= Denzinger, 195).
29. Mussner, *Gal.*, 400, n. 29.
30. Ibid., 400.
31. Ibid., 402.
32. Ibid., 400.
33. Ibid., 401; my italics.
34. Here we cannot go into further detail on the problem of the relation between work(s) and judgement according to works in Paul. On this subject see most recently Donfried, 'Justification and Last Judgement in Paul', *ZNW* 67, 90-110 (with detailed literature listed there).
35. Mussner, *Gal.*, 401.
36. Bultmann, art., καυχάομαι, *TWNT* III.649.25ff. (E.T. III.649.22ff.); my italics.
37. In my view it is characteristic that Bultmann in Section C.1.a nowhere refers to Gal 6.4 although he too does not distinguish between the statements in Gal and Rom! Thus this

passage perhaps does not fit into the context drafted on the basis of Romans. Bultmann does indeed then range Gal 6.4 under the heading 'Apostolic Self-Boasting' (ibid., 651.33ff. E.T. 650.22f.). But our passage has nothing to do with this subject.

38. Mussner, *Gal.*, 400.
39. Ibid., 401.
40. Ibid., 401.
41. Schlier, *Gal.*, 274.
42. K. Weiss, art., φορτίον, *TWNT* IX.88.35f. (E.T. IX.86.15f.); Weiss's italics.
43. Oepke, *Gal.*, 149; also Schlier, *Gal.*, 274, uses the term 'responsible' in this connection.
44. On this see Oepke, *Gal.*, 149.
45. Burton, *Gal.*, 332, rightly says: 'A protasis may be mentally supplied, "if his work shall be proved good"...'; but for Burton this supposition is just one of two possible ones. Thus he continues, '...or τὸ καύχημα may mean in effect, "his ground of glorying, whatever that be", the implication in such a case being that he who examines himself will not fail to find something (!) of good in himself.'
46. On the question how the present form οἱ περιτεμνόμενοι should be understood, see the commentaries! As the reading περιτεμνόμενοι is certainly original, Lietzmann's solution initially seems most plausible: the preachers who are agitating for circumcision are Gentile Christians who have been persuaded as to circumcision (*Gal.*, 44f., depending on E. Hirsch, *ZNW* 29, 192ff.). But does the present participle necessarily have to be understood as a passive form, as is generally assumed? Is it not possible to take it as a middle: those who circumcise (others) *in their own interest*? (thus also Jewett, 'The Agitators and the Galatian Congregation', *NTS* 17, 202f.). Otherwise, if we do not wish to regard the agitators as Gentile Christians, as Lietzmann does, we shall be obliged along with Schlier, *Gal.*, 281, to suppose that οἱ περιτεμνόμενοι are 'those who are in a circumcised condition', 'those who practise circumcision', 'the circumcision party', i.e., specifically the Jewish Christian opponents of the apostle (this translation perhaps implying that Schlier also thinks a middle form should be supposed) – without reflecting on the fact that the opponents themselves are already circumcised (see also Mussner, *Gal.*, 413, n. 23: 'timeless' participle). I do not find the view convincing that in 6.13a another subject should be assumed than that in 6.13b (e.g., Lipsius, *Gal.*, 62, rejected by Sieffert, *Gal.*, 366).
47. Thus for instance Oepke, *Gal.*, 159: If they preach Christ without the Law, 'then the whole might of Judaism – which in the world of that day was already immense – will turn against them, ostracise them in religion and in politics, deprive them of the protection of the *religio licita*, cast suspicion on them with the Roman authorities and so on.' Jewett, 'The Agitators and the Galatian Congregation', *NTS* 17, 198-212, seeks to be more specific still here: he suggests that the agitators were under pressure from the Zealots.
48. Mussner, *Gal.*, 412.
49. See Section 1.2 of this study.
50. On τῷ σταυρῷ τοῦ Χριστοῦ 'Ιησοῦ see the commentaries.
51. It neither competes with, nor contradicts, this to read the beginning of v. 12, freely translated, as: 'All those concerned about a favourable image in the sight of men...' For they wish to escape persecution on the basis of this image as zealous *Jewish* missionaries. Cf. Schlier, *Gal.*, 280: 'In a certain sense, being persecuted is of course the opposite of εὐπροσωπῆσαι. But vanity and fear can also be yokefellows.' However, neither such a juxtaposition in the psyche nor a contrast is involved here.
52. cf. Mussner, *Gal.*, 411: Paul 'overdoes his portraiture...of the opponents again in the style of "heresy-hunting".'
53. Mussner, *Gal.*, 414.
54. Schlier, *Gal.*, 481: 'Σταυρός here is an ideogram for the event of redemption.'
55. On Gal 6.14f. see also H.-W. Kuhn, 'Jesus als Gekreuzigter', *ZThK* 72, 38.40f.

56. Cf. the explanatory sentence in v. 5 with the reference to the eschatological judgement.

57. See n. 47 of Section 2.2.

58. Δικαιοσύνη τε καὶ ἁγιασμὸς καὶ ἀπολύτρωσις should be regarded epexegetically as an 'explanatory apposition' to σοφία, with J. Weiss, *1 Kor.*, 41; also Conzelmann, *1 Kor.*, 68 (E.T. 52) manifestly has this view of it, though he does not come out with it directly.

59. Conzelmann, *1 Kor.*, 68 (E.T. 52).

60. Paul's oldest letter, 1 Thess, takes ἁγιασμός as moral behaviour (4.3ff.), as does the later letter to the Romans (6.19, 22). We should then suppose that this also holds good for 1 Cor.

61. J. Weiss, *1 Kor.*, 43: 'Paul has not merely compressed but also reshaped the idea which is expressed in greater detail in the LXX text of Jeremiah.'

62. See also Sand, *Der Begriff 'Fleisch'*, 150 f.

63. Bultmann, art., καυχάομαι *TWNT* III.648ff. (E.T. III. 648ff.).

64. On 2 Cor 10ff. see above all H. D. Betz, *Der Apostel Paulus und die sokratische Tradition*.

65. On this see the *TWNT/TDNT* article by Bultmann already mentioned and the corresponding sections in his commentary on 2 Cor.

66. To different effect we have Käsemann, *Röm.*, 64 (E.T. 69): ἐπαναπαύεσθαι not used in its secondary censorious sense.

67. Lipsius, *Röm.*, 92.

68. Michel, *Röm.*, 75.

69. However, in Romans the idea is no longer stated explicitly that the obligation is to obey the Law *totally* because of circumcision; see Sections 2.1 and 2.4.

70. Bill. I.119; but see also GenR 48 (30a) there: R. Levi (around 300!) said: 'The time will come when Abraham will sit at the entrance to Gehenna (Gehinnom) and not let anyone from Israel who is circumcised go down there. But what will he do with those who have sinned to excess? He will take the foreskins of children who died before circumcision, and put them on these people and then cast them down into Gehenna.'

71. Michel, *Röm.*, 76, n. 4, assumes too much as an axiom that the principle quoted was already being maintained in Paul's day. The passage from Wis 15.2 quoted in many commentaries in this connection is neither in the context of circumcision nor in that of the Law. Besides the emphasis is on v. 2b!

72. Contrary to Michel, *Röm.*, 75.

73. Cranfield's exposition of Rom 2.17 in his *Romans*, I. 164 is not apposite: 'The Jew is absolutely right to be seriously concerned with God's law...and to rely on it as God's true and righteous word. But the trouble is that he follows after it ἐξ ἔργων instead of ἐκ πίστεως (cf. 9.32), and relies on it in the sense of thinking to fulfil it in such a way as to put God in his debt or (!) imagining complacently that the mere fact of possessing it gives him security against God's judgement.' Only the final comment here is right. However the idea that Paul here has in mind reliance on God's Law on the basis of faith is simply read into the text. It does not fit into the line of *this* argument in Romans at all.

74. So among others Lipsius, *Röm.*, 98: 'προητιασάμεθα... viz., 1.18ff., 2.1ff.'; Lietzmann, *Röm.*, 47; Michel, *Röm.*, 83; van Dülmen, *Theologie*, 82.

75. On ἁμαρτία as a power see especially Michel, *Röm.*, 84f.; Käsemann, *Röm.*, 80 (E.T. 86).

76. The matter has a somewhat different aspect in the accusation against the Gentile world: God abandoned the Gentiles to vices (thrice-repeated παρέδωκεν αὐτοὺς ὁ θεός: 1.24, 26, 28) on the grounds, *of course*, of their godlessness for which they are responsible and which is thus culpable!

77. Van Dülmen's objection (*Theologie*, 160) to Kümmel's statement that in Paul *hamartia* is always an objective power, viz., the principle of sin, is quite simply false.

78. On this see Hübner, 'Existentiale Interpretation der "Gerechtigkeit Gottes" ', *NTS* 21, 462-488, esp. 474ff.

79. See Section 2.3 of this study: see also Nygren, *Röm.*, 109 (E.T. 143): 'Paul answers that sin may be unmasked and man brought to a consciousness of it. And this means more than the unmasking of individual sins which man commits. In other words, the issue is not sins in a moralistic sense, but sin as a power, a dynamic force.'

80. On individual questions in this section, see Käsemann, *Röm.*, 84ff. (E.T. 91ff.) and the literature cited there; see also Stuhlmacher, 'Zur neueren Exegese von Röm 3,24-26' = *Jesus und Paulus*, 315-333. In my opinion it is to mistake the drift of the statement in Rom 3.25 if we say that Paul naturally by his interpretation διὰ πίστεως there is only logically extending and enlarging his tradition (ibid., 330f.). However I cannot discuss this essay in detail here.

81. Lipsius, *Röm.*, 101.

82. Lipsius, *Röm.*, 101: 'With διὰ ποίου νόμου Paul sums up the old and the new order of salvation under the common term of the νόμος and speaks of a νόμος πίστεως in the figurative sense occasioned by the contrast to the Mosaic Law, cf. 8.2; Gal 6.2'; similarly most other exegetes, e.g., Lietzmann, *Röm.*, 52; Bultmann, *Theologie*, 260 (E.T. I. 259f.); Michel, *Röm.*, 95; Kuss, *Röm.*, 176; Käsemann, *Röm.*, 95 (E.T. 104f.); van Dülmen, *Theologie.*, 87; Cambier, *L'Evangile* I, 148ff.: 'une note caractéristique de la nouvelle période religieuse, une manière religieuse de vivre' (p. 151f.).

83. *ThZ* 10, 401-417.

84. Ibid., 415.

85. E.g., Lohse, ὁ νόμος τοῦ πνεύματος τῆς ζωῆς = *Neues Testament und christliche Existenz*, 281; Cranfield, *Romans*, I. 220. Simply to say that Peter von der Osten-Sacken, *Römer 8*, 245ff., also takes the 'law of faith' in Rom 3.27 as the Torah in so far as there 'is a correspondence to it in faith', or as 'the Torah made effective through faith' fails to do justice to the specific contribution made by this important book. But we cannot enter into a debate here with von der Osten-Sacken. This must be postponed till a later date. Hans Wilhelm Schmidt, *Röm.*, 73f., is still undecided: 'The idea of a law of faith sharply contrasts with the law of works...but perhaps also shows that the apostle is *not* concerned with elimination of the *nomos* altogether; he rejects the Law only where it is proffered as a law of works in the sense of a power for salvation.' Wilckens in *Röm.*, 245, is unambiguous: in Rom 3.27 νόμος πίστεως 'must be understood strictly as "Law", Torah; God ties the Law to faith alone, as νόμος πίστεως, as against the Law which ties man's justification to his works.'

86. According to Wilckens, 'Zu Römer 3,21-4,25; Antwort an G. Klein' = *Rechtfertigung als Freiheit*, 50-76, 51f. and 52, n. 4, Rom 3.27f. says nothing of a *renunciation* of 'glory' on the part of the believer. Ἐξεκλείσθη in his view relates in fact not to the individual believer's decision which has to be taken on each occasion, but to a decision which has been taken in the Christ-event regarding his destiny, with eschatological validity. The expressions 'law of works' and 'law of faith' were intended to define the pre-condition which provides the very basis of the human behaviour concerned. This objectivistic interpretation by Wilckens fails to persuade me. Even if Paul may sometimes speak objectivistically – thus already in Gal 3.22ff. of πίστις – this mode of talking taken in the total context of Pauline thought implies human behaviour. On this see the excellent comments in Luz, *Geschichtsverständnis*, 146-156 and *passim*! Close to our interpretation too is that of Otto Michel: 'By the term νόμος τῶν ἔργων Paul means an *understanding* of the Law which atomises obedience into individual acts and *misunderstands* the will of God. Corresponding to the νόμος τῶν ἔργων there are on man's side the ἔργα νόμου (Rom 3.20). The Jewish understanding of the Law necessarily evokes man's self-glorying' (*Röm.*, 95; my italics). That there are shades of difference in Michel's view from what here is submitted as the interpretation of Rom 3.27 is of no consequence in contrast to the fact that he too takes the 'law of works' as an expression which linguistically describes the Torah from a specific standpoint which is, too, a negative one.

87. Wilckens, 'Was heisst bei Paulus: "Aus Werken des Gesetzes wird kein Mensch gerecht"?' = *Rechtfertigung als Freiheit*, 77-109, 82; quotation of Bultmann, *Theologie*, 268 (E.T. I. 267) (where the text runs somewhat differently; Wilckens is quoting from the third impression).

88. With Käsemann, *Röm.*, 97 (E.T. 105), Rom 3.31 is to be taken here as a transitional passage leading into c. 4. But even Cranfield, who does not take 3.31 as the start of the Abraham midrash but as the conclusion of 3.27ff. (in his *Romans*, I. 223), interprets this midrash as a confirmation of what has been said in c. 3, though initially with some limitations: 'The function of this section is to confirm the truth of what is said in the first part of 3.27' (ibid., 224; see also ibid., 227). The whole trend of his exegesis of Rom 4 shows however that he too takes this chapter as a proof from scripture for Rom 3.27f.

89. Bultmann, *Theologie*, 264 (E.T. I. 263).

90. See further the commentaries.

91. *Realis*: Lipsius, *Röm.*, 102; Wilckens, 'Aus Werken des Gesetzes...' = *Rechtfertigung als Freiheit*, 95f.; *irrealis*: Bultmann, art., καυχάομαι, *TWNT* III. 649, n. 36 (E.T. III. 649, n. 36); Kuss, *Röm.*, 181; Klein, 'Römer 4 und die Idee der Heilsgeschichte' = *Rekonstruktion und Interpretation*, 151, n. 25; Cranfield, *Romans*, I. 228; undecided: Käsemann, *Röm.*, 99 (E.T. 106).

92. Clearly there has to be a supplementation in terms of the meaning; ...ἔχει καύχημα (πρὸς ἄνθρωπον), ἀλλ' οὐ πρὸς θεόν.

93. Bill., III. 186ff.

94. Wilckens, 'Aus Werken des Gesetzes...' = *Rechtfertigung als Freiheit*, 96.

95. Ibid., 96.

96. Kuss, *Röm.*, 181; my italics.

97. Joest, *Gesetz und Freiheit*, 139: 'But Christ is not an emergency solution to vicarious effect...'

98. A possible hint that in Hellenistic Greek καύχημα may perfectly well stand for καύχησις means nothing here, as in Rom 4.2 καύχημα as the accusative object of ἔχει can only mean 'glory'.

99. cf. Barrett, *Romans*, 88: 'It follows that since Abraham had righteousness *counted* to him, he cannot have done works, but must have been the recipient of grace.' This is correct, though of course *only* from the time of the *terminus a quo*, i.e., the moment of his justification. The same is true of the statement we find shortly thereafter: '...and Abraham is to be found among those who do not perform works with a view to justification but put their trust in God himself' (ibid., 88).

100. Michel, *Röm.*, 101.

101. Käsemann, *Röm.*, 103 (E.T. 110). The sense is 'to have to do with works' (Translator's note).

102. Michel, *Röm.*, 95.

103. Bultmann, *Theologie*, 264f. (E.T. I. 263f.); Bultmann's italics.

104. Ibid., 268 (E.T. I. 267).

105. Wilckens, 'Aus Werken des Gesetzes...' = *Rechtfertigung als Freiheit*, 97f.: 'The aphoristic formulation of 4.4f. which corresponds to that of the statement in 3.28 which 4.4f is meant to interpret must not mislead us into seeing here a general rejection in principle of the works of the Law altogether, as ἐργάζεσθαι in the sense of the "principle of performance", in favour of the principle of gratuity.'

106. Cf. Bultmann, art., καυχάομαι *TWNT* II. 650.9ff. (E.T. II. 650.15f.).

107. Klein, 'Röm. 4 und die Idee der Heilsgeschichte' = *Rekonstruktion und Interpretation*, 153.

108. Ibid., 158.

109. Once again, see my reservation stated in n. 80 against Stuhlmacher.

110. Käsemann, *Röm.*, 123f. (E.T. 133); quotation: 124 (E.T. 133); Schlatter, on whom Käsemann depends, writes: 'Paul banished that "glorying" which glorifies man; it is the adversary of faith and must disappear for faith to become possible. But as man cannot live without "glory" he immediately emphasises that when faith is there glorying comes into being, but not now as something celebrating man and his actions but as giving the man of faith his hope' (*Gottes Gerechtigkeit*, 178).

111. For older literature (up to 1933) see Schrenk, art., δικαιοσύνη, *TWNT* II. 194 and in the notes there 204ff. (E.T. II. 192 and 202ff.).

112. Bultmann, *Theologie*, 273 (E.T. I. 272).

113. Ibid., 274 (E.T. I. 273).

114. Ibid., 275 (E.T. I. 274).

115. Ibid., 280f. (E.T. I. 279-281).

116. Ibid., 284 (E.T. I. 284).

117. Ibid., 285 (E.T. I. 285).

118. Ibid., 285 (E.T. I. 285).

119. Käsemann, 'Gottesgerechtigkeit bei Paulus' = *EVB* II, 181-193 (E.T. 168-182).

120. Ibid., 188 (E.T. 176).

121. For, or tending towards, Bultmann: e.g., Klein, 'Gottes Gerechtigkeit als Thema der Paulus-Forschung' = *Rekonstruktion und Interpretation*, 225-236; Lohse, *Theologie*, 86; to some extent Conzelmann, *Theologie*, 243 (E.T. 215f.); for, or tending towards, Käsemann: e.g., Stuhlmacher, *Gerechtigkeit Gottes*: Müller, *Gottes Gerechtigkeit*.

122. Stuhlmacher, *Gerechtigkeit Gottes*, *passim*; see e.g., the summary in regard to the writings of apocalyptic Judaism, ibid., 174f.

123. Ziesler, *Righteousness*, esp. 147ff.

124. Ibid., 212.

125. But see criticism by Watson, Review Article, *NTS* 20, 217-228.

126. On this especially Käsemann, 'Erwägungen zum Stichwort "Versöhnungslehre im Neuen Testament"' ' = *Zeit und Geschichte*, 49f.; Stuhlmacher, *Gerechtigkeit Gottes*, 77, n. 2.

127. Käsemann, *EVB* II, 182 (E.T. 169); but when Käsemann considers the δικαιοσύνη θεοῦ 'identified with Christ in 1 Cor 1.30 (a quotation from a Christian hymn)' he has surreptitiously introduced the genitive θεοῦ into the passage. However this is not to contest that 1 Cor 1.30 is moving *in the direction of* the δικαιοσύνη θεοῦ view of Romans.

128. Käsemann, *Röm.*, 19 (E.T. 22); otherwise Klein, 'Gottes Gerechtigkeit als Thema der Paulus-Forschung' = *Rekonstruktion und Interpretation*, 231f.: for the characteristic of power in the δικαιοσύνη of God, he says, the term δύναμις in Rom 1.16 cannot be put forward as this is predicated of the Gospel rather than of the righteousness of God. As far as it goes this is correct – at least as long as 1.16f. is given a purely immanent interpretation. But if we consider how Paul handles his terms, we can see *how greatly what the individual terms are trying to describe is affected by the conceptual field of these terms in any given instance*.

129. Käsemann, *Röm.*, 25 (E.T. 28).

130. Lyonnet, *Exegesis Epistulae ad Romanos*, 80-107d, especially 107a.

131. Käsemann, *Röm.*, 24 (E.T. 27).

132. Ibid., 26 (E.T. 29); my italics.

133. 'Merely' to pronounce someone *dikaios* is in fact not 'forensic' in Paul's sense.

134. Käsemann, 'Gottesgerechtigkeit bei Paulus' = *EVB* II, 187 (E.T. 175).

135. Those who know Luther will at once think of his polemic against Aristotle, e.g., *WA* 56, 172.8ff. For the passages in Aristotle in question see ibid., n. on 1. 9.

136. But it is too constricting if like Goppelt, *Theologie* II, 468, we define the righteousness of God in Paul in terms of God's faithfulness to his promise to which the Old Testament testifies. Yet we must remember that Goppelt's comments on justification remain fragmentary on account of his very sudden death.

137. Käsemann, *Röm.*, 73 (E.T. 79): ἀπιστία = breaking with the covenant.

138. The idea expressed positively in 2.14 - *positively in regard to the Jews* but not to the Gentiles if the discussion with Judaism starts already at 2.1 (e.g., Käsemann, *Röm.*, 49 (E.T. 53); Cranfield, *Romans*, I. 138f.; see also n. 75 in Section 2.3 of this study) - the idea that Gentiles do τὰ τοῦ νόμου because they are a law unto themselves is one which flows in the opposite direction into the theological judgement of 3.9 by which all, including therefore all the Gentiles, live under the power of sin. The presupposition behind this basic theological judgement of Paul's is his conviction that even the Gentiles know *God's* Law and therefore - despite their partial righteousness of works - are shown up as unrighteous. They too have totally failed to attain the purpose of the Law.

139. See also Section 3.3 of this study.

140. Ziesler, *Righteousness*, 190: 'forensic statement'.

141. See Käsemann, *Röm.*, 85 (E.T. 92f.).

142. Kertelge, *Rechtfertigung*, 95f., rightly emphasises that δικαιοσύνη θεοῦ in Rom 10.3 is to be explained both by contrast with ἰδία δικαιοσύνη and in terms of the summons to submission. Thus, he says, 'at least a double orientation of the term δικαιοσύνη θεοῦ can be assumed'. However in my view he has over-interpreted the Pauline idea, ibid., 97, when he says that one's 'own righteousness' can be spoken of only after the 'righteousness of God' has appeared. Exegesis of 10.3 in isolation, or perhaps even an exegesis within the complex constituted by cc. 9-11, may lead to this result. Only it is not compatible with cc. 3 and 4. For according to Romans, Abraham, as has been shown in the course of this study, had already perverted the Law of God into a law of works before he was justified by God, and thus set forth his 'own righteousness'! On the other hand we may agree with Kertelge when at p. 98 he takes Christ to be 'the personified righteousness of God'; Christ appears as its 'bearer and representative'.

143. Stuhlmacher, *Gerechtigkeit Gottes*, 91.

144. Ibid., 92.

145. Ibid., 92f.

146. Ibid., 93.

147. In Stuhlmacher's last-mentioned passage do we not detect some misunderstanding of what existential interpretation can achieve? For my reservations about his view of existential interpretation see Hübner, 'Existentiale Interpretation der paulinischen "Gerechtigkeit Gottes" ', *NTS* 21, 485, n. 3. It is probably significant that Stuhlmacher, loc. cit., 93, uses the term 'individualistic' though he probably means that Rom 10.3 should not be expounded with reference to the individual believer and so should not be expounded with an orientation on the individual (nor, of course, in a subjective, 'individual' way).

148. Käsemann, *Röm.*, 269 (E.T. 281); my italics.

149. Käsemann, 'Gottesgerechtigkeit' = *EVB* II, 183 (E.T. 170): 'The gift itself has thus the character of power. The meaning of this in concrete terms is quite clear. Paul knows no gift of God which does not convey both the obligation and *the capacity* to serve. A gift which is not authenticated in practice and passed on to others loses its specific content' (my italics); cf. also Käsemann, *Röm.*, 25 (E.T. 28).

150. Stuhlmacher, *Gerechtigkeit Gottes*, 93.

151. Käsemann, *Röm.*, 38f. (E.T. 43).

152. *WA* 57, 332.4f.; he does admittedly continue significantly as follows: '...*sicut iniustitia incredulitas cum operibus suis etiam bonis et sanctis* (!).'

153. Käsemann, *Röm.*, 170 (E.T. 180), depending on J. Weiss; Kertelge, *Rechtfertigung*, 269 and 269, n. 91, depending on Sickenberger.

154. Kertelge, *Rechtfertigung*, 270.

155. To different effect, Cranfield, *Romans*, I. 322, paraphrasing εἰς δικαιοσύνην as 'to final justification'; ibid., 322, n. 4: 'That δικαιοσύνη here has its forensic, rather than its

moral, sense is clear from the contrast with θάνατος.' Similarly also Michel, *Röm.*, 135: Here righteousness means God's eschatological pronouncement.

156. Lipsius, *Röm.*, 121: 'εἰς δικαιοσύνην: the object of ὑπακοή is the new *righteousness of life*' (my italics).

157. Käsemann, *Röm.*, 170 (E.T. 180).

158. Michel, *Röm.*, 135, n. 4, naturally does not understand death in 6.16 'in the same sense...as in Rom 5.12ff.'. He is forced into this because he interprets εἰς δικαιοσύνην in a forensic, eschatological way.

159. Lipsius, *Röm.*, 121, already spoke with reference to 6.18 of the new relationship of service to δικαιοσύνη as the objective *power of life* governing the Christian.

160. Lipsius, *Röm.*, 121, makes an even sharper differentiation of the two: 'εἰς ἁγιασμόν conversely signifies the object striven for by δικαιοσύνη as the power of life, so it is better rendered "for holiness"...than "for sanctification" '. Käsemann, *Röm.*, 174 (E.T. 183), puts it well: 'Sanctification means a *being for God manifesting itself bodily* in the secular world and in face of temptation, because in Christ God graciously sets us in his lordship and is there for us' (my italics). According to Käsemann Paul is concerned about the whole man in all his possibilities, 'and therefore in his worldly reality, since God wills and creates a new world'. Sanctification therefore means *this* specific 'intention and dimension of justification' which has to be championed individually and in exemplary fashion (*individuell und exemplarisch*).

161. Kertelge, *Rechtfertigung*, 271, expresses this reservation with reference to the whole of Rom 6. But he comes very close to our view when he writes, 'Δικαιοσύνη in vv. 16 and 18 and also in the subsequent vv. 19 and 20 denotes nothing other than it does in the previous chapters of Romans' (ibid., 271). But unlike us here he is not concerned with the question whether Paul uses 'righteousness of God' and 'righteousness' synonymously.

162. Ziesler, *Righteousness*, 201.

163. Bultmann, *Exegetica*, 49.

164. Ibid., 50.

165. Bultmann, *Theologie*, 273, 278 (E.T. I. 272, 276f.); O. Merk follows his teacher, W. G. Kümmel (*Röm 7 und die Bekehrung des Paulus*, 100) in his *Handeln aus Glauben*, 35, where he rightly criticises Bultmann's position. Merk also agrees with H. Windisch, 'Das Problem des paulinischen Imperativs', *ZNW* 23, 265ff., who considers that even freedom from sin lies within the sphere of what is discernible on earth. I cannot see that Bultmann, as Merk, ibid., 35, thinks, has in his *Theologie des Neuen Testaments* (*Theology of the New Testament*) 'appropriately corrected' his earlier view. What Bultmann is doing here is to expound what he said earlier in terms of existential interpretation.

166. Käsemann, *Röm.*, 166 (E.T. 43).

167. Ziesler, *Righteousness, passim*: 'ethical righteousness'.

168. Cf. Schlatter, *Gottes Gerechtigkeit*, 217.

169. Käsemann, *Röm.*, 39 (E.T. 43).

170. Ibid., 39 (E.T. 43).

171. Hübner, 'Existentiale Interpretation der paulinischen "Gerechtigkeit Gottes" ', *NTS* 21, 474.

172. There is of course in 5.12ff. some placing in parallel of *hamartia* and *nomos*. In v. 12 we have: ἡ ἁμαρτία... ἦλθεν, indicating that it is quasi-personified and so is a power. In v. 20 we have: νόμος...παρεισῆλθεν. Thus linguistically *nomos* and *hamartia* are given the same treatment. Yet this parallel cannot have enough weight as evidence that the reader is already taking the Law as a power in 5.20. On the other hand if he looks back from 6.14 to 5.20 he will re-evaluate the expression about the Law's 'coming in' which here occurs so casually. See further on 5.20 in Section 2.3 of this study.

173. Bultmann, *Der Stil der paulinischen Predigt und die kynisch-stoische Diatribe*, 67 and 67, n. 2.

174. Ibid., 67f.: 'In some circumstances objections do also arise which are the expression of really hostile intentions...' But Bultmann seems to evaluate the objection in 7.7 rather as a genuine expression of Paul's. In the sentence just quoted he goes on characteristically as follows: '...but almost always the fictitious opponent represents not a hostile view but draws false conclusions from Paul's view.' But where does Bultmann get his knowledge that this is so?

175. On Rom 8.21 see Balz, *Heilsvertrauen und Welterfahrung*, 50f.

176. Failing as it does to take into account the Pauline statements on the Spirit (Rom 8!) such a formulation is of course not merely infuriating but sheer nonsense.

177. Güttgemanns, '"Gottesgerechtigkeit" und strukturale Semantik, Linguistische Analyse zu δικαιοσύνη θεοῦ' = *studia linguistica neotestamentica*, 80, contests on linguistic grounds that δικαιοσύνη θεοῦ involves a technical term: 'A technical term does indeed have a synsemantic associated field, but it does not allow of any syntactical alteration which often also affects the entire syntactical structure of the sentence framework, e.g., the word order.' But does this remain true if an author takes over a *terminus technicus* and integrates it into his thought?

178. Klaus Koch in his essay 'Die drei Gerechtigkeiten, Die Umformung einer hebräischen Idee im aramäischen Denken nach dem jesaja-Targum' = *Rechtfertigung*, 245-267) attempts to show how a single Hebraic idea expressed by the stem *sdq* is *developed conceptually* and terminologically in Aramaic using three stems, *zkj*, *sdq* and *qst*. In New Testament research we might ask of this attempt whether that development might not make the various aspects in the content of δικαιοσύνη or δικαιοσύνη θεοῦ more clearly discernible, particularly in Romans.

179. On Gal 3.21 see Section 1 of this study *passim*.

180. There is no need to consider here Lütgert's thesis that Paul is fighting on two fronts.

181. See already Sieffert, 'Bemerkungen zum paulinischen Lehrbegriff', *JDTh* 14, 263: '...and here too it is the loss of freedom which the apostle is anxious to prevent in seeming to warn against an excess of freedom.'

182. Friedrich, 'Das Gesetz des Glaubens Röm 3.27, *ThZ* 10, 415; Lohse follows him in 'ὁ νόμος τοῦ πνεύματος τῆς ζωῆς' ₅ *Neues Testament und christliche Existenz*, 281.

183. To different effect Wilckens, 'Zu Röm 3,21-4,25' = *Rechtfertigung als Freiheit*, 52, n. 4.

184. Bultmann, *Theologie*, 260, (E.T. I. 259).

185. Käsemann, *Röm.*, 95 (E.T. 103).

186. This is brought out, e.g., in the Vulgate by its translation '*per legem fidei*' in v. 27 and '*per fidem*' in v. 28.

187. Käsemann, *Röm.*, 96 (E.T. 103).

188. Klein, 'Römer 4 und die Idee der Heilsgeschichte' = *Rekonstruktion und Interpretation*, 149.

189. Ibid., 149.

190. Ibid., 148; however Klein's evaluation of it is that it is 'reflective' inasmuch as 'man' in v. 27 is used in a 'generic sense' (ibid., 148f.).

191. Michel, *Röm.*, 97; likewise Cranfield, *Romans*, I. 223.

192. Cambier, *L'Evangile* I, 160.

193. Ibid., 162.

194. Bacher I.170f.; II.186ff.

195. Ibid., I.170.

196. Levy I.211f.; also Men 99b *bittulah shel torah*, listed by Levy, ibid., 212, under the heading *bittul*, has no relevance to this context.

197. I am grateful to my colleague Klaus Haacker for the suggestion that in the wider context of JMeg 1.70d, where *btl* stands for the cessation of the prophetic books or non-cessation of the Torah, there is the verb *qum* (statement in Est 9.31: that the days of Purim

should be observed, '*l*^e*qayyem*'). But at the same time he points out that the connection is not so close as in Ab 4.9. Thus as regards that passage we will have to keep hold of the point that here too the two verbs are not used as an idiomatically contrasting pair– quite apart from the fact that the niphal form does not express human activity of any kind, whether it is to be taken exegetically or otherwise (on the passage, see Levy I. 211). But see O. Hofius, 'Das Gesetz des Mose und das Gesetz Christi", *ZThK* 80 (183), n. 57.

198. Wilckens, 'Die Rechtfertigung Abrahams nach Röm 4' = *Rechtfertigung als Freiheit*, 42; ibid., 42: 'The Law established as γραφή testifies to the Christ-event as the fulfilment of God's history of election': see also Lietzmann, *Röm.*, 52; Michel, *Röm.*, 97: 'He (i.e., Paul) in fact hears the voice of the Gospel in the Old Testament itself (...3.21...)...'; Cranfield, *Romans*, I. 224; but see also Bornkamm, 'Wandlungen im alt- und neutestamentl. Gesetzesverständnis', *Ges. Aufs.* IV.111, where he adduces this interpretation as a *consequence* of what is about to be mentioned under point 2.

199. Bornkamm, 'Wandlungen im alt- und Neutestamentl. Gesetzesverständnis' = *Ges. Aufs.* IV.111; my italics.

200. Delling, art., καταργεῖν, *TWNT* I.453.29ff. (E.T. I.453).

201. Klein, 'Röm 4 und die Idee der Heilsgeschichte' = *Rekonstruktion und Interpretation*, 166f.

202. Wilckens, 'Die Rechtfertigung Abrahams nach Röm 4' = *Rechtfertigung als Freiheit*, 43.

203. This of course follows clearly for an exegesis which understands by 'law of faith' in 3.27 faith as a standard or ordinance.

204. Käsemann, *Röm.*, 97 (E.T. 105).

205. Friedrich, 'Das Gesetz des Glaubens Röm 3.27', *ThZ* 10, 416.

206. Michel, *Röm.*, 99; see also Michel, *Paulus und seine Bibel*, 53 and frequently.

207. Grundmann, art., ἵστημι, *TWNT* VII.640.23ff. (E.T. VII.641.28ff.).

208. Ibid., 645.43f. (E.T. 647.1).

209. Thus too despite differences on detail in his viewpoint we have Michel, *Röm.*, 161 (on Rom 8.4) saying: 'The salvation event serves the purpose of establishing and implementing the authority of the Law (Rom 3.31; 6.13).'

210. Cf. Käsemann, *Röm.*, 209 (E.T. 219): 'The slogan φρονεῖν denotes the direction not merely of thought but of total existence, which on the Semitic view is always orientated consciously or unconsciously to a goal.'

211. Lohse, 'ὁ νόμος τοῦ πνεύματος τῆς ζωῆς' = *NT und christliche Existenz*, 284; most exegetes take it differently: as in 3.27 *nomos* means principle, ordinance or standard; e.g., Lipsius, *Röm.*, 131: The law of the spirit of life in Christ Jesus is 'the new ordinance of life by which the divine Spirit rules in the believer (thus νόμος here too is figuratively used...).' 'This *Spirit* has freed you...' (my italics). For our understanding of νόμος in Rom 8.2 as Torah we must above all mention Jüngel, *Paulus und Jesus*, 54f. (though his interpretation of Gal differs from ours here); Schmidt, *Röm.*, 136 says, 'However, the idea of *nomos* in both formulations (viz., in Rom 8.2) is to be related to the Old Testament *nomos* in which of course the two possibilities are ready to hand, of its becoming a "law of sin" or a "spiritual law". The carnal man, held prisoner by sin, encounters the Old Testament Law in a false way as νόμος ἔργων and thus as νόμος ἁμαρτίας. But where the man in Christ receives the Spirit the Law discloses itself in its real nature (7.14); the veil is removed from the Law and Christ becomes manifest in the Spirit as the 'Law' (2 Cor 3.14); the Law becomes the νόμος πίστεως, the νόμος πνευματικός.' Von der Osten-Sacken, *Römer 8*, 226f. (see on this the note in n. 85 of Section 3.1.3); Wilckens, *Röm.*, 245.

212. But of course only figuratively, as our study shows in Section 2.3.

213. The difference between the perversion of the Torah into a 'law of works' in 3.27 and its perversion into a law that brings death in c. 7 must naturally not be suppressed. In the first

instance the perversion occurs through man, but in the second through *hamartia*. But here again we also have to take into account that dialectic which Paul brings out particularly in 5.12: sin is fate but also a responsible act of man.

214. There may be an initial intimation of this idea in 1 Cor 15.56: 'the sting of death is *hamartia*, but the *dunamis* of *hamartia* is the *nomos*', if 1 Cor is in fact to be placed after Gal. This sentence would then have to be interpreted thus: *hamartia* gains its *dunamis* through the *nomos*, which it misuses. J. Weiss, *1 Kor.*, 380, considers the verse to be 'a theological gloss which wholly departs from the inspired level but presupposes an exact acquaintance with Pauline theology'. For a contrary view see Conzelmann, *1 Kor.*, 350 (E.T. 293).

215. Bultmann, *Theologie*, 260 (E.T. I. 259).

216. Bruce, 'Paul and the Law of Moses', *BJRL* 57, 272; my italics.

217. Lohse, 'ὁ νόμος τοῦ πνεύματος τῆς ζωῆς' = *NT und christliche Existenz*, 286.

218. Bruce, 'Paul and the Law of Moses', *BJRL* 57, 272.

219. E.g. Michel, *Röm.*, 158; Käsemann, *Röm.*, 206 (E.T. 216).

220. E.g., Cranfield, *Romans*, I. 379.

221. Käsemann, *Röm.*, 204, 207 (E.T. 214, 217f.).

222. Ibid., 207 (E.T. 217f.).

223. Paulsen, *Überlieferung und Auslegung in Röm 8*, p. 65.

224. Käsemann, *Röm.*, 208 (E.T. 218).

225. Ibid., 207 (E.T. 218).

226. Hübner, 'Existentiale Interpretation der paulinischen "Gerechtigkeit Gottes" ', *NTS* 21, 462-488.

227. Bruce, 'Paul and the Law of Moses', *BJRL* 57, 272.

228. Ibid., 275.

229. Ibid., 275f.

230. It is in *this* light that we must understand what Schrage, *Einzelgebote*, 232, rightly says: viz., that Paul 'in fact...made an absolutely clear distinction between the way of salvation and a standard for life in regard to the moral demands of the Law, and rejected the Law only in the former sense, but in the second sense affirmed it as a standard for the moral life, and appeals to it. The holy and just Law which is good and spiritual (Rom 7.12,14), as the revelation of the will of God which is valid for all time, remains the standard to which even the Christian is tied...'; see also Bultmann, 'Christus des Gesetzes Ende' = *GuV* II, 52f. (E.T. 60f.).

231. Jüngel, *Paulus und Jesus*, 61.

232. Ibid., 61.

233. Ibid., 61.

234. Ibid., 61.

235. Limbeck, *Von der Ohnmacht des Rechts*, 99, makes this assessment: 'So that the Law could become powerful, God sent his Son into sin's sphere of power.' This *can* be interpreted unexceptionably. But unlike what we find with Paul, who speaks of the legal demands of the Law in the context of the Spirit of God, with Limbeck the Law is given too much independent weight.

236. Hahn, 'Gesetzesverständnis', 59.

237. Ibid., 35f.

238. Ibid., 48.

239. Ibid., 49.

240. Ibid., 51f.

241. Ibid., 52.

242. Schlier, *Gal.*, 136f.

243. Hahn, 'Gesetzesverständnis', 55.

244. Ibid., 56, n. 84.

245. Ibid., 62f.

246. Such a project might be tackled from the standpoints alluded to in Hübner, 'Biblische Theologie und Theologie des Neuen Testamentes", *KuD* 27 (1981), 2-19.
247. Sanders, *Paul, the Law, and the Jewish People*, 18.
248. Ibid., 18.
249. Ibid., 20.
250. Ibid., 20.
251. Ibid., 18.
252. Ibid., 18.
253. Ibid., 51, n. 16.
254. Ibid., 21.
255. Ibid., 215.
256. Ibid., 22.
257. Ibid., 22.
258. Ibid., 22.
259. Räisänen, *Paul and the Law*, 5.
260. Ibid., 6.
261. Ibid., 7.
262. Ibid., 7.
263. Ibid., 8f.

BIBLIOGRAPHY

Of works cited or referred to generally
(Abbreviations as in RGG³)

Apophoreta, Festschrift for E. Haenchen, ed. W. Eltester and F. H. Kettler, *BZNW* 30, Berlin 1964.

Bacher, W., *Die exegetische Terminologie der jüdischen Traditionsliteratur*, 2 Teile, Darmstadt 1965 (= Leipzig 1899 and 1905).

Balz, H. R., *Heilsvertrauen und Welterfahrung: Strukturen der paulinischen Eschatologie nach Röm 8, 18-39, BEvTh* 59, Munich 1971.

Bammel, E., Νόμος Χριστοῦ = *StudEv III*, 1964, 120-128.

Bandstra, A. J., *The Law and the Elements of the World: An Exegetical Study in an Aspect of Paul's Teaching*, Kampen 1964.

Barrett, C. K., *A Commentary on the Epistle to the Romans*, Black's *NTC*, London 1975 (= 1962).

–, 'The Allegory of Abraham, Sarah and Hagar in the Argument of Galatians' = *Rechtfertigung*, 1-16.

Barth, K., *Kirchliche Dogmatik IV: Die Lehre von der Versöhnung 1*, Zürich 1960 (= *Church Dogmatics*, IV/1: *The Doctrine of Reconciliation*, Edinburgh 1956).

Barth, M., 'Zur Einheit des Galater- und Epheserbriefs', *ThZ* 32, 1976, 78-91.

Baur, F. C., 'Über Zweck und Veranlassung des Römerbriefs und die damit zusammenhängenden Verhältnisse der römischen Gemeinde', *Tübinger Zeitschrift für Theologie*, 1838, Heft 3, 59-178; now in: Baur, F. C., *Ausgewählte Werke in Einzelausgaben*, ed. K. Scholder, 1 Bd., Stuttgart-Bad Cannstatt 1963, 147-266.

Becker, J., *Untersuchungen zur Entstehungsgeschichte der Testamente der Zwölf Patriarchen, AGaJU* 8, Leiden 1970.

Behm, J., Art. διαθήκη, *TWNT* II, 127-137 (= *TDNT* II, 124-134).

Berger, K., *Die Gesetzesauslegung Jesu, Ihr historischer Hintergrund im Judentum und im Alten Testament I: Markus und Parallelen, WMANT* 40, Neukirchen 1972.

Betz, H. D., *Der Apostel Paulus und die sokratische Tradition: Eine exegetische Untersuchung zu seiner 'Apologie' 2 Korinther 10-13, BhTh* 45, Tübingen 1972.

–, 'Geist, Freiheit und Gesetz', *ZThK* 71, 1974, 78-93.

–, 'The Literary Composition and Function of Paul's Letter to the Galatians', *NTS* 21, 1974/75, 353-379.

Bläser, P., *Das Gesetz bei Paulus*, Münster 1941.

Blass, F., *Grammatik des neutestamentlichen Griechisch*, revised by

A. Debrunner, Göttingen 1970[13].

Blass, F./Debrunner, A./Rehkopf, A., *Grammatik des neutestamentlichen Griechisch*, Göttingen 1976[14].

Bornkamm, G., *Paulus*, Urban Tabu 119, Stuttgart 1969 (= *Paul*, London 1975).

–, *Das Ende des Gesetzes: Paulusstudien*, *Ges. Aufs. I*, *BETh* 16, Munich 1958 (= *Early Christian Experience*, London, 1969); *Geschichte und Glaube*, Zweiter Teil = *Ges. Aufs.* IV, Munich 1971.

–, 'Sünde, Gesetz und Tod (Röm 7)' = *Ges. Aufs. I*, 51-69 (= 'Sin, Law and Death (Romans 7)' = *EXtn Exp*, 87-104).

–, 'Paulinische Anakoluthe' = *Ges. Aufs. I*, 76-92.

–, 'Die Häresie des Kolosserbriefes' = *Ges. Aufs. I*, 139-156.

–, 'Wandlungen im alt- und neutestamentlichen Gesetzesverständnis' = *Ges. Aufs. IV*, 73-119.

–, 'Der Römerbrief als Testament des Paulus' = *Ges. Aufs. IV*, 120-139.

Borse, U., *Der Standort des Galaterbriefes*, *BBB* 41, Cologne 1972.

Brandenburger, E., *Adam und Christus: Exegetisch-religionsgeschichtliche Untersuchung zu Römer 5, 12-31 (1 Kor 15)*, *WMANT* 7, Neukirchen 1962.

Bring, R., *Christus und das Gesetz: Die Bedeutung des Gesetzes des Alten Testaments nach Paulus und sein Glauben an Christus*, Leiden 1969.

Bruce, F. F., 'Paul and the Law of Moses', *BJRL* 57, 259-279.

–, *The Epistle of Paul to the Romans: An Introduction and Commentary*, Tyndale NTC, London 1969[5].

–, *Paul: Apostle of the Heart Set Free*, Michigan 1977 (= American edition of Bruce, F. F., *Paul: Apostle of the Free Spirit*, Exeter 1977).

Free Spirit, Exeter 1977).

Bultmann, R., *Der Stil der paulinischen Predigt und die kynisch-stoische Diatribe*, Göttingen 1910.

–, *Theologie des Neuen Testaments*, ed. O. Merk, Tübingen 1977[7] (= *Theology of the New Testament*, London 1952).

–, *Glauben und Verstehen II*, Tübingen 1962[3] (= *Essays philosophical and theological*, London, 1955 [=*GuV II*].

–, 'Christus des Gesetzes Ende' = *GuV II*, 32-58 (= 'Christ the End of the Law', *Essays*, 36-66).

–, *Exegetica: Aufsätze zur Erforschung des Neuen Testaments*, ed. E. Dinkler, Tübingen 1967.

–, 'Römer 7 und die Anthropologie des Paulus' = *Exegetica*, 198-209 (= 'Romans 7 and the Anthropology of Paul', *Existence and Faith*, London 1961, 147-157).

–, 'Glossen im Römerbrief' = *Exegetica*, 278-284.

–, 'Ursprung und Sinn der Typologie als Hermeneutischer Methode' = *Exegetica*, 369-380.

–; 'Adam und Christus nach Röm 5' = *Exegetica*, 424-444.

–, *Der zweite Brief an die Korinther* (Meyer VI), Göttingen 1976.

–, Art. πείθω, *TWNT II*, 1-12 (= *TDNT II*, 1-11).

-, Art. καυχάομαι, *TWNT* III, 646-654 (= *TDNT III*, 645-654).

Burton, E. de Witt, *A Critical and Exegetical Commentary on the Epistle to the Galatians*, *ICC*, Edinburgh 1975 (= 1921).

Cambier, J., *L'Evangile de dieu selon l'épître aux Romains, Exégèse et Théologie biblique 1, StNeotest* 3, Bruges 1967.

Clemen, C., *Die Chronologie der paulinischen Briefe aufs neue untersucht*, Halle 1893.

-, 'Die Reihenfolge der paulinischen Hauptbriefe', *ThStKr* 70, 1897, 219-270.

Conzelmann, H., *Grundriss der Theologie des Neuen Testaments*, Munich 1967 (= *An Outline of the Theology of the New Testament*, London 1969).

-, *Der erste Brief an die Korinther* (Meyer V), Göttingen 1969.

Cranfield, C. E. B., 'St. Paul and the Law', *SJTh* 17, 1964, 43-68.

-, *The Epistle to the Romans I*, *ICC*, Edinburgh 1975⁶ (entirely rewritten).

Cullmann, O., *Petrus, Jünger - Apostel - Märtyrer: Das historische und das theologische Petrusproblem*, Zürich/Stuttgart 1960² (= *Peter, Disciple, Apostle, Martyr: a historical and theological study*, London 1953).

Dahl, N. A., 'Widersprüche in der Bibel, ein altes hermeneutisches Problem', *StTh* 25, 1971, 1-19.

Davies, W. D., *Paul and Rabbinic Judaism: Some Rabbinic Elements in Pauline Theology*, London 1962.

-, *Torah in the Messianic Age and/or the Age to Come*, JBL MS VII, Philadelphia 1952.

-, 'Paul and the People of Israel', *NTS* 24, 1977/78, 4-39.

Deissmann, A., *Paulus: Eine kultur- und religionsgeschichtliche Skizze*, Tübingen 1925² (= *St. Paul: A Study in Social and Religious History*, London 1912).

Delling, G., Art. καταργέω, *TWNT* I, 453-455 (= *TDNT* I, 452ff.).

Denzinger, H., *Enchiridion Symbolorum Definitionum et Declarationum de rebus fidei et morum*, ed. C. Rahner, Freiburg 1952²⁸.

Dibelius, M., *Die Geisterwelt im Glauben des Paulus*, Göttingen 1905.

Dietzfelbinger, C., *Paulus und das Alte Testament: Die Hermeneutik des Paulus untersucht an seiner Deutung der Gestalt Abrahams*, ThExh 95, Munich 1961.

-, *Heilsgeschichte bei Paulus? Eine exegetische Studie zum paulinischen Geschichtsdenken*, ThExh 126, Munich 1965.

Dilthey, W., 'Die Entstehung der Hermeneutik' = *Ges. Schriften V*, 317-338, Göttingen 1968⁵.

Dinkler, E., *Signum Crucis: Aufsätze zum Neuen Testament und zur Christlichen Archäologie*, Tübingen 1967.

-, 'Der Brief an die Galater, Zum Kommentar von Heinrich Schlier' = *Signum Crucis*, 278-282.

Donfried, K. P., 'Justification and Last Judgement in Paul', *ZNW* 67, 1976, 90-110.

Drane, J. W., 'Tradition, Law and Ethics in Pauline Theology', *NovTest* 16,

1974, 167-178.

–, *Paul, Libertine or Legalist? A Study in the Theology of the Major Pauline Epistles*, London 1975.

van Dülmen, A., *Die Theologie des Gesetzes bei Paulus, StuttgBM* 5, Stuttgart 1968.

Eckert, J., *Die urchristliche Verkündigung im Streit zwischen Paulus und seinen Gegnern im Galaterbrief, BU* 6, Regensburg 1971.

Eichholz, G., *Die Theologie des Paulus im Umriss*, Neukirchen 1972.

Ellis, E. E., *Paul's Use of the Old Testament*, Edinburgh/London 1957.

Foerster, W., 'Abfassungszeit und Ziel des Galaterbriefs' = *Apophoreta*, 135-141.

–, Art. ὄφις, *TWNT* V, 571-582 (= *TDNT* V, 571-582).

Flückiger, F., 'Die Werke des Gesetzes bei den Heiden (nach Röm 2, 14ff)', *ThZ* 8, 1952, 17-42.

Friedrich, G., 'Das Gesetz des Glaubens Röm 3, 27', *ThZ* 10, 1954, 401-417.

Fuchs, E., *Hermeneutik*, Tübingen 1969⁴.

Georgi, D., *Die Geschichte der Kollekte des Paulus für Jerusalem*, Hamburg-Bergstedt 1965.

Gnilka, J., *Der Philipperbrief (HThKNT* X, 3), Freiburg/Basle/Vienna 1968.

Goppelt, L., *Typos: Die typologische Deutung des Alten Testaments im Neuen*, Gütersloh 1939 = Darmstadt 1969 with appendix: *Apokalyptik und Typologie bei Paulus*.

–, *Theologie des Neuen Testaments II: Vielfalt und Einheit des apostolischen Christuszeugnisses*, Göttingen 1976 (= *Theology of the New Testament*, Grand Rapids 1981-2).

Greeven, H., Art. πλησίον, *TWNT* VI, 314-316 (= *TDNT* VI, 316-318).

Grundmann, W., Art. ἵστημι, *TWNT* VII, 637-652 (= *TDNT* VII, 638-653).

Güttgemanns, E., '"Gottesgerechtigkeit" und strukturale Semantik, Linguistische Analyse zu δικαιοσύνη θεοῦ' = *studia linguistica neotestamentica. Ges. Aufs. zur linguistischen Grundlage einer Neutestamentlichen Theologie, BETh* 60, Munich 1971, 59-98.

Gutbrod, W. and Kleinknecht, H., Art. νόμος, *TWNT* IV, 1029-1084 (= *TDNT* IV, 1022-1085).

Haacker, K., 'Die Berufung des Verfolgers und die Rechtfertigung des Gottlosen, Erwägungen zum Zusammenhang zwischen Biographie und Theologie des Apostels Paulus', *ThBeitr* 6, 1957, 119.

–, 'War Paulus Hillelit?' = *Das Institutum Judaicum der Universität Tübingen* 1971-1972, 106-120.

Haenchen, E., *Gott und Mensch, Ges. Aufs.*, Tübingen 1965.

–, 'Matthäus 23' = *Gott und Mensch*, 29-54.

Hahn, F., 'Gen 15, 6 im Neuen Testament' = *Probleme biblischer Theologie*, 90-107.

–, 'Das Gesetzesverständnis im Römer- und Galaterbrief', *ZNW* 67, 1976, 29-63.

Hanson, A. T., *Studies in Paul's Technique and Theology*, London 1974.

Harder, G., 'Der konkrete Anlass des Römerbriefes', *TheolViat* 6, 1959, 13-24.

Heidegger, M., 'Die Sprache im Gedicht' = *Unterwegs zur Sprache*, Pfullingen 1971[4], 35-82.

Hengel, M., *Judentum und Hellenismus: Studien zu ihrer Begegnung unter besonderer Berücksichtigung Palästinas bis zur Mitte des 2. Jh. v. Chr.*, WUANT 10, Tübingen 1969 (= *Judaism and Hellenism: Studies in their encounter in Palestine during the Early Hellenistic Period*, London 1974).

–, *Der Sohn Gottes: Die Entstehung der Christologie und die jüdisch-hellenistische Religionsgeschichte*, Tübingen 1975 (= *The Son of God: The Origin of Christology and the history of Jewish-Hellenistic religion*, London 1976).

Herold, G., *Zorn und Gerechtigkeit bei Paulus: Eine Untersuchung zu Röm 1, 16-18*, Berne/Frankfurt 1973.

Holsten, C., *Das Evangelium des Paulus I, 1*, Berlin 1880.

Holtz, T., Review of U. Wilckens, *Rechtfertigung als Freiheit*, *ThLZ* 101, 1976, 264-266.

Horst, F., *Hiob, BK* XVI/1, Neukirchen 1968.

Hübner, H., *Rechtfertigung und Heiligung in Luthers Römerbriefvorlesung*, Witten 1965.

–, *Das Gesetz in der synoptischen Tradition: Studien zur These einer progressiven Qumranisierung und Judaisierung innerhalb der synoptischen Tradition*, Witten 1973.

–, *Politische Theologie und existentiale Interpretation: Zur Auseinandersetzung Dorothee Sölles mit Rudolf Bultmann*, Witten 1973.

–, 'Gal. 3, 10 und die Herkunft des Paulus', *KuD* 19, 1973, 215-231.

–, 'Existentiale Interpretation der paulinischen "Gerechtigkeit Gottes"', Zur Kontroverse Rudolf Bultmann - Ernst Käsemann', *NTS* 21, 1974/75, 462-488.

–, 'Das ganze und das eine Gesetz, Zum Problemkreis Paulus und die Stoa', *KuD* 21, 1975, 239-256.

–, 'Mk 7, 15 und das "judisch-hellenistische" Gesetzesverständnis', *NTS* 22, 1975/76, 319-345.

–, 'Das Gesetz als elementares Thema einer Biblischen Theologie?', *KuD* 22, 1976, 250-276.

–, Art. γραφή, *Exegetisches Wörterbuch zum Neuen Testament I*, 628-638.

Jeremias, G., *Der Lehrer der Gerechtigkeit*, StUNT 2, Göttingen 1963.

Jeremias, J., 'Paulus als Hillelit' = *Neotestamentica et Semitica: Studies in Honour of Matthew Black*, ed. E. E. Ellis and M. Wilcox, Edinburgh 1969, 88-94.

Römerbriefes', *StTh* 25, 1971, 61-73.

Jesus Christus in Historie und Theologie, Festschrift for H. Conzelmann, ed. G. Strecker, Tübingen 1975.

Jesus und Paulus, Festschrift for W. G. Kümmel, ed. E. Earle Ellis and Erich Grässer, Göttingen 1975.

Jewett, R., 'The Agitators and the Galatian Congregation', *NTS* 17, 1970/71, 198-212.

Joest, W., *Gesetz und Freiheit: Das Problem des tertius usus legis bei Luther und die neutestamentliche Paränese*, Göttingen 1961³.

Jonas, H., 'Philosophische Meditation über Paulus, Römerbrief, Kapitel 7' = *Zeit und Geschichte*, 557-570.

Jüngel, E., 'Das Gesetz zwischen Adam und Christus, Eine theologische Studie zu Röm 5, 12-21', *ZThK* 60, 1963, 42-74.

–, *Paulus und Jesus: Eine Untersuchung zur Präzisierung der Frage nach dem Ursprung der Christologie*, Tübingen 1964².

Kasting, H., *Die Anfänge der christliche Mission*, BEvTh 55, Munich 1969.

Käsemann, E., 'Erwägungen zum Stichwort "Versöhnungslehre im Neuen Testament"' = *Zeit und Geschichte*, 47-59.

–, *Exegetische Versuche und Besinnungen I/II*, Göttingen 1960 (= *Essays on New Testament Themes*, London 1964 [= *EVB* I]).

–, 'Das Problem des historischen Jesus' = *EVB* I, 187-214 (= 'The problem of the historical Jesus' in *ENNT*, 15-47).

–, 'Gottesgerechtigkeit bei Paulus' = *EVB* II, 181-193 (= '"The Righteousness of God" in Paul' in *NTQT*, 168-182).

–, *An die Römer*, *HNT* 8a, Tübingen 1973 (= *Commentary on Romans*, London 1980).

Kertelge, K., *'Rechtfertigung' bei Paulus: Studien zur Struktur und zum Bedeutungsgehalt des paulinischen Rechtfertigungsbegriffs*, Münster 1971².

–, 'Exegetische Überlegungen zum Verständnis der paulinischen Anthropologie nach Römer 7', *ZNW* 62, 1971, 105-114.

Kierkegaard, S., *Philosophisch-theologische Schriften*, ed. H. Diem and W. Rest, Cologne/Olten 1956².

Klein, G., *Rekonstruktion und Interpretation: Ges. Aufs. zum Neuen Testament*, BEvTh 50, Munich 1969.

–, 'Galater 2, 6-9 und die Geschichte der Jerusalemer Urgemeinde' = *Rekonstruktion und Interpretation*, 99-128.

–, 'Der Abfassungszweck des Römerbriefs' = *Rekonstruktion und Interpretation*, 129-144.

–, 'Römer 4 und die Idee der Heilsgeschichte' = *Rekonstruktion und Interpretation*, 145-169.

–, 'Individualgeschichte und Weltgeschichte bei Paulus' = *Rekonstruktion und Interpretation*, 180-224.

–, 'Gottes Gerechtigkeit als Thema der Paulusforschung' = *Rekonstruktion und Interpretation*, 225-236.

Knierim, R., *Die Hauptbegriffe für Sünde im Alten Testament*, Gütersloh 1967².

Koch, K., 'Die drei Gerechtigkeiten, Die Umformung einer hebräischen Idee im aramäischen Denken nach dem Jesaja-Targum' = *Rechtfertigung*,

245-267.

Kühner, R./Gerth, B., *Ausführliche Grammatik der griechischen Sprache II/I*, Darmstadt 1966 (= 1898³).

Kümmel, W. G., *Römer 7 und die Bekehrung des Paulus*, Leipzig 1929; now in: *Römer 7 und das Bild des Menschen im Neuen Testament: Zwei Studien*, Munich 1974 (= *Man in the New Testament*, London 1963).

–, *Einleitung in das Neue Testament*, Heidelberg 1976 (= 18th completely new and revised edition of *Einleitung in das Neue Testament* by Paul Feine and Johannes Behm = *Introduction to the New Testament*, London 1966).

Kuhn, H.-W., 'Jesus als Gekreuzigter in der frühchristlichen Verkündigung bis zur Mitte des 2. Jahrhunderts', *ZThK* 72, 1975, 1-46.

Kuhn, K. G., Art. προσήλυτος *TWNT* VI, 727-745 (= *TDNT*, VI, 727-744).

Kuhn, K. G./Stegemann, H., Art. 'Proselyten', *PW Suppl.* IX 1962.

Kuss, O., 'Nomos bei Paulus', *MThZ* 17, 1966, 173-227.

–, *Der Römerbrief* (1. und 2. Lieferung), Regensburg 1957.

Kutsch, E., Art. bᵉrit, *Verpflichtung*, *ThHAT* I, 338-352.

Lang, F., 'Gesetz und Bund bei Paulus' = *Rechtfertigung*, 305-320.

Levy, J., *Wörterbuch über die Talmudim und Midraschim*, 4 Bd., Darmstadt 1963 (= Berlin and Vienna 1924²).

Lietzmann, H., *An die Galater*, *HNT* 10, Tübingen 1971⁴.

–, *An die Römer*, *HNT* 8, Tübingen 1971⁵.

Limbeck, M., *Die Ordnung des Heils: Untersuchungen zum Gesetzesverständnis des Frühjudentums*, Düsseldorf 1971.

–, *Von der Ohnmacht des Rechts: Zur Gesetzeskritik des Neuen Testaments*, Düsseldorf 1972.

Lipsius, R. A., *Briefe an die Galater, Römer, Philipper*, *HCNT* II, 2, Freiburg 1891.

Lohse, E., 'ὁ νόμος τοῦ πνεύματος τῆς ζωῆς, Exegetische Anmerkungen zu Röm 8, 2' = *Neues Testament und christliche Existenz*, 279-287.

–, *Grundriss der neutestamentlichen Theologie*, *ThW* 5, Stuttgart 1974.

–, Art. Mission II. Jüdische Mission, *RGG*³ IV, 971-973.

Lüdemann, G., *Paulus der Heidenapostel: Studien zur Chronologie*, *FRLANT* 123, Göttingen 1979 (= *Paul, Apostle to the Gentiles. Studies in Chronology*, Philadelphia 1984).

Lütgert, W., *Gesetz und Geist: Eine Untersuchung zur Vorgeschichte des Galaterbriefes*, *BFchTh* 6, Gütersloh 1919.

Luther, M., *Werke, Kritische Gesamtausgabe*; 56. Bd., Weimar 1938; 57. Bd., Weimar 1939.

Luz, U., *Das Geschichtsverständnis des Paulus*, *BEvTh* 49, Munich 1968.

Lyonnet, S., *Exegesis Epistulae ad Romanos, Cap. I ad IV*, Rome 1963³.

MacGorman, H. W., 'Problem Passages in Galatians', *SouthWestJTh* 15, 1972, 35-51.

Maier, J., *Die Geschichte der jüdischen Religion, Von der Zeit Alexander des*

Grossen bis zur Aufklärung mit einem Ausblick auf das 19./20.Jahrhundert, Berlin/New York 1972.

Marböck, J., 'Gesetz und Weisheit, Zum Verständnis des Gesetzes bei Jesus Ben Sira', *BZ* 20, 1976, 1-21.

Marxsen, W., *Einleitung in das Neue Testament: Eine Einleitung in ihre Probleme*, Gütersloh 1963 (= *Introduction to the New Testament: An approach to its problems*, Oxford 1968).

–, 'Der ἕτερος νόμος Rm 13, 8', *ThZ* 11, 1955, 230-237.

Maurer, C., *Die Gesetzeslehre des Paulus nach ihrem Ursprung und ihrer Entfaltung dargelegt*, Zürich 1941.

Melanchthon, P., *Werke in Auswahl II. Band, 1. Teil, Loci communes von 1521, Loci praecipui theologici von 1559 (1. Teil)*, ed. H. Engeland, Gütersloh 1952.

Menge, H., *Langenscheidts Großwörterbuch Griechisch-Deutsch unter Berücksichtigung der Etymologie*, Berlin/Munich/Zürich 1973[22].

Merk, O., *Handeln aus Glauben: Die Motivierungen der paulinischen Ethik*, *MThSt* 5, Marburg 1968.

–, 'Der Beginn der Paränese im Galaterbrief', *ZNW* 60, 1969, 83-104.

Meyer, R., Art. περιτέμνω, *TWNT* VI, 72-83 (= *TDNT* VI, 72-84).

Michel, O., *Der Brief an die Römer*, (Meyer IV), Göttingen 1957[11].

–, *Paulus und seine Bibel*, Darmstadt 1972 (= Gütersloh 1929).

–, Art. συγκλείω, *TWNT* VIII, 744-747 (= *TDNT* VIII, 744-747)

–, *Paulus und seine Bibel*, Darmstadt 1972 (= Gütersloh 1929).

–, Art. συγκλείω, *TWNT* VII, 744-747.

Müller, C., *Gottes Gerechtigkeit und Gottes Volk: Eine Untersuchung zu Römer 9-11*, *FRLANT* 86, Göttingen 1964.

Munck, J., *Paulus und die Heilsgeschichte*, *Acta Jutlandica XXVI, 1, Teol. S. 6*, Copenhagen 1954 (= *Paul and the Salvation of Mankind*, London 1959).

Mussner, F., *Der Galaterbrief*, *HThKNT* IX, Freiburg/Basle/Vienna 1974.

Neues Testament und christliche Existenz, Festschrift for H. Braun, ed. H. D. Betz and L. Schottroff, Tübingen 1973.

Neusner, J., *The Rabbinic Traditions about the Pharisees before 70*, 3 parts, Leiden 1971.

Niederwimmer, K., *Der Begriff der Freiheit im Neuen Testament*, Berlin 1966.

Noth, M., '"Die mit des Gesetzes Werken umgehen"' = *Gesammelte Studien*, *ThB* 6, 155-171.

Nygren, A., *Der Römerbrief*, Göttingen 1959[3].

Oepke, A., *Der Brief des Paulus an die Galater*, *ThHNT* 9, Berlin 1960[2].

–, Art. διά, *TWNT* II, 64-69 (= *TDNT* II, 65-70).

–, Art. μεσίτης, *TWNT* IV, 602-629 (= *TDNT* IV, 598-624).

Osten-Sacken, P. von der, *Römer 8 als Beispiel paulinischer Soteriologie*, *FRLANT* 112, Göttingen 1975.

Paschen, W., *Rein und Unrein: Untersuchung zur biblischen Wortgeschichte*, *StANT* 24, Munich 1970.

Paulsen, H., *Überlieferung und Auslegung in Römer 8, WMANT* 43, Neukirchen 1974.

Probleme biblischer Theologie, Festschrift for G. von Rad, ed. H. W. Wolff, Munich 1971.

Prümm, K., *Die Botschaft des Römerbriefes: Ihr Aufbau und Gegenwartswert*, Freiburg 1960.

Quell, G./Schrenk, G., Art. δίκη κτλ., *TWNT* II, 176-229 (= *TDNT* II, 174-225).

von Rad, G., 'Die Anrechnung des Glaubens zur Gerechtigkeit'= *Gesammelte Studien zum Alten Testament, ThB* 8, Munich 1961, 130-135.

Rechtfertigung, Festschrift for E. Käsemann, ed. J. Friedrich and others, Tübingen/Göttingen 1976.

Ritschl, A., *Die Entstehung der altkatholischen Kirche: Eine kirchen- und dogmengeschichtliche Monographie*, Bonn 1850[1], 1857[2].

–, *Die christliche Lehre von der Rechtfertigung und Versöhnung*, 2. Bd., Bonn 1882[2], 1889[3].

Sand, A., *Der Begriff 'Fleisch' in den paulinischen Hauptbriefen, BU* 2, Regensburg 1967.

Sanders, E. P., *Paul and Palestinian Judaism: A Comparison of Patterns of Religion*, London 1977.

Schäfer, P., 'Die Torah der messianischen Zeit', *ZNW* 65, 1974, 27-42.

Schenke, H.-M./Fischer, K. M., *Einleitung in die Schriften des Neuen Testaments I*, Berlin 1978.

Schlatter, A., *Gottes Gerechtigkeit: Ein Kommentar zum Römerbrief*, Stuttgart 1935.

–, *Der Evangelist Matthäus: Seine Sprache, sein Ziel, seine Selbständigkeit*, Stuttgart 1973[2].

Schlier, H., *Der Brief an die Galater*, (Meyer VII), Göttingen 1962[12].

Schmidt, H. W., *Der Brief des Paulus an die Römer, ThHNT* 6, Berlin 1972[3].

Schmithals, W., *Paulus und Jakobus, FRLANT* 85, Göttingen 1963.

–, *Paulus und die Gnostiker: Untersuchungen zu den kleinen Paulusbriefen, ThF* 35, Hamburg-Bergstedt 1965.

–, 'Die Häretiker in Galatien' = *Paulus und die Gnostiker*, 9-46.

–, Review of J. Eckert, *Die urchristliche Verkündigung im Streit zwischen Paulus und seinen Gegnern nach dem Galaterbrief, ThLZ* 98, 1973, 747-749.

–, *Der Römerbrief als historisches Problem*, Gütersloh 1975.

Schoeps, H.-J., *Paulus: Die Theologie des Apostels im Lichte der jüdischen Religionsgeschichte*, Darmstadt 1972 (= Tübingen 1959).

Schrage, W., *Die konkreten Einzelgebote in der paulinischen Paränese: Ein Beitrag zur neutestamentlichen Ethik*, Gütersloh 1961.

Schrenk, see Quell.

Schweitzer,A., *Die Mystik des Apostels Paulus*, Tübingen 1930 (= *The Mysticism of Paul the Apostle*, London 1931).

Schweizer, E., 'Die "Elemente der Welt"', Gal 4, 3.9; Kol 2, 8.20' = *Verborum Veritas*, 245-259.

Sieffert, F., 'Bemerkungen zum paulinischen Lehrbegriff, namentlich über das Verhältnis des Galaterbriefs zum Römerbrief', *JDTh* 14, 1869, 250-275.

–, *Der Brief an die Galater*, (Meyer VII), Göttingen 1886[7] (I have made use of the 7th edition, not the 9th (1899). This is justifiable in view of the fact that the changes in the 9th edition, as against the 7th, are quite insignificant.)

–, 'Die Entwicklungslinie der paulinischen Gesetzeslehre nach den vier Hauptschriften des Apostels' = *Theologische Studien*, Göttingen 1897, 332-357.

Suhl, A., *Paulus und seine Briefe: Ein Beitrag zur paulinischen Chronologie*, Gütersloh 1975.

Strack, H. L./Billerbeck, P., *Kommentar zum Neuen Testament aus Talmud und Midrasch*, 4 Bände, Munich 1965[4].

Strecker, G., 'Das Evangelium Jesu Christi' = *Jesus Christus in Historie und Geschichte*, 503-548.

–, 'Befreiung und Rechtfertigung, Zur Stellung der Rechtfertigungslehre in der Theologie des Paulus' = *Rechtfertigung*, 479-508.

Strobel, A., 'Das Aposteldekret in Galatien: Zur Situation von Gal 1 und 2', *NTS* 20, 1973/74, 177-190.

Stuhlmacher, P., *Gerechtigkeit Gottes bei Paulus*, FRLANT 87, Göttingen 1966[2].

–, 'Zur neueren Exegese von Röm 3, 24-26' = *Jesus und Paulus*, 315-353.

Theologische Studien, Festschrift for B. Weiss, Göttingen 1897.

Ulonska, H., *Die Funktion der alttestamentlichen Zitate und Anspielungen in den paulinischen Briefen*, Diss. Münster 1963.

Verborum Veritas, Festschrift for G. Stählin, Wuppertal 1970.

Vielhauer P., 'Gesetzesdienst und Stoicheiadienst im Galaterbrief' = *Rechtfertigung* 543-555.

Watson, N. M., Review Article, *NTS* 20, 1973/74, 217-228.

Wedderburn, A. J. M., 'The Theological Structure of Romans v. 12', *NTS* 19, 1972/73, 339-354.

Weinfeld, M., Art. b^{c}rit, ThWAT I, 781-808 (= *TDOT* II 253-279).

Weiss, J., *Der erste Korintherbrief*, Göttingen 1970 (= Meyer V, 1910[9]).

Weiss, K., Art. φορτίον, TWNT IX, 87f (= *TDNT* IX, 84-87).

Wendland, P., *Die hellenistisch-römische Kultur in ihren Beziehungen zum Judentum und Christentum*, HNT 2, Tübingen 1972[4] (= 1912[2]).

Westermann, C., *Genesis I*, BK I/1, Neukirchen 1974.

Whiteley, D. E. H., *The Theology of St. Paul*, Oxford 1974[2].

Wilckens, U., *Rechtfertigung als Freiheit: Paulusstudien*, Neukirchen 1974.

–, 'Die Rechtfertigung Abrahams nach Röm 4' = *Rechtfertigung als Freiheit*, 33-49.

–, 'Zu Römer 3, 21-4, 25, Antwort an G. Klein' = *Rechtfertigung als Freiheit*,

50-76.

–, 'Was heisst bei Paulus: "Aus Werken des Gesetzes wird kein Mensch gerecht?" ' = *Rechtfertigung als Freiheit*, 77-109.

–, 'Über Abfassungszweck und Aufbau des Römerbriefes' = *Rechtfertigung als Freiheit*, 110-170.

–, Art. σοφία, *TWNT* VII, 497-529 (= *TDNT* VII, 496-528).

–, 'Christologie und Anthropologie im Zusammenhang der paulinischen Rechtfertigungslehre', *ZNW* 67, 64-82.

–, *Der Brief an die Römer I, EKK VI/1*, Neukirchen 1978.

Wilson, R. McL., 'Gnostics - in Galatia?', *StEv IV/1* (= *TU* 102), Berlin 1968, 358-367.

Windisch, H., 'Das Problem des paulinischen Imperativs', *ZNW* 23, 1924, 265-281.

Zahn, T., *Der Brief des Paulus an die Römer*, Leipzig 1910².

Zeit und Geschichte, Festschrift for R. Bultmann, ed. E. Dinkler, Tübingen 1964.

Ziesler, J. A., *The Meaning of Righteousness in Paul: A Linguistic and Theological Enquiry*, *SNTS MS* 20, Cambridge 1972.

INDEX OF AUTHORS

INDEX OF REFERENCES